D1592981

Andean Journeys

Pachamama (Earth Mother)
S. D. Nelson

Andean Journeys

Migration, Ethnogenesis, and the State
in Colonial Quito

Karen Vieira Powers

University of New Mexico Press
Albuquerque

Portions of this material appeared previously and excerpts here are from Karen Powers, "Resilient Lords and Indian Vagabonds: Wealth, Migration, and the Reproductive Transformation of Quito's Chiefdoms, 1500–1700," *Ethnohistory*, 38:3, pp. 225-49. Copyright Duke University Press, 1991, and Karen Powers, "Indian Migration in the Audiencia of Quito: Crown Manipulations and Local Co-optations," In *Migration in Colonial Spanish America*, ed. David J. Robinson, 313–323. Copyright Cambridge University Press, 1990. Reprinted with permission. The publication of this book was supported in part by a grant from the National Endowment for the Humanities.

Library of Congress Cataloging-in-Publication Data

Powers, Karen Vieira, 1950-
    Andean journeys : migration, ethnogenesis, and the state in colonial Quito / Karen Vieira Powers. — 1st ed.
        p. cm.
    Includes bibliographical references and index.
    Contents: Demographic chaos: Spanish invasion and Andean migration — Fleeing toward the enemy: seventeenth-century migration patterns — Colonial state formation and the politics of Andean demography — Migration and the reproduction of the cacicazgo — Decline of the cacicazgo and the reconstitution of Andean society — Conclusion.
    ISBN 0-8263-1600-X
    1. Quito (Audiencia)—Population—History. 2. Migration, Internal—Ecuador—Quito (Audiencia)—History. 3. Ecuador—History—To 1809. 4. Quito (Audiencia)—History. I. Title.
    HB3570.Q58P69 1995
    304.8'09866'13—dc20   94-18696
                                    CIP

To Stephen Nelson

and

In memory of Warren Dean

Contents

Maps

Figures

Tables

Acknowledgments

This book is the result of an odyssey that began as a childhood passion for the Spanish language in Yonkers, New York, and ended in the archives of the far reaches of the Ecuadorean highlands. Along the way, I have had the privilege to meet many special people whose advice, encouragement, and example have contributed immeasurably to this project's realization. First, I would like to thank the directors and general staffs of the archives of Ecuador and Spain. I am especially grateful for the unfailing assistance of Grecia Vasco de Escudero and Dr. Juan Freile Granizo, the current and former directors of the Archivo Nacional in Quito, and for the extraordinary generosity and trust exhibited by many of Ecuador's provincial archivists. In addition, my research at the Archivo General de Indias in Seville was especially productive, not only owing to the efficiency of the staff, but to the collaboration and collegiality of its scholarly community.

Second, I owe a special intellectual debt to the late Warren Dean and to Herbert Klein who made incisive critiques of the project when it was in the dissertation stage. Indispensable, however, has been the advice, support and patience of my mentor and friend, Nicolás Sánchez-Albornoz, who introduced me to the wonders of the Andean world and gave me the benefit of his demographic expertise. I would also like to acknowledge my debt to Frank Salomon, Robson Tyrer, and the late Thierry Saignes, whose pioneering works have made my journey smoother and shorter.

Several institutions have also contributed to both the successful completion of this book and to my formation as a scholar. I would like to thank: the City University of New York for providing me with a tuition-free, undergraduate education; New York University for much-needed, graduate school funding; the Fulbright-Hays Commission and the Social Science Research Council for financing extensive research in Ecuador and Spain; and Northern Arizona University for its support during the project's revision stages.

Over the years, I have gotten by "with a little help from my friends" and it is to them that I am most deeply indebted. In Quito, I would like to thank

Carmen Guanoluisa, María Mogollón, Kate Fleming, Jackie Kann, Nora McVeigh, Teri Hein, and Ursula Poeschel for their friendship and for seeing me through a serious illness. I am also grateful to Christiana Borchart de Moreno and Segundo Moreno Yánez for their archival advice and for opening their home to me, to Kenneth Andrien for his encouragement, and to Anton Rosenthal for being there.

In Seville, I had the good fortune to be accompanied by Tom Abercrombie, Mary Dillon, Nancy van Deusen, Efraín Trelles, Rafael Varón, Margarita Suárez, Antonio Acosta, and Kendall and Margie Brown. I thank them all for their personal kindness and scholarly collaboration.

At New York University, I would like to thank the Center for Latin American and Caribbean Studies for providing a warm, friendly atmosphere and its director, Christopher Mitchell, for his encouragement throughout the years. I am also grateful to Deborah Levenson who was my comrade-in-arms during graduate school and to Deborah Truhan for her steadfast friendship and for having faith in me when I doubted. At Northern Arizona University, I thank my friend and colleague, Susan Deeds, for her intellectual and emotional support and for her careful assessment of parts of the manuscript. On the homefront, I am grateful to my sister, Barbara, for her help during a critical time and to my parents for having expectations. Lastly, I would like to take this opportunity to express my deepest appreciation to my compañero, Stephen Nelson, without whose love and support the author's life would be incomplete.

Andean Journeys

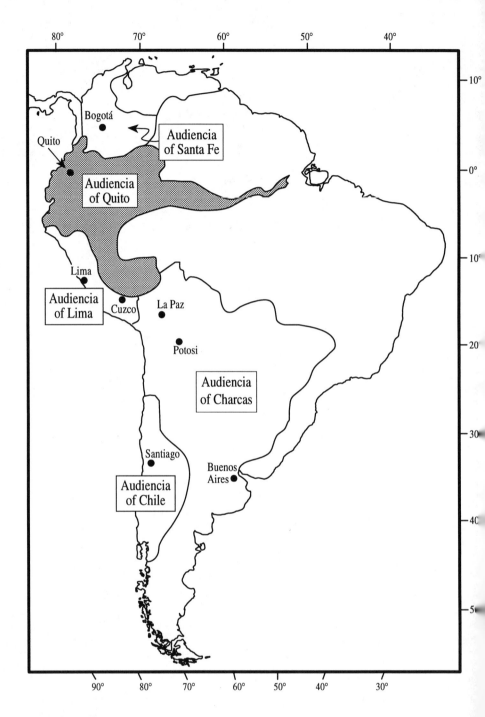

Map 1. The Audiencia of Quito, c. 1650

Introduction

In recent years, the project of ethnohistorical research has been to confer history on historically neglected peoples; in the Americas, much of this effort has focused on uncovering the processes through which native Americans have survived as distinct non-Western cultures. A poignant case is the Andean region where, despite the destructurating effects of Spanish colonization and contemporary modernization, indigenous peoples still represent 40 to 70 percent of the populations of Ecuador, Peru, and Bolivia. Of these three nations, Ecuador has received the least scholarly attention; therefore, I decided to center my research on the use of migration as a colonial survival strategy among the ethnic groups of the Audiencia of Quito. The outcome has been surprisingly productive, resulting in both a revisionist treatment of Quito's demographic history and a clearer understanding of North Andean ethnogenesis.[1]

The growing literature on the cultural and ethnic preservation of Amerindian peoples serves as a significant point of departure for this book. Because my research focuses on Quito, the northernmost part of the Inca empire, I have limited most of my historiographical comments to works that treat the descendants of America's high civilizations—that is, those of Mesoamerica and the Andes.

Eric Wolf, in *Europe and the People without History,* challenges historians "not to be content with writing only the history of victorious elites or with detailing the subjugation of dominated ethnic groups," and urges them "to uncover the history of the people without history."[2] Latin American historiography, however, anticipates Wolf's mandate by almost two decades with the publication of Charles Gibson's *The Aztecs under Spanish Rule.*[3]

In 1964, Gibson broke important ground when he provided us with a monumental and carefully documented treatise on how the pre-existing political structures of the Aztec empire informed the construction of Spain's colony in Central Mexico. Of particular significance were the adaptations of the indigenous tribute and labor systems for colonial purposes and the strategies devised by the Mesoamericans, themselves, to preserve their pre-

Hispanic political organization. This key study of Amerindian ethnohistory, however, would have to wait several years to be followed by other attempts to give voice to the "people without history."

Also of import in the 1960s and 1970s were the structural analyses of the dependency and world systems theorists who included colonized peoples in history, but emphasized their role as an exploited class within a global economic structure.[4] For historical purposes, it is a model that divides the universe into the descendants of the conquerors and the descendants of the conquered, into the actors of world history and those who have been acted upon.

The dependency model generated numerous works across disciplines that attempted to delineate the historical (though unintended) contributions of Latin America's unchronicled peoples to the formation of the modern world economy. These scholars reasoned that it was, after all, the labor of native Americans and Africans in the silver mines and on the plantations of the New World which fostered the capital accumulation necessary for Europe's industrial revolution. Prominent among these works are Eduardo Galeano's classic, *Open Veins of Latin America,* which traces the plunder of the region from Columbus's arrival to the present, and Stanley and Barbara Stein's *The Colonial Heritage of Latin America,* which uncovers the colonial roots of Latin America's economic dependence.[5]

Eventually, these structural analyses came under criticism for portraying colonized peoples as little more than a peripheral milch cow from whom a surplus was extracted and sent back to a center or metropolis. Though powerful tools for understanding the interconnected nature of world history, these interpretations told us little about the unique historical actions of the ancestors of today's Third World peoples, as they struggled to survive in a world increasingly defined by Europe's agenda.[6]

The dependency theorists, however, were paralleled in Latin American historiography by another interdisciplinary group of scholars whose works represent an auspicious beginning to writing a "history of the people without history." New methodologies, such as the translation of native chronicles and the textual analysis of conquest plays, reenacted annually by indigenous peoples, enabled scholars like Miguel León-Portilla and Nathan Wachtel to tell the story of the conquest through Amerindian eyes.[7] While of utmost importance to the field, these histories focus largely on subjugation and the effects of subjugation on native societies.

Building on these works, however, historians and anthropologists of the 1980s and 1990s have made a concerted effort to search for Amerindian agency. This has resulted in a historiography that emphasizes the survival strategies, or adaptive resistance, of native peoples vis-à-vis the Spanish regime. Some representative examples of this trend are the works of Nancy Farriss, Luis Miguel Glave, Grant Jones, Brook Larson, Galo Ramón, Thierry Saignes, Karen Spalding, and Steve Stern.[8] These works illuminate the myriad ways in which the conquered struggled to save their lives, their communities, and their cultural identities. Indigenous peoples are depicted in these works as indefatigable litigants who learned to operate rapidly and effectively within the Spanish judicial system. They defended their lands, herds, and other resources. They defended themselves against the unscrupulous acts of royal officials, the extortions of private Spaniards, the abuses of Spanish priests, and even against the self-aggrandizement of their own caciques (Amerindian leaders). They are shown as participants in largescale uprisings, local rebellions, millenarian movements, and acts of a more passive aggressive nature, such as infanticide, the maiming of male children, the sale of fraudulent death certificates, and migration to avoid the tribute and labor exactions of the Spanish state. In short, these are works in which native peoples are active players, not only in their own cultural survival, but in the forging of the larger colonial world.

Of course, it has been singularly difficult to uncover this new history of Amerindian agency. New sources and methodologies were needed and a variety of experiments were undertaken. They included: further discovery and translation of native texts; studies of Amerindian civil and criminal litigation; analyses of notarial records in which indigenous peoples appear in last wills and testaments, dowries, labor contracts, and land transactions; and the use of historical demography for ethnohistorical extrapolation.

Most prominent among those based on native texts are the works of James Lockhart and several of his students.[9] Using Nahuatl language sources, they have been able to uncover much about the inner world of Central Mexico's indigenous population during the colonial period. Their works have both revised and enriched existing historical accounts, though their claims for far more sociopolitical continuity of Mesoamerican societies than was previously thought has been criticized for its lack of attention to political economy and demography. Other Mexicanists have attempted to combine the latter with concern for cultural history, but without a philological approach.[10]

Due to the relative absence of native language sources in the Andes, scholars of that region have had to depend on alternative methodologies that would give voice to the "people without history." One of the most effective methods to date has been the use of historical demography. As Sánchez-Albornoz, a prominent figure in this field, has stated: "los números cantan" ("the numbers sing") and sometimes quite eloquently.

The significance of population studies for the field of ethnohistory derives from Cook and Borah's 1963 demographic analysis of the central Valley of Mexico. By analyzing Aztec and later Spanish tribute records, they posited that the area once known as the Aztec empire had been inhabited by 25.2 million people upon Cortes's arrival. Their study also revealed that the central Mexican population had dwindled to 1.075 million by the year 1605—a short 80 years—a depopulation rate of 96 percent.[11]

The findings of what came to be known as the Berkeley or California School of historical demographers, though tempered by subsequent estimates, generated numerous demographic studies of other areas of Latin America. Using both similar and more varied methods, most scholars uncovered the same startling depopulation rates.[12] This gave rise to new questions about Amerindian civilizations and eventually stimulated an interest in using colonial censuses as important sources for ethnohistory—an interest which was encouraged in Andean studies by the works of John Murra, Waldemar Espinosa Soriano, and others.[13]

In 1978, with the publication of *Indios y tributos en el Alto Perú,* Nicolás Sánchez-Albornoz gave historical demographers pause for thought. Contrary to traditional historiography which posed a static colonial order of urban-based Spanish overlords and stationary Amerindian communities, he found that the colonial Andes were characterized by constant human movement.[14] The Spanish invasion of the New World set in motion a dynamic migration of native peoples that began as a survival strategy, but ended up having a determinant effect on the evolution of both indigenous and Spanish colonial societies.

Throughout the sixteenth and seventeenth centuries, the imposition of the new regime and its attendant abuses generated mass migrations of Amerindians away from their communities of origin. Because tribute and forced labor were levied on their communal villages, indigenous peoples often evaded these exactions by fleeing to Spanish cities, textile mills, and haciendas, to other native villages, and to inaccessible places. They lost themselves in urban and frontier settings or entered the employ of Spanish entrepreneurs and Amerindian lords, many of whom were eager to harness extra official labor.

As the colonial period progressed, these population movements accelerated, owing to the increasing divestment of native communities and the ensuing search for subsistence. So widespread was migration in the

Viceroyalty of Peru that by the end of the seventeenth century, foreign Amerindians, called forasteros, comprised up to 80 percent of some Andean towns.[15] Once outside their communities of origin, these migrants and their descendants were usually exempt from tribute and the *mita* (forced labor system) because they did not have formal access to communal lands.

Sánchez-Albornoz and others have been quick to point out the problem that forasteros present for the demographic history of early Spanish America. Native depopulation has frequently been assessed by studying tribute records in which forasteros were often not represented, thereby casting shadows on the conclusions of some earlier population studies.

In recent years, however, the migrations themselves have become a focus of research; a new historiography has begun to emerge that uses the study of migration as a vehicle for uncovering socioeconomic and political changes in both indigenous and Spanish colonial societies.[16] In addition, by combining analyses of population movements with qualitative data derived from judicial proceedings and notarial records, a few historians and anthropologists have begun to grasp a clearer understanding of the interior meanings of indigenous life and to produce rich studies of Andean ethnogenesis.[17]

My work falls into this incipient genre since it traces Andean population movements in the Audiencia of Quito from 1534 to 1700 with an eye to extrapolating the region's ethnohistory. Using data from censuses, lawsuits, correspondence, official decrees, and fiscal records, it has three objectives: (1) a revision of Quito's anomalous population history; (2) an analysis of the effects of Andean demography and human agency on colonial state formation; and (3) an assessment of the impact of migration and human agency on the ethnogenesis of Quito's indigenous societies.

With relation to the first objective, existing historiography suggests that, compared with other areas of Spanish America, colonial Quito had an unusual demographic curve. Reportedly, the region's population, after an initial post-conquest decline, exhibited remarkable stability and even growth until the end of the seventeenth century. Robson Tyrer's pioneering analysis posits a demographic explosion in the central and north-central highlands between 1590 and 1660. Using tribute records, he demonstrates that the tributary population of some central sierran *corregimientos* tripled and even quadrupled during those seventy years. In her recent epidemiological history, Suzanne Alchon concurs with Tyrer's projected increase, though she arrives at slightly different figures.[18]

Quito's seventeenth-century growth is an aberration in the Viceroyalty of Peru where the rest of the indigenous population experienced steady decline until approximately 1730.[19] What is even more puzzling is that subsequent research, including my own, confirms that Quito's native peoples were indeed subject to the same depopulating events as those of other areas. Sources abound that point to a history of epidemics, natural disasters, and abusive labor conditions in the Audiencia.[20]

In the search for an explanation of Quito's demographic contradiction, Sánchez-Albornoz's work has figured prominently. He suggests that the precipitous population decline extrapolated from tribute records for the southern Andes might be attributed, in part, to native migration.[21]

The significance of these findings for the study of Quito is that if migration could skew downward the population statistics presented in tribute records, then, under varying circumstances, it could also skew them upward. Indeed, it is the central hypothesis of Chapter One that the seventeenth-century rise exhibited in Quito's demographic curve was not the result of natural growth, but rather of sixteenth-century migrations from marginal areas to the center of the audiencia. These migrants and their descendants were then incorporated into the tributary base in the seventeenth century, along with Amerindians who had been hidden by their caciques. Analyzing the contradictory content of bureaucratic reports on Quito's demographic state, native petitions and litigation over Andean absenteeism, and Spanish census-taking procedures, it has been possible to delineate the migrations and administrative practices that produced the seventeenth-century "population explosion."

Once Quito's demographic anomaly was resolved, the study of migration was used as a vehicle for understanding the constantly mutating colonial world that emerged from the interaction of Andeans and Spaniards. Native migration was singularly important in bringing these two groups into closer contact and producing the cultural conflicts and adaptations, economic transformations, and sociopolitical struggles that determined the evolution of both Andean and Spanish colonial societies.

Through computer analysis of censuses and absentee lists, Chapter Two measures the migratory flow from the Indian to the Spanish sphere of the colony—that is, from native communities to Spanish cities, textile mills, and haciendas. The study determines that by late seventeenth century a considerable population shift had taken place that left the Indian sphere half-emptied and the Spanish sphere inflated. This movement had serious consequences for the politico-economic structures of both the Indian and Spanish republics.[22] This impact is the subject of the rest of the book, though the emphasis is clearly on the evolution of indigenous society.

Chapter Three analyzes the effects of Andean demography and human agency on colonial state formation. Using mostly official correspondence and reports, it traces the evolution of administrative practices regarding population counts and poses an intimate relationship between Andean migration and statistical manipulation on the one hand and the balance of power among various colonial sectors on the other. The major hypothesis of this chapter is that the forasteros became a swing factor in the ebb and flow of political power both between crown and colonists and among local interest groups. Interwoven into the analysis is a vivid portrayal of the Andean-Spanish tug of war over "demographic accuracy." This was a century-long struggle in which Andean leaders resisted Spanish efforts to uncover the true numbers of their subjects by engaging in various forms of demographic subterfuge.

The project's third objective, to measure the impact of migration and human agency on Andean ethnogenesis, has received little attention, even in the more researched southern Andes. What exactly transpired inside native communities as a result of the migratory phenomenon has been difficult to ascertain. Existing historiography falls into two categories—works that pose migration as an important agent of destructuration in Andean communities and those that posit, in opposition to this view, that caciques frequently used migration and *forasterismo* as adaptive strategies for community survival.

Various works by Sánchez-Albornoz reveal that migration accelerated socioeconomic differentiation among Andean peoples and that forasteros who remained in the Indian sphere suffered ostracism and low status.[23] Apropos of this, Ann Wightman posits that, while migration undermined communal landholding, altered traditional patterns of reciprocity, and facilitated the spread of Spanish norms, Cuzco's forasteros nonetheless became a stable sector of indigenous society.[24] Finally, the late Thierry Saignes proposed several interesting theories about the role of migration and the forasteros in the reproduction of native societies in Alto Perú. The most noted are: (1) that forasteros who lived in the Indian sphere supplemented the labor forces of the communities where they resided; (2) that migration did not necessarily imply an Andean's rupture with his or her community of origin; and (3) that caciques frequently placed their subjects in the Spanish sphere in order to use their wages as community inputs.[25] Luis Miguel Glave, in his recent work on the southern Andes, concurs with this view.[26]

Chapters Four and Five are shaped by this debate and suggest that the answer in the northern Andes lies in periodization, as well as in the application of the conceptual frame of ethnogenesis—a continuous cultural process that is simultaneously reproductive and transformative. Utilizing the latter approach, I have concluded that migration reproduced the indigenous societies of Quito, but in an increasingly transformative manner as time went on. Based largely on the demographic and political content of six-teenth- and seventeenth-century suits between Andean leaders, these chapters examine the effects of migration on the north Andean *cacicazgo* (chiefdom). Chapter Four delineates the early colonial caciques' strategies for the maintenance of power—strategies which utilized the forastero mass as a supplementary labor supply and translated into the successful reproduction of Andean society during the sixteenth and early seventeenth centuries. During the remainder of the seventeenth century, however, migration was increasingly directed toward the Spanish sphere, causing this adaptive strategy to break down. Chapter Five then traces the downward spiral of the early colonial cacicazgo and poses out-migration and related ills as major catalysts for its weakening as an Andean institution. It also suggests that, from this point on, the work of cultural reproduction was carried out by Amerindian commoners who reconstructed Andean social organization inside the sites to which they migrated—cities, haciendas, obrajes, etc.

This part of the analysis is situated in Sahlins's "structure of the conjuncture"—a theory that posits that culture is determined by a dialectical relationship between existing structures and historical events.[27] As cultures reproduce themselves, the interaction of existing internal structures and external historical forces results in a gradual but continual adjustment of cultural forms in order to deal with new imperatives. Thus, the cultural survival strategies delineated in Chapters Three, Four, and Five have been examined as part of the larger process of ethnogenesis. They have been treated not as discrete reactive phenomena or mechanisms to maintain pre-Hispanic culture in pristine form, but rather as integral elements of an evolving indigenous culture whose trajectory was affected, but not determined, by Spanish colonialism.[28]

Before venturing into Chapter One, some terms, concepts and categories need to be clarified. In the documentation, the term *Quito* may refer to the city, the corregimiento, or the audiencia. When used alone, it usually refers to the audiencia. If not, it will be qualified by its administrative unit or the meaning will be clear from the context. In addition, the term *Spanish sphere* refers to Spanish urban centers and Spanish enterprises, like haciendas and textile workshops; the *Indian sphere* includes Andean communities and Andean enterprises, whether they belong to the community or to the caciques.

The terms *migration* and *absentee* also need further explanation. This study has determined that migration patterns varied significantly throughout the colonial period depending on local conditions. Some movements were interregional (long-distance); others took place within the same corregimiento (administrative unit); and still others were so localized as to be almost imperceptible. In addition, though most migrations of the seventeenth century were directed toward the Spanish sphere, inter-community migration within the Indian sphere continued, although at increasingly reduced rates as Andean towns lost their economic viability and caciques their authority. Nevertheless, all these movements were significant for their contributions, whether as adaptive or transformational agents, to the colonization process. Thus, since the study of physical movement is used here as a vehicle for measuring continuity and change, all movements will be referred to as "migration," regardless of their geographic range or lack thereof.

In similar fashion, there were many variations on absenteeism. First, the documentation on the Audiencia of Quito, contrary to census materials for other parts of the Viceroyalty of Peru, usually lists Andean migrants and their descendants as *ausentes* (absentees) in their communities of origin and not as forasteros in their communities of residence. It is, therefore, the ausentes who become the most important unit of analysis.

By midseventeenth century, there were three types of ausentes: *camayos,* absentees whose whereabouts were known, and absentees about whom nothing was known at all. The camayos were members of economic colonies who lived extra-territorially in order to exploit resources for their communities. For this reason, they will be singled out as a distinct category of absentee and not included in absentee rates. The latter two categories of absentees were sometimes referred to as *ausentes seguros* (secure absentees) and *ausentes perdidos* (lost absentees); at other times the people in the first category were not recorded as officially absent, but rather their extra-community residences were matter-of-factly listed in specific cities or haciendas. The cacique's knowledge of their whereabouts may indicate that these absentees still had some attachment to the community, no matter how tenuous, and that the cacique may have attempted to collect tributes from them. The other group of absentees, those whose location was unknown, appear to have severed ties with their towns. What these two groups have in common, however, is that their labor was not available to the community, hence they are treated together under the rubric of "absentee rates," although the *ausente perdido* was the category most inimical to the reproduction of the Indian sphere.

Native leaders are described as *caciques* instead of the more common Andean term, *kurakas.* The former was chosen owing to the relative absence of the quechua term "kuraka" in the documentation of the audiencia. Even local ethnic lords usually described themselves as caciques, as opposed to kurakas, in the records of the period. This may be a manifestation of Quito's linguistic diversity, its brief experience with Inca rule, and its distinctiveness from better-studied groups to the south. Lastly, the traditional Andean kinship group is referred to as the *ayllu,* a term of southern Andean origins, instead of the pre-Hispanic Ecuadorean term, *llajta,* because it is used consistently in colonial documentation and is more readily identifiable to Latin Americanists.

I have tried to present in the following pages a history that recognizes the constant interaction of two forces: (1) the actions of the colonizers, as witnessed by the ideological and material aspirations of a European people seeking to establish and maintain hegemony in Europe by expanding markets, extracting surplus, and winning adherents to Catholicism abroad; and (2) the counteractions of a multiplicity of Andean peoples, only recently conquered by the Inca, and more recently divested of their dreams for autonomy by a Spanish regime that some of them had helped bring to power. These two forces, while certainly not equivalent in coercive potential were indeed contending forces whose interaction produced a colonial world with a distinctive character. In short, this work is about the colonization process, but a process in which the colonized peoples of Ecuador not only resisted, adapted, and survived, but reinvented themselves as a culture.

1
Demographic Chaos: Spanish Invasion and Andean Migration

In the opening years of Spanish rule, Quito's ethnic peoples had already experienced one of the most tumultuous cultural and demographic histories of South America. From 1400 to 1534, the region was visited by successive waves of conquest, giving rise to population upheavals whose radical nature nearly defies demographic analysis.

Upon the arrival of the Inca, Quito consisted of six aboriginal chiefdoms, whose members resided in its inter-Andean valleys. They were, from north to south, the Pasto, the Cara, the Panzaleo, the Puruhá, the Cañari, and the Palta.[1] Although often described as the historic tribes of Quito, there is substantial archaeological evidence that some of them were lowlanders who had conquered highland areas as recently as the fifteenth century.[2] All six enjoyed an intimate relationship with lowland tribes to the east and west.

As early as 1455 the Inca, Tupac Yupanqui, began to make incursions into the southern region of Quito. Forty years later his son, Huayna Capac, completed the conquest, making Ecuador the northern border of the Inca empire on the eve of Spanish arrival. Unlike the Aztecs, who were content to collect tribute from subjugated peoples, the Inca sought to integrate them into an imperial construct of unifying political, religious, and economic practices. They achieved this by sending colonies of loyal subjects to newly conquered areas in both a military and didactic role and by removing resistant native elements to distant regions.

These institutionalized population transfers occurred on a grand scale in Quito; Quitos, Caranquis, and even Pastos were forcibly resettled as far south as Lake Titicaca, while a large colony of Cañaris found themselves in the Yucay Valley outside of Cuzco. The Cayampis of northern Quito were sent south to the Peruvian coca plantations of Ancara and to Huánuco, while several contingents of loyal Chachapoyas, Wayakuntus, and Huamachucos from northern Peru were sent to various locations in Quito.[3]

On the heels of Inca conquest followed the disease catastrophes of the 1520s and 1530s. Several years before Pizarro's band of gold-hungry expeditionaries set foot on Inca soil, the microbes they and their cohorts

harbored were already wreaking havoc on the unsuspecting populations of
the Andes. Besides the staggering mortality usually engendered by smallpox and measles in nonimmune populations, such epidemics also gave rise
to general flight.[4] In addition the Inca, Huayna Capac, succumbed to this
invisible enemy, as did his designated heir, throwing the empire, and especially the Quito region, into a protracted war of succession. The demographic result was more death and displacement. By the time the Spaniards
arrived, then, a significant population shift had already taken place in the
Ecuadorean highlands.

With barely enough time to consolidate their holdings in Quito, the Inca
were swept off their feet in 1534 by the Spaniards and their Andean allies.
In the wake of Spanish victory came yet another wave of population movements. Both the Battle of Quito and secondary expeditions of conquest
caused widespread displacement of native peoples. Throughout the rest of
the sixteenth century, civil wars and rebellions, the labor demands of the
mines and *obrajes* (textile workshops), Spanish resettlement policies, and
spontaneous migration to escape colonial exactions also contributed to
ongoing population shifts.

In short throughout the fifteenth and sixteenth centuries, the aboriginal, Incaic, and Spanish conquests of the Ecuadorean sierra and their resultant population movements created a demographic setting that can only
be described as pandemonium. The perplexing overlay of peoples and cultures that ensued has made it singularly difficult for scholars to define, let
alone resolve, the demographic and ethnohistorical problems of the area.

The Migration Phenomenon

Quito's legacy of human movement continued unabated throughout the
sixteenth century. What was already a critical demographic situation in 1534
was exacerbated by the Spanish invasion and the subsequent activities of
the new regime. Andean population movements in the colonial period can
be divided into two categories: Spanish-directed and Andean-directed migrations. Some examples of Spanish-directed, or forced, migration are: the
conscription of native troops, the coerced relocation of *encomienda* Indians, and the incorporation of large numbers of Andeans into the mita, or
forced-labor system.

Forced migrations and the painful displacements that accompanied them,
however, were paralleled by Andean-initiated movements that often assumed
the characteristics of carefully designed survival strategies. As the native

population contracted due to war, illness, and abuse, those who survived were left with the awesome burden of tribute and participation in the mita. In order to escape the excessive demands of the Spanish state, indigenous peoples began to move to areas where they would not be recognized as community members. They became forasteros, or outsiders, who were not obliged to pay tribute or perform the mita, presumably because they no longer enjoyed access to communal lands. These movements included both the spontaneous migrations of individuals and the planned movements orchestrated by indigenous leaders in the interests of community survival.

Although not a heavily researched topic, interested historians and anthropologists have ascertained that Amerindian-directed migration was a well-known phenomenon in nearly every area of colonial Spanish America. So widespread was migration in the Viceroyalty of Peru that by the middle of the eighteenth century the forasteros represented one-half the population of La Paz and one-third that of Cuzco.[5]

That migration—both Spanish- and Andean-directed—occurred on a large scale in the Audiencia of Quito is unmistakable. Sixteenth- and seventeenth-century sources abound with references to indigenous peoples who were no longer residing in their communities of origin. As early as 1559, the *visita* (official inspection and census) of Francisco Ruiz's encomienda (grant of indigenous tribute and labor) recorded 64 "units" of forasteros. If one considers that "units" probably referred to households, then the total number of forasteros present was closer to 250. According to the visita testimony, these forasteros had resided there since 1544, by permission of the local cacique, or lord.[6]

By 1585 Andean migration had created such widespread displacement that the Audiencia of Quito issued a decree recommending that Andeans pay tribute where they lived and not where they were born; although intended to reduce the tribute collectors' work load, it was not implemented. Officials also complained that some towns of the audiencia had already been half-emptied, because their inhabitants had become residents in other *pueblos* (towns).[7]

In 1592 the "Relación de Zaruma" reported that there were more than two thousand Andean vagabonds of tributary age residing in the highlands.[8] By 1601 the city of Quito was reported to have six thousand "vagabonds who do not have encomenderos and who do not pay tributes because they are from different regions, nor do they serve anyone, but instead commit a thousand crimes on the highways and in the towns."[9] Note that the figure six thousand only represents vagabonds of tributary age; it does not include women, children, and the elderly. Neither does this estimate include the many forasteros who were attached to Andean communities and worked for the caciques, nor those who lived in the service of Spaniards, both in urban areas and on haciendas. Considering these omissions, the total forastero population of the sierra must have been considerable at the turn of the seventeenth century. What follows is an analysis of the sixteenth-century movements that produced this large number of "outsiders."[10]

From 1534 to 1600, the migratory behavior of the indigenous population was informed by the conquest, civil wars between Spanish leaders, epidemics, the exigencies of the new market economy, and land pressure in the sierra. The result was a series of radical population movements that sent indigenous society into temporary disarray and obstructed the consolidation of the colonial regime.

Quito was a nucleus for the diffusion of the northern conquest and a stopover for hundreds of Spaniards in search of gold and cinnamon. Spanish forces abducted waves of Amerindians from the region and pressed them into service as warriors, porters, concubines, and servants. During the first decades of Spanish rule, constant tension existed between expeditionaries and city council members, who feared that Quito was teetering on the brink of demographic collapse.[11] A poignant example is Gonzalo Pizarro's 1541 foray into the Amazon, which drained Quito of between six and ten thousand native inhabitants.[12] Expeditions such as this were a constant source of vexation to the *cabildo* (municipal council), since they carried Andeans off to distant places, often never to return.

The Spanish civil wars and Andean rebellions were also occasions for migration. In 1544 for example, Quito became the center for the war between Gonzalo Pizarro and the viceroy, Blasco Núñez Vela; local peoples were forced to serve in both the loyal and rebel troops and compelled to suffer the fate of the faction with which they served.[13] Depopulation and demographic shifts also resulted from punitive expeditions against rebellious tribes; the indigenous population of Popayán, for example, was seriously undermined by such campaigns.[14]

As conquest and colonization expanded to new zones of economic opportunity, Quito's indigenous population suffered an even greater drain. Some Spaniards, in their search for fame and fortune, were prompted to move from Quito, often taking whole encomiendas with them. In 1537 Pizarro ordered that Quito's peoples were not to be transferred to newly founded towns, because the region was on the verge of depopulation. However, as late as 1562, Andrés Contero forced a thousand highland Andeans to migrate to the newly established settlements of Quijos, in the eastern lowlands.[15]

The discovery of gold in the southern regions of the audiencia also had dire consequences for Quito's population. The mines of Zangurima, Zamora, and Zaruma became the "final destination" for thousands of Andean peoples. Constantly in need of fresh human supplies, the mines served both to depopulate the southern highlands and to syphon off Andean labor from the central and northern sierra. Loja, Cuenca, and Zamora, all mining regions, experienced the most precipitous decline of the entire audiencia between 1570 and 1591 (table 1). Mining also aggravated the demographic drain on the region's core, since labor gangs were sent to the goldfields from encomiendas as far north as Otavalo (250 miles away).[16]

Without a doubt, however, the single most disruptive event of the sixteenth century was the introduction of Old World diseases. Scholars have identified five major epidemics, mostly of smallpox and measles, which ravaged Quito in 1524–27, 1531–33, 1546, 1558–60, and 1585–91.[17] Alchon poses that this epidemiological onslaught produced a depopulation rate of 85–90 percent within a brief seventy years (1520–90).[18] In addition to high mortality, the societal destructuration and psychological disorientation that accompanied these disease episodes must also be considered important catalysts for subsequent population movements.

In the early years of the colony, secondary expeditions of conquest, Spanish civil wars, extrasierran colonization, and the pull toward the southern mines generated Spanish-directed or forced migrations that undermined the Andean population of the central and north-central highlands. These movements, in combination with the death and displacement brought about by the great sixteenth-century pandemics, resulted in population shortages there. Subsequently it will be shown how the sierran caciques compensated for these shortages and stimulated yet a new wave of movements—this time Andean-directed.

Movements from Marginal Areas to the Center

In the first half of the sixteenth century, the destabilizing events of Spanish colonization diffused Quito's indigenous population. The wanton acts of expeditionaries and unrestrained *encomenderos* (grantees of encomiendas) resulted in the forced migration of thousands of Andeans to scattered locations. Spontaneous and orchestrated flight to peripheral areas of the audiencia also occurred, as individuals and groups sought safety from the savage invader. As a result the eastern and western *montaña* regions (subtropical slopes), traditional places of refuge and staging areas for resis-

Table 1: Indigenous Population of Audiencia of Quito, 1561–1591

Province	1561		ca. 1570	1586	1590	1591	1570–1591
	Tributaries	Total Population	Tributaries	Total Population	Tributaries (Relación de Zaruma)	Tributaries (Morales Figueroa)	Percentage Change Tributary Population
Quito	48,134	240,670	42,000–43,000	118,141	21,250	24,380	-43
Cuenca	—	—	8,000	—	3,000	1,472	-82
Loja	3,647	9,495	6,000	16,000	—	2,849	-52
Zamora	6,093	11,222	5,000	8,100	—	685	-86
Jaen	—	—	8,000–10,000	11,397	—	2,654	-73
Quijos	—	—	—	10,000	—	—	—
Guayaquil	2,280	4,742	3,000	7,355	—	2,198	-27
Puerto Viejo	1,377	2,297	1,500	4,102	—	1,253	-16

Source: Robson Brines Tyrer, La historia demográfica y económica de la Audiencia de Quito: Población indígena e industria textil, 1600–1800 (Quito: Banco Central del Ecuador, 1988), p. 27.

Note: The censuses of 1570 and 1591 were selected to calculate percentage changes because each shows statistics for at least seven of the eight provinces.

tance, experienced a temporary demographic inflation between 1534 and 1560.[19] These were also the years during which the conquest expanded to the montañas—Quijos, Yumbos, Cayapas, Macas, Yaguarzongo, and the Jíbaro region of Popayán. Not surprisingly, then, this period witnessed a large-scale movement of indigenous peoples, both forced and voluntary, away from the central valley floors and toward these marginal zones.

In contrast the dispersion of Quito's indigenous population gave way, in the second half of the sixteenth century, to a marked reconcentration in the sierran corregimientos of Otavalo, Quito, Latacunga, Ambato, and Riobamba—the heartland of the audiencia. Although demographic centralization was due, in part, to the Spanish reducciones of the 1560s and 1570s, much of the movement from the periphery to the center can be squarely attributed to autonomous native decisions.

Although data does not permit quantitative analysis, the magnitude of the periphery-to-center movement can be assessed through a revisionist interpretation of the existing record. Demographic historians have traditionally held that Quito's population enjoyed an unusually privileged history in the late sixteenth and seventeenth centuries. When most New World populations were still in the throes of the hemisphere's most devastating loss, that of Quito is said to have experienced an anomalous growth.[20] This study suggests, however, that such growth was more apparent than real.

Despite reliance on works that are limited to the heartland, there is a general historiographical impression that the Audiencia of Quito boasted a stable and even growing population during the last decade of the sixteenth and throughout the seventeenth century. A closer look at both primary and secondary sources, however, reveals two problems that are worth investigating: (1) contradictory data, even for the central and north-central highlands, the area that has received the most scholarly attention; and (2) considerable regional variation of demographic experience throughout the audiencia.

The contradictions of the record are especially evident for the seven sierran corregimientos of Ibarra, Otavalo, Quito, Latacunga, Riobamba and Chimbo. Alchon and Tyrer's studies of this heartland area posit that the indigenous population began to level out in the late sixteenth century and increased substantially in the seventeenth.[21] Although this pattern coincides remarkably with what occurred in Mesoamerica, it is unusual within the Viceroyalty of Peru, where the population declined from the time of the conquest until approximately 1730 and then recovered rapidly. In Quito there was reportedly a striking sixteenth-century decline, followed by rapid increase in the seventeenth century, and then severe depopulation at the turn of the eighteenth century, followed by stabilization (table 2).[22]

Table 2: Indigenous Population of Highland Ecuador, 1520-1828

Year	Tributary Population	Total Population	Source
1520	216,000	1,080,000	Alchon[a]
1534	75,000–114,000	375,000–570,000	Alchon
1559	54,000	270,000	Alchon
1572	42,000–43,000	200,000	Alchon
1590/91	35,800	168,260	Tyrer[b]
	30,000	112,500	Alchon
1598	29,000	105,000	Alchon
1660s&	51,012	230,000	Tyrer
1670s	71,155	300,000	Alchon
1690	60,700	273,000	Tyrer
1700/10	40,000	164,000	Tyrer
	44,500	150,000	Alchon
1740	——	200,000	Minchom[c]
1780	——	217,000	Alchon
1789	44,000—48,000	220,000	Tyrer
1825/28	48,000	197,000	Tyrer, Minchom

Sources: [a]Alchon, Native Society, pp. 47, 80, and 115.
[b] Tyrer, Historia demográfica, pp. 33, 45, and 78–79
[c] Martin Minchom, "Demographic Change in Ecuador during the Eighteenth Century," Cultura 24 (1986): 465-68.
Note: Figures for the years up to and including 1598 encompass the entire highlands of Ecuador (from Ibarra in the north to Cuenca in the south); figures from the 1660s onward exclude Cuenca.

While waves of epidemics, natural disasters, and the decline of the textile industry induced the demographic crisis at the end of the seventeenth century, the unprecedented growth of the central and north-central sierra at the beginning of that century has not been adequately explained. Other demographic research has pointed to natural increase, the absence of a mining mita, the lessening virulence of disease, Andean immigration from other parts of the viceroyalty, a dispersed settlement pattern, and a cheap and abundant food supply as possible reasons for Quito's enviable position vis-à-vis other South American populations.[23] Nevertheless these conditions are not sufficiently different from those of many neighboring Andean regions to have made seventeenth-century Quito exempt from demographic decline; nor did they protect the region from extreme depopulation in the sixteenth and eighteenth centuries. Clearly this mystery is in need of more unraveling; perhaps an examination of the qualitative record will provide some clues.

The population history of Quito's heartland is punctuated by simultaneous evidence for both growth and decline.[24] An impressive number of late sixteenth-century bureaucrats reported an increase of the native population in the sierra. As early as 1571, Pedro Rodríguez de Aguayo gave the following assessment: "In the province of Quito the natives have grown in greater number after the Conquest than in any other part of Peru." Authorities in the city of Quito attributed demographic growth in 1573 to the "good life" the Indians were leading under Spanish rule. In 1576 the royal treasury reported that in the Province of Quito "the number of natives rises every day." Cuenca, Quito (city), and Santo Domingo de Chunchi all related population increases in 1582. And by the beginning of the seventeenth century, the royal officials of the audiencia consistently reported that the native population was expanding in the sierra.[25]

Table 3: Indigenous Population Increase in Chillos Valley, 1559–1591

Llajta	Visita of 1559 Persons	Census of 1591 Total Population	Percentage Change
Puembo	282	456	+62
Pingolquí	383	287	-25
El Ynga	177	498	+181
Urin Chillo (Zangolquí)	1,156	1,551	+34
Anan Chillo (Amaguaña)	1,088	1,194	+10
Uyumbicho	481	1,184	+146
Total:	3,567	5,180	+45

Sources: AGI, Justicia 683, as quoted in Salomon, Native Lords, pp. 175–77; RAH/M, Muñoz Collection, "Relación de Morales Figueroa . . . ," 1591.

A comparison of the visita of 1559 and the Morales Figueroa census of 1591 also points to explosive demographic growth for some towns in the highlands.[26] Although the 1559 visita is arranged by "units" and "persons," while the 1591 census is arranged by "tributarios," the latter can be converted to "total population" figures by using a factor of 4.7, making a comparison plausible (table 3).[27]

In thirty-two years, the population of these six sierran communities made an impressive leap, at a time when most of the indigenous populations of

Spanish America were still declining. Because Toledo's resettlement policy was implemented in the 1570s, however, other communities may have been incorporated into these six at that time, thus accounting for at least part of the increase.

Tyrer and Alchon's demographic analyses of the central and north-central sierra present an even more convincing case of population increase in the highlands. Tyrer estimates that the tributary population of this area rose from 30,700 to 51,012 between 1591 and 1660; Alchon calculates an increase from 26,563 to 71,155 (more than 2.6 times) between 1590 and 1670 (table 2). By comparing the Morales Figueroa census and the Relación de Zaruma of 1590–91 with Tyrer's and Alchon's projections for the 1660s and 1670s, one can extract population growth for specific areas of the central and north-central highlands (table 4).

Table 4: Tributary Population Increase in Heartland, 1590--1670s
(averages in parentheses)

Corregimiento	1590–91 Zaruma/Morales (tributaries)			1660s and 1670s Tyrer/Alchon (tributaries)			Percentage Change
Ibarra	3,313	3,464	(3,388)	2,435	3,044	(2,739)	-19
Otavalo	3,125	2,491	(2,808)	6,800	8,500	(7,650)	+172
Quito	5,125	3,777	(4,451)	13,070	19,265	(16,167)	+263
Ambato	2,125	1,987	(2,056)	4,178	6,011	(5,094)	+147
Latacunga	5,875	6,524	(6,199)	11,337	14,171	(12,754)	+105
Riobamba	5,625	2,709	(4,167)	10,430	17,500	(13,965)	+235
Chimbo[a]	1,375	396	(885)	2,131	2,664	(2,397)	+170

Sources:"Relación de Zaruma," in Jiménez de la Espada, Relaciones geograficas 3: 265–90; RAH/M, Muñoz Collection, "Relación de Morales Figueroa . . . ," 1591; Tyrer, Historia demográfica, p. 45; Alchon, Native Society, p. 80.
Note: Percentage changes are impressionistic since they were calculated by averaging the Zaruma and Morales figures for 1590 and 1591 and the Tyrer and Alchon figures for the 1660s and 1670s.
[a]Tyrer (p. 31) notes that the Morales Figueroa Census of 1591 omitted several towns in the Corregimiento of Chimbo, thereby underreporting the number of tributarios there.

Most heartland populations experienced, at least on paper, a dramatic increase, particularly those of Quito and Riobamba. Evidence for demographic growth in the highlands, however, is paralleled by just as convincing data for serious depopulation. Alchon's epidemiological history, for example, posits a population loss of more than 50 percent between 1559 and 1590. Her work and those of Robson Tyrer, Gualberto Arcos, Linda Newson, and Aquiles Pérez point to the severe epidemics of the years 1585–91 as the principal culprits.[28] Ironically these were the years (1570s, 1580s, and 1590s) during which numerous bureaucrats and civilians insisted that the indigenous population was proliferating.

Indeed a deeper analysis of the demographic record shows that this paradox resulted partly from population replenishment through migration. As the Andeans of the central and north-central highlands died off during the depopulating events of the sixteenth century, they were replaced systematically by migrants. Using this model the precipitous demographic decline of the period 1520 to 1598 (tables 1 and 2) represents a real loss of sierran tributaries, while the bureaucrats' insistence on a population increase is attributed to the presence of large numbers of migrants, or forasteros, in the sierra.[29]

One of the most pressing questions regarding this model is where would such a migration have originated?[30] The answer lies in regional differentiation. The positive curve described by previous historians is based on the demographic experience of the heartland, while only casual mention has been made of the simultaneous depopulation of peripheral areas.[31] Traditionally treated as two dissociated trends, this study suggests that there was a causal relationship between them. Thus Quito's perplexing demographic problem can be explained by a periphery-to-center migration.

Throughout the sixteenth and early seventeenth centuries, a population shift took place from peripheral areas to the center of the audiencia. This migration was partly responsible for emptying the northern and southern highlands as well as the adjacent montaña regions all along the intermontane corridor. At the same time, it also had the effect of creating an illusion of demographic growth in the central and north-central sierra.

As demonstrated more thoroughly in chapter 3, caciques succeeded in hiding much of the migrant population from the census takers; as a result, they did not appear in sixteenth-century demographic statistics. Throughout the seventeenth century, the Spaniards made a concerted effort to convert the forasteros and other hidden segments of the population to tributaries, artificially inflating the highland statistics of the 1660s and 1670s.

In order to prove this hypothesis, I will analyze specific periphery-to-center migrations, starting with those that originated in the montaña regions—traditional refuge areas for many Andean peoples. In 1576 royal officials described the temperate sierra as densely populated and the coastal areas, the eastern lowlands of Quijos and Yaguarzongo, and the southern mining regions as depopulated.[32] In 1582 another account expressed the dichotomy more succinctly: "The indigenous population of the temperate zones is increasing tremendously, while that of the hot regions is rapidly diminishing."[33] It was not abnormal for lowland populations to decrease at more alarming rates than those in the highlands, as witnessed by the early decimation of Peru's coastal groups. Epidemics spread more easily in warmer climates and took a heavier toll there. In the Ecuadorean case, however, highland groups proliferated at the same time that the lowlanders were nearing demographic collapse. While disease was, in part, responsible for lowland depopulation, vertical migration (that is, movement to higher, contiguous zones) also played a significant role.

By the 1570s the demographic situation of the lowlands had become critical. The coastal populations were the first to be decimated. When Cieza de León arrived in Guayaquil in the early 1550s, he reported that the Indians had died out. In 1576 officials depicted Guayaquil and Puerto Viejo as ghost towns.[34] The eastern and western montañas remained densely settled until the late sixteenth century, at which time they also experienced a precipitous decline.

The montaña regions figure significantly in vertical migration and sierran population replenishment. Provinces such as Yumbos, to the west, and Quijos and Yaguarzongo, to the east, were sources for a systematic movement to the central and north-central sierra. They lie adjacent to important highland centers, with which they were politically and economically affiliated.

Was the demographic pool of the eastern and western slopes large enough to generate a prolonged lowland-to-highland movement?[35] John Phelan estimates a pre-Hispanic eastern population of two hundred thousand, while Salomon suggests that the western region of Yumbos sustained a pre-Incaic population comparable to that of its sierran counterpart.[36] Indeed at a cabildo meeting in 1538, Gonzalo Díaz de Pinera defended his intention to conquer Yumbos, pointing out that Quito was devoid of Indians, while Yumbos was densely populated.[37]

Evidence also suggests that the populations of the eastern and western lowlands became inflated as a result of both the Inca and Spanish conquests. Incaic military architecture implies that the Inca feared incursions from the east, probably not only from Amazonian groups but also from highlanders who had retreated there.[38]

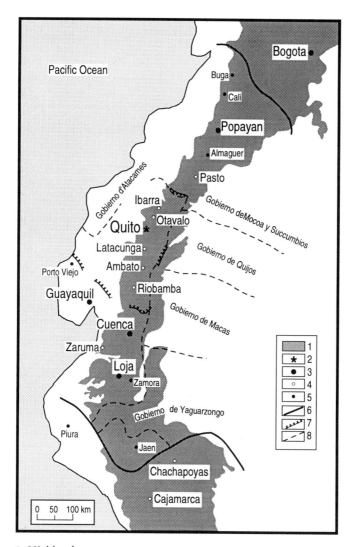

1. Highlands,
2. Seat of the Audiencia,
3. Spanish City,
4. Urban Center,
5. Town,
6. Boundaries of the Audiencia,
7. Boundaries of the Municipal District of Quito,
8. Boundaries of Gobiernos.

Map 2. Administrative Organization of Audiencia of Quito. Sixteenth Century

After the Spanish conquest, a similar swelling of adjacent lowland populations occurred. Upon their defeat in the highlands of Quito (1534), the Inca and their supporters retreated to Yumbos in the west and Quijos in the east.[39] Still in 1569 Andrés Contero, while exploring the upper River Daule in the western lowlands, heard news of Inca residents who had escaped there after the Spanish invasion.[40] The province of Esmeraldas, west of the northern sierra, was also a refuge for various highland groups. The Malabá, purportedly a Puruhá group, were discovered residing there in the seventeenth century.[41]

Conquest-induced flight created a population reserve in contiguous lowland areas from which highland caciques could draw in times of demographic crisis. Eventual Spanish expansion to these areas of refuge may also have prompted a return migration to the sierra. Highlanders had no reason to continue living in exile, once the whole region had suffered the same fate. Furthermore Spanish consolidation in these areas translated into the distribution of encomiendas and, as commonly reported, conditions in lowland encomiendas were exceptionally abysmal, especially in Quijos, Yaguarzongo, and Guayaquil.[42]

Still this movement had its primary roots in a pre-Hispanic lowland-highland relationship that stemmed from the requirements of the region's microvertical economy. Like most Andean societies, those of Quito benefited from an economy based on vertically contiguous but distinct ecological zones that included the *páramos,* the inter-Andean valleys, and the eastern and western lowlands.[43] Although some of these niches, or *pisos,* produced a wide range of products, none was self-sufficient enough to furnish an acceptable standard of living. Unlike the far-flung economic archipelagos of the southern Andes, however, Quito's compact but varied geography gave rise to a microvertical economy. A multiplicity of pisos were located within short distances of one another—a few days' journey at most. The close proximity of complementary ecological zones and the necessity for an exchange between them generated intimate economic and political relationships between highland communities and their lowland counterparts.[44] It was this intricate web of politico-economic alliances that formed the infrastructure for the lowland-to-highland movements of the early Spanish colony.

The breadth of pre-Incaic affiliations between the sierra and the eastern and western lowlands was impressive (figure 1). Note that lowland alliances have been uncovered for each of Quito's sierran tribes except the Puruhá; the latter did, however, develop the region's most extensive network of lowland colonies under the Inca.

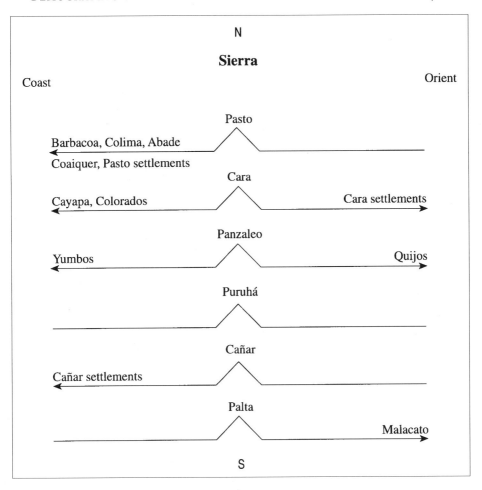

Figure 1. Aboriginal Lowland/Highland Political Affiliations.
Source: Murra, "Historic Tribes of Ecuador," 788–808.

A detailed examination of Panzaleo affiliations will be instructive. The Panzaleos controlled the central highland communities near the city of Quito and were linked to the Yumbos in the west and the Quijos in the east; the latter are described in the ethnographic literature as probable Panzaleo groups.[45] The Panzaleo-Yumbos connection is further borne out by inclusion of Yumbos in several sierran encomiendas. Salomon points out that the highlands around the city of Quito and the lowlands of Yumbos have traditionally been treated as a single political unit and that such unity may have its roots in the pre-Incaic past.[46]

According to Porras, remains classified as Cosanga-Píllaro have been found in both the Valley of Quijos and in the Panzaleo region of the sierra, placing the Panzaleo-Quijos connection as far back as 400 B.C. He interprets the presence of Cosanga artifacts in the sierra as evidence of an early lowland-to-highland migration.[47] Affiliation between these groups continued in the sixteenth century. In 1559 Gil Ramírez Dávalos conquered Quijos through the intercedence of Don Sancho Hacho, the cacique of Latacunga, a highland Panzaleo center; the latter was the brother-in-law of an important cacique of Quijos.[48]

Notably the Corregimiento of Quito, Panzaleo territory, experienced one of the most spectacular demographic growths of the audiencia in the late sixteenth and seventeenth centuries (see table 4). Clearly the Panzaleos' strong ties to Yumbos and Quijos prompted a migration from the eastern and western lowlands to the sierra. In previous works I have documented a significant movement from Quijos to the central highlands.[49] In light of the evidence presented above, however, an equally substantial migration from Yumbos to Quito is more than likely.

The region's numerous highland-lowland political affiliations were reinforced by important economic relations generated by the need for interzonal exchange. Since the pre-Hispanic mechanisms through which this exchange was made provided the infrastructure for a lowland-to-highland movement in the colonial period, they will be examined in some detail below.

Salomon's study of Quito's vertical economy discloses a multitude of indigenous strategies that facilitated mutual access to a variety of ecological resources. Among the mechanisms instrumental in promoting a lowland-to-highland movement were: barter between domestic units, kinship ties, and extraterritorial residence.

From the Corregimiento of Quito northward, highlanders often traveled two to four days into the western lowlands to exchange maize and other sierran foodstuffs for cotton, salt, and pepper. Salomon has documented this practice for the Quito-Yumbos area and also for Otavalo and its adjacent western lowlands.[50] Exchange between households was undoubtedly solidified by intercommunal marriage and child-loan, forming strong familial bonds between highland and lowland groups. Kinship ties may have facilitated a lowland-to-highland movement, particularly if the system of domestic exchange was disrupted by Spanish policies. Destructuration was evident in Quijos, for example, where the Spanish conquest of 1559 resulted in an initial breakdown of economic links with the sierra.[51] Likewise Spanish resettlement of several Yumbos pueblos in the 1580s must have altered that region's economy.

Economic mechanisms based on extraterritorial residence of highlanders in the lowlands were also instrumental in promoting a migration to the sierra. Through sharecropping arrangements and mixed colonies, highland groups often gained access to products requiring warmer climates, such as cotton, coca, fruit, and capsicum pepper. Thus the presence of substantial numbers of highland peoples in the lowlands created a demographic reserve there. Sierran caciques must have recalled these colonists when Spanish disruption obstructed vertical economies or when demographic crises occurred in the sierra.

Although Salomon documents extraterritorial residence of highlanders in the lowlands all along the intermontane corridor, the Puruhá were especially noted for a complex system of colonies that ranged from nearby tropical slopes to distant coastal plains. In 1557 the communities of Juan de Padilla's encomienda still maintained five cotton colonies, one salt colony, and one colony for capsicum pepper, most of which were located in Chimbo, on the western slopes. They also maintained maize and coca plantations in the eastern lowlands.[52]

Note that these were the operations of only one encomienda; there were at least four other large encomiendas in the Corregimiento of Riobamba during the second half of the sixteenth century—the period when return migrations would have taken place.[53] Furthermore, the Inca state maintained coca plantations in both Yumbos and Quijos, worked by Puruhá, which probably continued under local auspices well into the sixteenth century. In short the number of Puruhá living in the montaña regions was considerable.

The extraterritorial residence of numerous highlanders in the lowlands provided the infrastructure for a lowland-to-highland migration in the following ways. First, Spanish distribution of encomiendas and resettlement policies often disrupted native vertical economies, signaling the collapse of some colonies, whose inhabitants returned to their nuclear communities in the sierra. Second, demographic crises in the highlands must have made the maintenance of extraterritorial settlements untenable, compelling the recall of their members. Soon after the Spanish conquest, some Andean communities began to neglect the upkeep of distant colonies, particularly those cultivating coca. The Manchac abandoned their distant plantations at Huánuco, while Pacaibamba, east of Cuenca, was described as uninhabited in 1582; in the past it had been covered with coca fields.[54]

During the late sixteenth and early seventeenth centuries, the cotton lands were also abandoned in the Audiencia of Quito. In the early sixteenth century, natives made their attire exclusively from cotton and produced a large surplus for tribute.[55] By the early seventeenth century, the cotton lands of Yumbos and Quijos were severely depopulated. Tellingly the population of Chimbo, former site of numerous cotton colonies, also languished, while that of its highland counterpart, Riobamba, quadrupled between 1590 and 1660.[56]

Third, highland communities that did not exercise political control over the lands on which their colonies were established, but instead depended on agreements with lowland caciques, often experienced evictions after the Spanish conquest. In a cabildo session of January 1, 1551, it was reported that highland groups were being ejected from lands in subtropical zones that had been assigned to them by the Inca.[57] Once the Incaic veneer was lifted, some colonies were placed in jeopardy by the apparent hegemony of lowland caciques and their members forced to return to the sierra.

Having identified a significant population in the montaña, further demographic analysis bears out a causal relationship between depopulation in subtropical zones and population growth in the sierra. In 1578 Fray Pedro de la Peña, bishop of Quito, complained that he left Yumbos exhausted from administering to a dense population.[58] In the early 1580s, the tributary population of Yumbos was only 4,701;[59] by 1591 it had dwindled to 1,072.[60] Finally in the late seventeenth century, the Yumbos were declared extinct.[61] It is revealing that as Yumbos languished, its sierran counterpart, the Corregimiento of Quito, experienced substantial demographic growth (see table 4).

Some might attribute Yumbos's depopulation to its location in the unhealthy "hot lands" and to the high mortality of the 1585–91 pandemic. The demographic stability of the coastal areas during this period, however, suggests that either the spread of disease was not uniform in the lowlands or that epidemics were not the only reason for population decline in the montañas.[62] Indeed the prevalence of disease may have helped to trigger a migration to the healthier sierra.

In Yaguarzongo and Quijos, a similar demographic trend occurred during the same period. In 1545 the viceroy sent to Yaguarzongo to recruit soldiers for the War of Quito;[63] evidently it was densely populated. In 1578 the bishop reportedly confirmed over 15,000 Amerindians there.[64] In 1591 the caciques of Yaguarzongo and Jaen reported that their populations had declined from 30,000 to 1,000 during the epidemic of 1589.[65] Since a mor-

Table 5: Tributary Population of Gobernación of Quijos, 1559–1608

Town	1559	1577	1608	Percentage Change
Baeza	12,000	5,013	980	-92 (from 1559)
Avila		919	240	-74 (from 1577)
Archidona		871	215	-75 (from 1577)

Sources: Marcos Jiménez de la Espada, *Relaciones geográficas,* 1:74–78; Diego de Ortegón, "Descripción de la governación de Quijos, Sumaco y la Canela," *Cuadernos de Historia y Arquelogía* 33 (1973):16–26.

tality rate of 97 percent in one year is impossible, a good number of their subjects must have opted for migration.

Similarly when the Spaniards entered Quijos in 1559, they were met by 30,000 to 40,000 native peoples.[66] Conversely in 1603 the audiencia's president reported: "The Indians of Quijos and Yaguarzongo have been finished off" (table 5).[67] In short the late sixteenth and early seventeenth centuries witnessed the near total depopulation of the eastern and western lowlands.

As the population curve of the adjacent lowlands declined, that of the highlands reportedly rose. While official comments herald an increase in the sierra, the overall statistics of the sixteenth century do not corroborate it, showing instead a depopulation rate of nearly 50 percent between 1561 and 1591 (see table 1). Local records, however, indicate stability and even growth for specific highland regions, making it possible to analyze particular lowland/highland dichotomies and to trace population movements within vertically contiguous areas.

The demographic record of 1586 can be compared with that of 1591 for the corregimientos of the central and north-central sierra. Dividing the total population of 1586 by Tyrer's factor of 4.7 results in a tributary population of 25,000 in the heartland (see table 1). This figure's close approximation to Morales Figueroa's 1591 undercount of 24,380 tributaries indicates that the population of the central and north-central sierra remained statistically stable between 1586 and 1591. Enigmatically these were years of severe epidemics that reportedly had a decided impact on Quito's sierra.

The more specific case of Otavalo is also pertinent. In 1582 the province reported 2,360 tributaries; in 1591, the Morales Figueroa census cited 2,011, while the 1590 "Relación de Zaruma" claimed 2,500.[68] Thus between 1582 and 1591, Otavalo exhibited a curious demographic constancy. At the same time, the adjacent towns of Lita, Quilca, and Caguasquí on the western slopes declined from 700 to 572.[69] Notably these towns had important political and economic affiliations with Otavalo.

Similarly the encomienda of Francisco Ruiz in the Chillos Valley (Corregimiento of Quito) is an example of unexplained growth in the sierra. Between 1559 and 1591, its population increased by 45 percent (see table 3). Note that the site of the encomienda was contiguous with Yumbos to the west and Quijos to the east, both of which became depopulated prior to 1591.

In spite of severe epidemics and the abuses of the Spanish regime, the Andean populations of specific regions in the central and north-central highlands remained stable and often grew in the late sixteenth century; their contiguous lowland counterparts languished during the same period. Evidently some sierran communities were able to remain demographically stable because they were fed by the populations of the adjacent lowlands.

That population replenishment occurred in the sierra is implicit in a statement made by licenciado Francisco de Auncibay, a judge of the audiencia. In 1592 he described the Indian towns of the central and north-central sierra as overcrowded and marveled: "When an epidemic hits and kills part of the population, within a very brief time, it returns to its previous size."[70]

More concrete documentation also exists for specific lowland-to-highland movements, some of them planned by the native leadership. The visita of 1559 listed sixty-four "units" (households) of forasteros resident in the communities of Ruiz's highland encomienda; thirty-one emanated from Sigchos, Tomavela, and Chimbo, all located on the western slopes.[71] Similarly between 1571 and 1581, 1,000 Tomavelans moved to Ambato, Quito, and Pelileo, in the central sierra. This was apparently a planned migration; the caciques of Tomavela kept track of their number and location and continued to tax them.[72] Likewise thousands of Quijos moved from the eastern lowlands in the 1560s and joined sierran communities.[73] Over time many of these forasteros were statistically detached from their original pueblos and integrated into the sierran population.

In addition to organized lowland-to-highland movements, many Andeans also migrated spontaneously. Independent migrants came from all parts of the audiencia, including the lowlands. In 1592 the author of the

"Relación de Zaruma" described the thousands of vagabond Indians resident in the sierra as emanating from both temperate and hot zones.[74]

The highland population was further inflated by a return migration of
mitimaes, those who had been relocated by the Inca. Just as some foreign
mitimaes stationed in Quito returned home shortly after the Spanish conquest, others whom the Inca had removed to various parts of the empire
eventually made their way back to Quito. The case of the Cañari is instructive. In 1582 the "Relación de Cuenca" reported that the number of Cañari
had risen since the conquest from 3,000 to 12,000.[75] Conversely the population of the Yucay Valley near Cuzco, where numerous Cañari had been
transferred by the Inca, declined from 3,000 in 1530 to 780 in 1558.[76] Return migration is undoubtedly a partial explanation.

The reducciones of the 1570s also contributed to population growth in
the sierra. In some cases montaña peoples were resettled in the nearby highlands. Those who moved peaceably were often rewarded with a ten-year
exemption from tribute and the mita.[77] The author of the "Relación de
Cuenca" reported, for example, that only 80 of the 190 tributaries of San
Bartolomé de Aroczapa were native to the area; the rest were brought from
the montaña on the other side of the cordillera.[78] In seventeenth-and eighteenth-century records, a *parcialidad* (administrative unit of Andeans) called
Macas appears in Azogues, as does an ayllu (Andean kinship group) of
Quijos in Tumbaco, outside the city of Quito.[79] Whether these incorpora-
tions were the result of Spanish reducciones or Andean-directed movements
is uncertain. It is, however, noteworthy that both Macas and Quijos were
lowland regions contiguous to the highland towns in which these peoples
were found.[80]

Vertical migration, then, is a viable explanation for the paradoxical demographic stability of the sierra. During the second half of the sixteenth
century, the adjacent lowlands, both east and west, provided human rein-
forcements to the highlands, perhaps on a systematic basis. In order to fill
population shortages in the sierra, Andean leaders undoubtedly orchestrated part of this movement; highland caciques, for example, reportedly
lured the Quijos to the "fertile" lands of Quito.[81]

It may seem absurd that indigenous peoples migrated toward, instead of
away from, the central and north-central highlands—regions that were
under even more solid Spanish control than the areas they vacated. Nevertheless Quito's compact geographical setting did not lend itself well to long-
distance "escape" movements, since to move just a little too far west or too
far east was to end in the Pacific Ocean or the Amazonian jungles. Unlike

areas of the southern Andes, where inhabitants could travel fairly far and still be in the same ecological zone—the altiplano, for example—the ethnic peoples of Quito were limited by the microverticality of their economies and by the abbreviated extension of habitable space. The lowland-to-highland movement was also facilitated by the less-extreme climatic variations between the region's major ecological zones. In comparison with Peru and Bolivia, both the lower elevation of its major peaks and its position on the equator determine that Quito's sierran climate is milder and hence more amenable to the migratory adaptation of humans.[82]

The lowland-to-highland migrations analyzed above were not, however, the only periphery-to-center movements of the second half of the sixteenth century. Rather they were paralleled by intrasierran migrations from the northern and southernmost reaches of the highlands to the center of the audiencia. Throughout the colonial period, but most especially during the early years of Spanish rule, a substantial migration occurred from the Gobernación of Popayán in the north to points south. At the same time, a lesser and shorter-lived movement took place from the southern mining regions (Cuenca, Zamora, and Zaruma) to the heartland.

Sixteenth-century sources for Popayán are characterized by a constant barrage of official complaints about vast depopulation. In 1564 during an official investigation of the governor, Pedro de Agreda, one witness testified that the district of Popayán originally had an indigenous population of sixty thousand that had since dwindled to eight or nine thousand. In addition he claimed that the towns of Cali, Cartago, and Enzerma were inhabited at the time of their foundations by eight, ten, and twelve thousand Andeans, but now had only one thousand, fifteen hundred, and two thousand, respectively. A more appalling example was the town of Carma, which boasted a population of twenty thousand at the time of the conquest and which by 1564 had scarcely eight hundred inhabitants.[83] More disinterested accounts reported similarly startling depopulation rates. Ecclesiastical and official reports of the late sixteenth century claimed that twenty thousand Andeans were registered in the city of Pasto during the visita of 1559, while in 1583 only eight thousand remained.[84]

The precipitous decline of Popayán's population was attributed to numerous factors, many of which are summarized in the following quote from the investigation of 1564:

> The *vecinos* and encomenderos exonerate themselves of all blame, saying that sickness, pestilence and tribal wars are responsible for the disappearance of the Indians, but they are wrong. The Indians have been visited by a new pestilence, not known to them before,

which has ended in their ruination, and that pestilence is the Spaniard. The Spaniards have consumed the Indians and this is the
pestilence and the war of which they speak . . . [85]

According to a panoply of sources on sixteenth-century Popayán, the
Spanish pestilence to which this witness testified included forced labor in
the mines, personal service, Indian slavery, and battle deaths in the persistent warfare between resistant Andean groups and the colonial administration. The perils of mining work in Popayán were notorious and caused
widespread death and flight from the area. According to an account of 1570,
caciques were required to deliver 10 percent of their subjects to the mines
for periods of eight months and were obliged to replace runaways systematically with other subjects from their jurisdictions. Personal service or
unpaid labor, although outlawed by the New Laws of the 1540s and repressed
in most of the viceroyalty by the 1560s, was still in full swing in Popayán in
1598 and continued into the seventeenth century.[86]

In Popayán as well as in other remote areas, such as Quijos, Yaguarzongo
and Macas, abuses of the indigenous population were more extreme. Distance from colonial power centers led to autonomous bureaucracies and
uncontrolled civilian populations. Both often engaged in unbridled exploitation, giving rise to a type of "free-for-all" ambience that central authorities found difficult to hold in check. One incredulous audiencia president
reported in 1564:

> In the gobernación of Popayán which is located at quite a distance
> from any audiencia, there have been many excesses against the
> Indians including abuses in the mines and personal service. There is
> no order or moderation there as witnessed by the sale of whole
> repartimientos of Indians as though they were flocks of sheep. Even
> the governors of the province have been responsible for selling
> Indians to whomever would pay the highest price . . . [87]

The consequences of these abuses were not limited to mortality, as some
authors imply, but also included a rather sizable population movement to
points south, most especially of peoples from the region of Pasto. The
Pastuzos took up residence in numerous towns throughout the length and
breadth of the audiencia. And while their names appear in lawsuits and
censuses as far south as Loja, most migrated to the neighboring
Corregimiento of Otavalo, just south of Pasto territory.

This north-to-center movement was, in part, orchestrated by the caciques
of the Corregimientos of Otavalo and Quito. In 1557 Francisco Ponce, an
official of Popayán, reported that many Indians had left the domains of
their caciques to become subjects of other caciques, who hid them. Pre-

tending to defend the interests of the Andean leadership, he requested a royal provision ordering them to return to their native lands to be christianized and pay their tributes.[88]

In 1568 the president of the audiencia forwarded a report, signed by all the vecinos of Pasto, to the Council of the Indies describing the flow of these migrations:

> The city of Pasto [gobernación de Popayán] is contiguous to the city of Quito where there are many natives who speak the same language as the Pasto Indians. For this reason, the natives of the jurisdiction of Pasto, in order to avoid resettlement and indoctrination in the Catholic Faith, have left their lands and pueblos and have gone and continue to go each day to the jurisdiction of the city of Quito and to other places where they hide themselves among the natives of the provinces of that city. And because they are all of the same language, the latter hide them, and if this problem is not resolved, the city of Pasto will become so depopulated that it will collapse. I request that your majesty send a royal decree demanding that all Indians who have left their towns and are in the district of the city of Quito and other areas return to their lands and towns with their wives and children and that the caciques, principales and other Indians who have them in their service relinquish them . . .[89]

Clearly a substantial north-to-center movement took place in the 1560s, whose specific flow was from the jurisdiction of the city of Pasto in the Gobernación of Popayán to that of Quito. At that time the district of the city of Quito included all territory north to the city limits of Pasto and south to the limits of Cuenca;[90] this means that the Pastuzos could have taken refuge in all the corregimientos located between these points— Otavalo, Quito, Latacunga, Ambato, and Riobamba. Their favorite target areas, however, were Otavalo and Quito, the closest corregimientos to Pasto territory.

That the caciques of Quito and Otavalo not only received the Pastuzos in their communities but also induced them to migrate is corroborated in the following letter, written by the Cabildo of Pasto to the king in 1571:

> . . . the repartimientos and towns of the city of Pasto border on those of the city of Quito and for this reason, many natives of the repartimientos of Pasto have moved and continue to move to those of Quito . . . where they are not enumerated and registered and since there is no accounting of them, the other Indians hide them from the priest and use their services . . . the Indians of the district of Quito are more intelligent and cunning than the Pastuzos and so they hold them in

servitude as though they were slaves and for this purpose they attract them and lure them to their towns and then hide them in forests and ravines where the priest never sees them . . . [91]

The steady flow from north to center decimated the Gobernación of Popayán and fed the populations and labor pools of the central and north-central sierra. Migration from Popayán to Quito, though difficult to quantify, was considerable and had a protracted history. In 1649 Don Juan de Salazar, governor of Popayán, reported that all 143 Indians of the encomienda of the deceased Don Joseph de Bolivar y la Redonda were found to be fugitives in the town of Otavalo, where they had escaped their tribute and mita responsibilities for years.[92] As late as 1707, a census recording land and house ownership was made of all the peoples of Pupiales (Gobernación of Popayán) resident in Otavalo, Quito, and Latacunga.[93] Apparently the north-to-center movement continued unabated, although an improved state apparatus was now able to track down forasteros for tax purposes.

While the corresponding south-to-center movement is not as well documented, inhabitants of the southern mining regions most likely fled north to escape the rigors of mining work. Sixteenth-century records for the towns around Cuenca and Loja show consistent depopulation and labor shortage.[94] Even the few local peoples who were distributed in encomiendas did not acquiesce easily to the demands of the mines. Spanish complaints abound regarding native resistance to mining, mortality, and flight to other regions.

Among the solutions proffered were slave imports, the resettlement of Andean vagabonds near the mines, and a mita that would draw upon the populous central and north-central provinces. In 1579 officials presented a plan to settle a substantial number of Puruhá in the area, but were staunchly opposed by Riobamba's encomenderos, who feared for their tributes. In 1586 Juan Sevillano, a miner of Cuenca, requested a license to import 600 slaves to work the mines of Zaruma, Zamora, and Santiago de las Montañas, because three-quarters of the Indians had died off.[95] Tellingly a royal judge, Licenciado Francisco de Auncibay, proposed in 1587 that 2,000–3,000 Indians from the central and north-central sierra be sent to Zaruma, because their populations were healthy, while those of the south had declined seriously.[96]

Severe depopulation of the southern highlands is also evident in sixteenth-century censuses. According to Morales Figueroa, the mining regions of Cuenca and Zamora were among the most depopulated of the audiencia in 1591 (see table 1). Although Newson attributes this to the pandemic of 1585–91, it is evident that migration accounted for a substan-

tial part of the decline.[97] A more empirical example is the 1581 inspection
of Cañaribamba and Garrochamba, Andean towns whose populations were
subject to labor in the mines of Zaruma. The bishop of Quito reported that
Cañaribamba's population had declined from 2,100 to 500 and that of
Garrochamba from 2,000 to 183 in six years. When asked about the missing inhabitants, the people replied that some were at the mines in Zaruma,
but that the majority had fled precisely because they did not wish to work
in the mines.[98]

Barring concealment of numerous residents, the two towns suffered,
within a six-year period, depopulation rates of 76 percent and 91 percent,
respectively. Since the years 1575 to 1581 were not witness to severe epidemics—the most serious periods of illness were both before and after these
years (1558–60 and 1585–91)—this decline cannot be wholly attributed to
mortality. Undoubtedly some Andeans died in the mines, but the inhabitants of both towns reported that fleeing also played a significant role in the
alarming drop in population.

A pressing question concerning the demographic decline and flight of
the southern highlanders is quite simply, where did they go? It would be
methodological folly to assume that they fled to the central and north-central sierra just because the latter's populations were increasing. Admittedly
there is little hard data with which to trace the movements of the resistant
miners; nevertheless bits and pieces show up occasionally in disperse locations. Cañari names, for example, appear in central-sierran censuses in the
seventeenth century. It is possible that the descendants of forasteros who
took refuge there during the sixteenth-century mining boom were later incorporated into the ayllus as *originarios* (original kin members)—a common administrative practice in the Audiencia of Quito.

Peoples from Cuenca and Loja also appear in seventeenth-century lawsuits and investigations as residents in the audiencia's heartland. Some
movement undoubtedly took place from south to center, although its magnitude and exact flows cannot be determined. Since the Andeans of the
southern highlands were substantially reduced in number by the Inca conquest, reprisals, and population transfers, the late-sixteenth-century movement to the central sierra must have been modest. It does, however, bear
out the centripetal tendency of population movements during the latter
half of the sixteenth century.

Whether emanating from the lowlands or from the northern and southern sierra, periphery-to-center migrations were shaped principally by the
exigencies of the Spanish economy. During the sixteenth and seventeenth
centuries, the majority of Spanish enterprises were located in the central

and north-central highlands and required sizable work forces. The labor-intensive nature of the obrajes and one of the highest tribute and mita levies of the colonial world must have combined to exert unusual demographic pressure on the indigenous peoples of Quito. How did highland caciques provide workers for all these sectors and still maintain enough labor to reproduce their communities in the face of depopulating events?

Indeed many chiefly lineages of Quito maintained their traditional positions of authority until well into the eighteenth century. Surely long-term retentions of power were not accomplished by failing the Spaniards in the one thing that mattered most, the provision of labor. The staffing of the obrajes, for example, remained fairly stable throughout the sixteenth and seventeenth centuries.[99] On the contrary the highland caciques of Quito were able to stave off an erosion of power by recruiting labor from among the forastero mass.[100]

Intra-heartland Migrations

The periphery-to-center movements of the second half of the sixteenth century both resulted in and were partially paralleled by short-distance movements within the central and north-central sierra itself. The temporary displacements of the early years not only depopulated the highlands but also left vacant extensive tracts of land upon which the Spaniards encroached. Thus the demographic reconcentration brought about by the return migrations of the 1560s through the 1580s, while at first prompted by land availability in the sierra, soon generated enormous pressure on the resources of certain regions. Since subsequent years (1574–1628) witnessed the steady growth of the Spanish population as well, the Andean migrants often found themselves competing, not only with established colonists who had taken over prime lands during their absence, but with a multitude of new Spanish immigrants who intruded on their resources with impunity.[101]

The resultant land shortage was most severe in the Corregimientos of Quito and Otavalo, where lands were logically more desirable, owing to their proximity to the audiencia's largest city and its market opportunities. There land scarcity set off another movement in the late 1570s, which intensified at the turn of the seventeenth century, this time of divested Andeans in search of either employment or subsistence lands.

Although some of these migrations were directed toward the Spanish sphere—that is, toward cities and haciendas—many were "musical chairs" movements; they occurred most often between Andean towns of contiguous provinces and had as their most important pull factor the lands of absentees. By 1600 nearly every Andean town had a substantial population of absentees, who fled to avoid tribute and forced labor. The caciques then rented out or offered their lands to the absentees of other pueblos in return for services, thus effecting an interprovincial exchange of population.

From 1580 to 1620, the Corregimiento of Quito experienced the audiencia's most serious land problems and hence the most out-migration. The Cabildo of Quito, in the early years, granted so much land to the first vecinos that by 1578, the city and towns in its district were completely hemmed in by privately held lands. Since most of these concessions were made to its own officers, their descendants monopolized extensive tracts of land to everyone else's detriment.[102] Consequently, both Spaniards and Andeans encroached on the *ejidos* (common pasturelands), building houses, planting crops, and raising livestock, throughout the sixteenth century.[103]

Land-grabbing by early vecinos was facilitated by the temporary absence of displaced Andeans; their eventual return, combined with the Spanish grantees' monopoly of resources, produced an agrarian crisis, especially in the environs of the city of Quito. Erosion caused by European livestock and further encroachment pushed the Andeans to marginal lands at a very early stage of colonization. Only eight years after the conquest, the cabildo ordered Diego Suárez to withdraw from his land grants because they prejudiced the indigenous peoples.[104] In 1598 the bishop of Quito, Fray Luis López de Solís, complained that land seizure in some areas had extended to "the doors of the Indians' houses."[105]

By the year 1551, other natural resources were being depleted as well, and the Andeans had already been squeezed out onto the timberlands. In protection of the peoples of Cotocollao and Pomasqui, north of the city of Quito, the cabildo prohibited the opening of new irrigation ditches. Deforestation, evident in the same year, prompted the cabildo to prohibit the Indians from clearing the forest under penalty of a hundred lashes.[106]

The case of Uyumbicho, an Andean community four leagues from the city of Quito, illustrates the pressure on natural resources. The land squeeze experienced by its inhabitants and the Spaniards' exasperation over deforestation are recorded in cabildo sessions spanning forty-three years. In 1553 the cabildo visited Uyumbicho and discovered that the Andeans had cleared the timberlands and were raising livestock and practicing slash-and-burn agriculture on them. It ordered that they be evicted and publicly whipped if they returned. Apparently they declined to move, for in 1563 the cabildo issued another warning.[107]

By 1596 deforestation had become so severe that the cabildo decided to take urgent action. Before charting its course, it interviewed the priest, caciques, and Spanish residents of Uyumbicho. Fray Joan de Paz testified that the Indians planted crops in the town's forest because they did not have sufficient subsistence lands. These lands could only be cultivated for two years before new clearings were required, with the result that Uyumbicho's peoples had occupied all the town's nearby slopes and the forest going toward Panzaleo. Ultimately the cabildo decided to forcibly evict them and assign them new lands. It was hard pressed to find land, however, and ironically ended by granting them lands in another forest.[108]

The dilemma of Uyumbicho was far from anomalous. In 1575 the cabildo reported that a new Indian town had illegally been established on the ejido of Chillogallo and that another town, Machángara, had spread out onto the same ejido.[109] In 1578 when the audiencia proposed to settle all the *yanaconas* (unattached Andeans) and vagabonds of the city in two pueblos, it had difficulty finding lands on which to establish them. Because the early cabildo had made such excessive grants, it was common for older vecinos to possess lands that covered three leagues. The audiencia subsequently ordered that lands be taken from Spaniards to build the new towns and that they be compensated with other lands.

As the land squeeze became exacerbated in the late sixteenth century, the rate of migration stepped up, as indigenous peoples sought ways to survive the dispossession of their resources. By 1600 officials already cited Spanish land encroachment as the most serious push factor for Andean migrations from the Corregimiento of Quito.[110] Again in 1609 the audiencia reported that the towns within five leagues of the city of Quito were severely depopulated, due to migrations caused by extreme land shortage.[111] In the same year, Don Sancho Díaz de Zurbano, a royal treasury official, announced that land divestment of the native population had given rise to excessive absenteeism in the forty-five towns in the district of Quito, resulting in serious tribute deficits, known as *rezagos*.[112]

Similar complaints also emanated from the Corregimiento of Otavalo, Quito's northern neighbor. In 1620 and 1623, the president of the audiencia, Antonio Morga, and General Pedro Ponce Castillejo cited the theft and illegal purchase of Andean lands as motives for out-migration and absenteeism, which in turn were responsible for the precarious fiscal state of Otavalo's crown repartimiento. Morga emphasized that there had been "no considerable mortality or consumption of Indians"; rather the principal cause of the province's downfall had been native migrations to other provinces.[113]

In short the years from 1580 to around 1620 saw an agrarian crisis in the Corregimientos of Quito and Otavalo that stimulated intrasierran population movements. Although land shortage and out-migration would subsequently become generalized problems, the corregimientos located farther from the audiencia's power center temporarily escaped this divestment. During the years under discussion, they often became places of refuge, where land was available in return for a fee or services paid to local caciques.[114]

Conclusion

The disruptive events of the early Spanish colony caused widespread population displacement away from the center and toward marginal areas of the audiencia. This, in combination with the traditional extraterritorial residence of Andean colonists in the lowlands, resulted initially in the demographic inflation of the eastern and western montañas. At the same time that the Spanish conquest expanded to include these traditional places of refuge and colonial activities lessened the effectiveness of vertical economies, the highlands suffered population shortages as a result of epidemic disease and the labor demands of the Spanish regime. This conjuncture then prompted a return migration to the central and north-central highlands. A simultaneous movement also occurred from the northern- and southernmost reaches of the sierra toward the center—a movement generated both by abysmal working conditions in the mines and the abuses typical of remote colonial centers. In the interim, however, Spaniards had encroached on Andean lands, especially in the environs of the city of Quito. Land shortage, then, became the major catalyst for subsequent intrasierran movements, as indigenous peoples searched for alternative resources.

Three major trends can be identified in the migration history of the sixteenth-century Audiencia of Quito: (1) an initial dispersion to marginal areas, brought about in part by Spanish action (1534–60); (2) demographic reconcentration in the central and north-central sierra, which resulted from Andean initiatives and was achieved both through the spontaneous migrations of individuals and the planned movements of the native leadership (1560–90); and (3) subsequent intrasierran exchanges of population as a consequence of land divestment in the Corregimientos of Quito and Otavalo (1580–1620). Put more succinctly, the movements of the sixteenth century can be characterized by demographic dispersion, reconcentration, and exchange.

More importantly the constant and widespread movement of the indigenous population of Quito during this first century of Spanish rule brings into question both the vast depopulation rates of the sixteenth century

(85–90 percent) and the remarkable demographic recovery of the seven-teenth century proposed by other historians. With relation to the first, it is also fair to conclude that the prevalence of migration casts aspersions on most studies of sixteenth-century population decline in Spanish America, especially those based on an overreliance on colonial census and tribute records. Lastly migration constitutes a form of Andean agency at its most rudimentary level and must be taken into account in any demographic his-tory of the Andean region. If it is not, scholars run the risk of writing popu-lation histories that do not tell us anything about indigenous peoples except that they died.

2

Fleeing Toward the Enemy
Seventeenth-Century Migration Patterns

The constant human movement described in chapter 1 continued unabated throughout the seventeenth century. As the vise of depopulation and colonial demands drew tighter, native peoples increasingly sought relief through migration and forasterismo. All over the Andes, the words *ausente* (absentee), *forastero* (outsider), and *rezagos* (tribute arrears) punctuated the desperate reports of colonial bureaucrats. Other Andeanists have posited that from one-third to two-thirds of the indigenous population were forasteros by the 1680s; as will be seen subsequently, the Ecuadorean highlands were not an exception to this high absentee rate.[1]

Literally all Andean migration studies of this period have focused on the southern Andes, where most movements revolved around mining operations at Potosí. There the mining mita was both the motive force behind native population movements and the determinant factor in migration flows; Andeans migrated either toward the mines to work for wages or away from obligated provinces to escape the mining mita. The study of seventeenth-century Quito, where there was no mining mita, provides a universe free of the immediate shadow of Potosí—although indirectly affected by it—and perhaps lends an opportunity for a varied and more nuanced analysis of Andean migration.

Native population movements of seventeenth-century Quito differed, both qualitatively and quantitatively, from those of the earlier colony and ended in the radical transformation of Andean and Spanish societies. As demonstrated in chapter 1, the lowland-to-highland and intrasierran movements of the sixteenth century occurred most often between Andean communities. Dispossessed and abused Amerindians searched for subsistence and were recruited by caciques desiring to fill labor shortages in their districts. These migrations, while disruptive to the balance of power among native leaders, served to retain the majority of the indigenous population in the Indian sphere, where its labor was available to the native economy. In contrast seventeenth-century movements were increasingly directed toward the Spanish sphere, a pattern that carried labor away from Andean communities and toward European enterprises.

Although native movement toward the Spanish sphere began at the inception of colonial rule, it was limited in the sixteenth century by encomenderos' interests and land availability in most regions. Some movement toward European cities and enterprises did occur, however, as witnessed by the continual complaints of Spanish officials and Andean caciques about the increasing incidence of *yanaconaje*.[2] Amerindians who were uprooted during the wars of the sixteenth century often became yanaconas, or retainers of the Spaniards they served, and continued to live detached from their communities. This group was surreptitiously inflated, however, by migrants who voluntarily entered the employ of Spaniards in order to escape tribute and forced labor.

Artisans and domestic servants also sought protected status by migrating to the Spanish sphere. The number of Andean artisans in the city of Quito expanded continually during the sixteenth century. López de Solís, bishop of Quito, complained in 1596 that "any Indian who wishes dedicates himself to artisanry and . . . is [therefore] exempt from the mita." He contended that there were so many migrant artisans that the Indian towns could not fulfill their labor quotas.[3] The number of Andeans, especially women, who left their communities, both voluntarily and forcibly, to become servants in urban centers was also sizable. Judging from royal decrees and local complaints, the kidnapping of young women, called *chinas,* for service in Spanish homes was a widespread practice in Quito.[4]

In addition to the yanaconas, artisans, and domestic servants, there were also the ubiquitous mitayos (forced laborers), who took up residence in the places of their tours of duty. Although Quito was not exposed to the pervasive abuses of the mining mita, as were other parts of the viceroyalty, its peoples were subject to an unending panoply of mitas for obrajes, agriculture, transport, domestic service, public works, timber and fodder, and *tambos* (supply stations).[5] The region also had the colony's highest labor quota—one-fifth of the tributary population instead of the customary one-seventh.

Caciques protested bitterly that their subjects never returned from these mitas and instead took up residence in Spanish urban centers or haciendas, where they frequently formed whole new communities. The "mitayo who stayed behind" was a perennial problem. In 1630 the cacique of Guaranda (Chimbo) attributed the depopulation of Chimbo to mitayos who remained in Ambato long after their tours of duty. Seventy-two years later, another Chimbo cacique, Don Manuel Lema of Pallatanga, complained that his subjects never returned from the mita in Riobamba. To support his claim he presented a 1645 decree calling for the forced return of Pallatangans from Riobamba, indicating that the population drain on Chimbo occasioned by truant or abducted mitayos had had a protracted history.[6]

During the sixteenth century, then, movement from the Indian to the Spanish sphere progressed from a trickle to a steady outflow, but it had not yet reached a magnitude prejudicial to the integrity of most Andean communities. The Corregimiento of Quito, however, was an exception to this rule, since there the exodus from the native sphere reached serious proportions sooner than in areas distant from the audiencia's political and economic center. In the city of Quito and its environs, land divestment and native displacement to the Spanish sphere were early and swift. Indeed sixteenth-century population movements in this region foreshadowed the pan-audiencia movements of the seventeenth century. This prototypical pattern was eventually repeated all along the intermontane corridor, with the same demographic results.

As the Spanish population increased and that of the indigenous peoples dwindled, the colonists appropriated the resources of more and more distant Andean communities. The production of textiles and agricultural goods, the mainstays of Quito's economy, passed to the Spanish sphere. As the new market economy eclipsed that of the Andeans, the latter engaged in more radical migrations, not only to earn wages for tributes, but merely to subsist. At this critical juncture, the steady outflow from Andean communities was converted, by the late seventeenth century, into a veritable exodus, causing a human deficit in the Indian sphere.

Through a comparison of mid- and late-seventeenth-century census materials, we will discern the progression and patterns of these intersphere movements, by examining rates of absenteeism in Andean communities, migration flows, and migratory styles. This analysis will elucidate for Quito two related historiographical debates opened by scholars of the southern Andes: (1) whether migration ended in the destructuration or reproduction of Andean communities; and (2) how ethnic groups have been able to maintain cultural cohesion up to the present day, in spite of widespread demographic disruption.

Mid-Seventeenth-Century Migration

Three midcentury censuses have been selected for detailed analysis: the census of the Repartimiento of Otavalo of 1645, that of the town of Guaca

Table 6: Andean Absenteeism in Repartimiento of Otavalo, 1645, by Town

Town	Total Population	Absent Population	%	Economically Active Population	Absent Active Population	%
Otavalo	1,276	550	(43)	580	302	(52)
Cotacache	1,866	1,141	(61)	885	618	(70)
Tontaquí	825	367	(44)	405	215	(53)
Ynta	370	170	(46)	172	84	(49)
Malchinguí	178	97	(54)	101	62	(61)
Urcuquí	263	138	(52)	137	83	(61)
Yacelga	436	343	(79)	203	164	(81)
Repartimiento Totals:	5,214	2,806	(54)	2,483	1,528	(61)

Sources: Juan Freile Granizo, *Numeraciones del repartimiento de Otavalo* (Otavalo: Instituto Otavaleño de Antropología, 1981); AN/Q, Indígenas: 4, 23-III-1645, "Visita, quenta y numeración de los indios del pueblo de Malchinguí . . . , 1646."

of 1650, and that of the town of Calpi of 1663. The first consists of several towns in the Corregimiento of Otavalo, while the other two are fairly typical Andean towns in the Corregimientos of Ibarra and Riobamba, respectively.[7] The selection was based on the physical state of the documents and the differing economic and political conditions of each locale, with an eye toward pointing up regional variations in migration patterns. Although each census was studied for all available data, special attention was given to absentee rates, migration flows, and the kin composition of migrating groups.[8]

Beginning with the census of Otavalo, the analysis reveals that more than half the repartimiento's recorded inhabitants were absent from their communities in 1645. When the economically active population—that is, people from ages eighteen to fifty—is considered as the unit of analysis, the percentage of absentees rises to slightly more than 60 percent.

Examining table 6, it becomes evident that rates of absenteeism varied depending on the town in question.[9] Considerable variation between towns and even between ayllus of the same town suggests that there was equivalent disparity in the resources that these groups had been able to maintain. The socioeconomic differentiation of ayllus, however, had its roots both in the pre-Hispanic past and in colonial developments; that is, in the level of wealth with which they started out and with the pace at which local Spaniards made inroads into their resources. The ayllu of Sarance, for example, was reportedly the elite ayllu of the entire region upon the Spanish arrival. That it exhibited a very low absentee rate (17 percent) in comparison with all other ayllus in the repartimiento is not surprising. Evidently this group's original wealth provided it with a cushion that minimized the need to emigrate in the face of Spanish demands.

Absentee rates also depended surprisingly on the availability of Spanish resources in the local area; for example, the town of Otavalo had the smallest absent population in the repartimiento (43 percent), most probably because it was the site of the large crown obraje. The latter employed five hundred workers and was reported to have been instrumental in keeping the town demographically intact. It was claimed that because the obraje provided employment in the town, the Andeans did not need to leave the area to earn their tributes.

Putting aside the many variations, there was no town in the repartimiento that exhibited an absentee rate of less than 43 percent of the total population, a significant figure when one considers that the labor of these people was lost to the economies of their communities. In addition many of those who remained behind were held responsible for the town's labor obligations to the Spanish state and were not available to the Andean economy either. Sadly this was just the beginning of a debilitating trend that would become exacerbated as the century progressed.

With more than half the indigenous peoples of the Repartimiento of Otavalo recorded as having left their towns of origin, a most compelling but simple question arises: Where did they go? Indeed one of the major objectives of this analysis has been to uncover the migratory flows of the native population and more specifically to determine what percentage of them ended up in the Spanish sphere.

The census of 1645 reveals that 71 percent of the absentees had migrated within the Corregimiento of Otavalo. Another 23 percent had strayed only as far as the neighboring provinces of Ibarra, to the north, and Quito, to the south. In short the overwhelming majority of "wandering" Otavaleños had taken up residence within the north-central sierra, with the bulk having remained in their home province.[10] If one examines table 7, which lists the absentees' towns of origin as well as their places of residence, the preponderance of this intra-corregimiento movement becomes boldly evident.

Two towns, Cotacache and Urcuquí, even exhibited local migration flows of over 80 percent. The smallest intra-corregimiento movements, those of Otavalo and Malchinguí, can easily be explained. A sizable percentage of Otavalo's absentees were diverted to Quito, probably owing to the very marketable skills they acquired in the crown obraje and the availability of well-paying jobs in the capital city's textile industry. As for Malchinguí, it was located on the border with the Corregimiento of Quito, so that its migrants had not actually moved any farther from home than their more northern counterparts.[11]

Table 7: Migratory Flows of Indigenous Population of Repartimiento of Otavalo, 1645 (percentages in parentheses)

Place of Origin by Town	Place of Residence by Corregimiento					
	OTAVALO	IBARRA	QUITO	POPAYÁN	OTHER	UNKNOWN
Otavalo	310	63	121	2	1	53
	(56)	(12)	(22)	—— a	——	(10)
Cotacache	917	111	66	7	3	37
	(80)	(9)	(6)	(1)	(1)	(3)
Tontaquí	226	93	23		7	18
	(62)	(25)	(6)		(2)	(5)
Ynta	100	35	20			14
	(59)	(21)	(12)			(8)
Malchinguí	43		35	1	9	9
	(45)		(36)	(1)	(9)	(9)
Urcuquí	113	21	3			
	(83)	(15)	(2)			
Yacelga	273	36	24	4	4	2
	(80)	(11)	(7)	(1)	(1)	——
Repartimiento Totals:	1,982	359	292	14	24	133
	(71)	(13)	(10)	——	(1)	(5)

Sources: Juan Freile Granizo, Numeraciones del repartimiento de Otavalo (Otavalo: Instituto Otavaleño de Antropología, 1981); AN/Q, Indígenas: 4, 23-III-1645, "Visita, quenta y numeración de los indios del pueblo de Malchinguí . . . , 1646."
aDashes indicate an insignificant percentage.

It is also significant that the caciques reported unknown locations for only 5 percent of the absent population; this indicates that native leaders knew the whereabouts of the vast majority of their "truant" subjects, implying that these movements were, if not organized, at least monitored in some way. Later in the century, the caciques would claim that they were totally ignorant of the residences of the absent population—a development that implies some radical political changes in the Indian sphere.[12]

In the main then, the seventeenth-century demography of the Repartimiento of Otavalo was characterized by exceedingly compact and semicontrolled migratory flows which might at first glance seem inconsequential. The real significance of these short-distance movements, however, lies not so much in their geographic range, but rather in which "republic" the migrants chose as their destination. Whether they ended their days in the Spanish or Indian sphere and in what numbers is a crucial question, since its answer will divulge much about the eventual politico-economic destructuration of native communities.

A sectoral analysis of the absentees' places of residence reveals that one-quarter had migrated within the Indian sphere, while three-fourths had relocated to Spanish urban centers and haciendas. Within the wider demographic context, this means that 12 percent of the total population of the repartimiento had moved to other native communities, while 37 percent was already working and residing in the Spanish sphere by the year 1645 (table 8).[13] This is a conservative estimate, considering that data on specific locations is missing for 227 absentees, many of whom were liable to have been in the Spanish sphere.

In addition it is highly probable that the figure of 37 percent does not include those Andeans who were performing the mita. Since the labor quota was set at one-fifth of the tributary population in the Audiencia of Quito and mitayos usually brought their wives and children with them on their tours of duty, it might be valid to add 20 percent to the number of Andeans in the Spanish sphere. The incorporation of mitayos and their families would then raise the figure to 57 percent of the total native population, signifying that by 1645 the majority of indigenous peoples were permanently dedicated to the Spanish economy and not available to that of the Indian sphere. Here lies the real import of Otavalo's midcentury migration patterns—patterns that were to intensify considerably during the remainder of the century.

Although the economic dislocations that this movement must have engendered contributed significantly to the destructuration of the Indian sphere, the migratory styles of Otavalo's peoples attenuated the socially disintegrative potential of the movement. The overwhelming majority of ab-

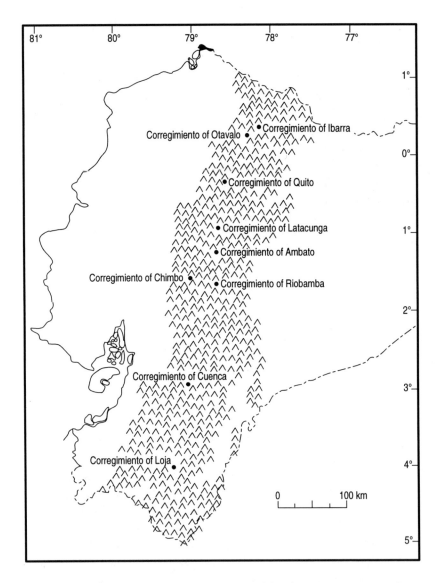

Map 3. Administrative Organization of Highland Quito. Seventeenth
Century

Table 8: Location Categories of Absentees from Repartimiento of Otavalo, 1645 (percentages in parentheses)

Town of Origin	Place of Residence				
	Spanish Sphere			Indian Sphere Communities	TOTAL ABSENT
	URBAN CENTER	HACIENDA	TOTAL		
Otavalo	56	249	305	170	475
% of absentees	(12)[a]	(52)	(64)	(36)	
% of total pop.	(4)[b]	(19)	(24)	(13)	
Cotacache	101	700	801	253	1,054
% of absentees	(10)	(66)	(76)	(24)	
% of total pop.	(5)	(37)	(43)	(13)	
Tontaquí	64	242	306	32	338
% of absentees	(19)	(72)	(90)	(10)	
% of total pop.	(8)	(29)	(37)	(4)	
Ynta	39	28	67	85	152
% of absentees	(26)	(18)	(44)	(56)	
% of total pop.	(10)	(8)	(18)	(23)	
Malchinguí	11	72	83	4	87
% of absentees	(13)	(83)	(95)	(5)	
% of total pop.	(6)	(40)	(47)	(2)	
Urcuquí	10	120	124	12	136
% of absentees	(7)	(84)	(91)	(9)	
% of total pop.	(4)	(46)	(46)	(7)	
Yacelga	33	231	264	73	337
% of absentees	(10)	(68)	(78)	(22)	
% of total pop.	(8)	(53)	(61)	(17)	
Reparti-miento Totals:	314	1,636	1,950	629	2,579
	(12)	(63)	(76)	(24)	
	(6)	(31)	(37)	(12)	

Sources: Freile Granizo, *Numeraciones,* and AN/Q, Indígenas 4, 23-III-1645.

Note: Although the total absent population of the repartimiento totaled 2,806 (table 6), the above total of 2,579 represents all absentees for whom locations were listed in the census.

[a]The first set of figures in parentheses is the percentage of all absentees for each town who are in the Spanish and Indian spheres.

[b]The second set of figures in parentheses is the percentage of the total population for each town that is in the Spanish and Indian spheres.

sentees migrated in kin groups, usually to the same place or at least within
the same vicinity (table 9). Conversely only 7 percent left their communities unaccompanied.[14]

A more detailed study of the migratory styles of one particular ayllu will
be instructive. Urcuquiango in the town of Urcuquí has been selected for
further analysis on the basis of its fairly typical absentee rate (52 percent)
and migration patterns.[15]

The kin composition of Urcuquiango's absent groups is fairly representative. Only 4 of its 138 absentees migrated alone; the rest migrated in family groups ranging in size from two to thirteen members. Most kin groups
migrated to the same location as a single unit, while two extended kin groups
migrated out to nearby but somewhat dispersed locations. The family
headed by Domingo Pinango (thirteen members), for example, ended up

Table 9: Migratory Styles in Repartimiento of Otavalo, 1645
(number of kin groups in parentheses)

Town	Lone Individuals	Kin Groups 2–5	Kin Groups 6–9	Kin Groups 10 or more	Total
Otavalo	58	233 (69)	178 (23)	81 (7)	550
Cotacache	72	582 (174)	301 (42)	186 (15)	1,141
Tontaquí	39	172 (56)	81 (10)	75 (6)	367
Ynta	17	41 (10)	51 (6)	61 (5)	170
Malchinguí	9	48 (17)	40 (5)		97
Urcuquí	4	62 (27)	48 (8)	24 (2)	138
Yacelga	12	154 (49)	121 (16)	56 (4)	343
Totals:	211	1,292 (402)	820 (110)	483 (39)	2,806
Percentages:	7	46	30	17	

Sources: Freile Granizo, *Numeraciones,* and AN/Q, Indígenas 4, 23-III-1645.

in four different places—Colimbuela, Puchimbuela, the hacienda of Doña Mariana de Villafuerte, and Ibarra—all of which were within close proximity of each other.

Five families had close relatives still residing in the town, with whom they must have carried on important relations. In addition it is probable that most of the migrants had kin relations in town who were not apparent from the census. The blood relationships of married women, for example, were lost in the format of the census, thereby obfuscating the true extension of family networks. The census taker also remained uninformed about many so-called "illegitimate," or natural, relationships.

Over 80 percent of Urcuquiango's absent population was still resident in the Corregimiento of Otavalo, and another 15 percent had migrated to neighboring Ibarra (table 7). In addition to this limited geographic range, further analysis of common destinations and the composition of the migratory group reveals even more concentrated, kin-based migration patterns. In Tontaquí, where fourteen people from Urcuquí resided, they were derived from two extended families; in Tumbaviro, sixteen Urcuquiangos composed three nuclear families and one extended family.

Among the Spanish haciendas in the vicinity of Urcuquí, the concentration is even more notable. Only 18 absentees were not concretely described as working for Spaniards; the other 120 were divided among eighteen local Spanish enterprises. In short, 46 percent of Urcuquí's total population was living on Spanish haciendas, not temporarily as rotational workers or mitayos, but permanently as resident farmhands.

What conclusions can be drawn, both from the microstudy of the Urcuquiango ayllu and from the larger study, about the Repartimiento of Otavalo's migration patterns at midseventeenth century? The movements of the region's peoples took place within an exceedingly compact area; few strayed far from home, and most remained within the corregimiento or moved short distances to nearby provinces. The proximity of the Andeans' new residences to their towns of origin may have enabled caciques to continue extracting tribute from their subjects, thereby appeasing the Spanish regime and retaining power. Nevertheless even if the caciques were able to fulfill their obligations to the Spanish state, the labor of these Andeans, now occupied for the most part in Spanish economic enterprises, was lost to them and to their communities. So although the Otavaleño movement can be described as constricted in physical or geographic terms, it represented, in economic terms, a distinct movement away from the Indian economy and toward a dominant Spanish economy.

This demographic analysis, combined with the rather unique political and economic circumstances of the Corregimiento of Otavalo, make it possible to zero in on the exact motives or push factors of the movement in a way that is not always feasible in other regions. That only 7 percent of the absentees migrated alone indicates that these migrations did not represent the flight of lone tributaries seeking relief from excessive demands and abusive treatment (see table 9). First Otavalo was a crown repartimiento, where tribute rates were characteristically low and where the majority of native tributes were paid by the profits of the obrajes in the towns of Otavalo and Peguche. Consequently the repartimiento had, at midseventeenth century, one of the better financial records of the audiencia, confirming that prompt tribute payment is not necessarily an indicator of demographic stability.

Second it is unlikely that the absentees left their communities in order to escape unusual abuses; surely there were abuses in Otavalo, but the short-distance character of the migrations indicates that poor treatment did not surpass that which was ordinarily internalized by colonized peoples. Furthermore contemporary reports insisted that Amerindians were treated better in Otavalo than in other regions, precisely because they belonged to the crown and were not distributed in private encomiendas. Clearly the principal motive for the region's migrations was the search for subsistence occasioned by resource divestment—euphemistically known as "the transfer of land from Indian to Spanish hands." Otavalo's proximity to agricultural markets in the city of Quito made it an early target of Spanish land encroachment.

More importantly, because of the corregimiento's unique political and financial position, the commonly cited reasons for migration—tribute and mita evasion and extreme abuse—can be all but eliminated as push factors. This clears the way for positing a direct correlation between absenteeism and resource divestment. Such a correlation makes it possible to measure the rate of resource transfer from indigenous peoples to the European colonists by measuring native population shifts toward the Spanish sphere. In this case the figure, 37 percent, which represents the minimal Andean population permanently resident in the Spanish sphere, would be roughly equivalent to the minimal rate of resource divestment in the year 1645.

Lastly the compact and familial nature of Otavalo's migrations facilitated the continuation of important social relationships among ayllu members. Nevertheless, although sociocultural continuity was possible under these new demographic circumstances, migration did undermine traditional political and economic structures.[16]

The consequences of midcentury population movements differed by region, ranging from severe destructuration to near preservation of the Indian sphere. If Otavalo occupies the median on a continuum of migration patterns, the town of Guaca in the Corregimiento of Ibarra may be considered its most negative point and the town of Calpi, in Riobamba, its most positive. Analyses of these towns' census records, while not as detailed as that of Otavalo, will highlight contrasting population trends.

The 1650 census of the people of Guaca reveals the demographic variations that existed in the audiencia, even between geographically contiguous provinces, such as Ibarra and Otavalo. Although Guaca's absentee rate was a full twelve points lower than that of the average town in Otavalo, its migration patterns left behind a much more deleterious legacy than those of the neighboring region (table 10).

There is considerable disparity both in the sizes and absentee rates of individual ayllus (see table 10). While some ayllus may have been larger than others owing to differentiated access to resources, it is puzzling that the smallest ayllus, Chuquín-Chuquín and Quatinpas, had the lowest absentee rates. When analyzed within the context of Ibarra's grim demographic

Table 10: Andean Absenteeism in Town of Guaca, 1650
(Corregimiento of Ibarra)

Ayllu	Total Population	Absent Population	%	Economically Active Population	Absent Active Population	%
Pu-Guachan	134	49	(37)	69	38	(55)
Puentestar	56	29	(52)	27	12	(44)
Chuquín-Chuquín	27	4	(15)	12	3	(25)
Chuquín-Chalacam	123	45	(37)	65	28	(43)
Ytul	66	28	(42)	31	16	(52)
Quatinpas	29	5	(17)	17	4	(23)
Chuquín-Tulcanasa	133	40	(30)	60	22	(37)
Guecaran	78	33	(42)	39	19	(49)
Pu-Chalacam	62	38	(61)	31	19	(61)
Camcam	93	51	(55)	38	22	(58)
Town totals:	801	322	(40)	389	183	(47)

Source: AN/Q, Indígenas 5, 20-VII-1650, "Traslado segundo de la numeración, quenta y discrepción de los yndios del pueblo de Guaca de las parcialidades del Pu i Chuquín de la Corona Real, 1650."

history, however, the riddle is resolved. Ibarra, noted for the labor demands of sugar production and its proximity to the Popayán mines, was, according to Tyrer, the only region of the audiencia to experience population loss throughout the seventeenth century. Clearly these small ayllus had already reached their nadir in previous years, either through out-migration or mortality, and are perfect illustrations of the destructurating impact occasioned by the region's depopulation.[17]

Aside from evidence of previous population disasters, the census also exhibits demographic trends that imply ongoing destructuration. The migratory flows from the town of Guaca are somewhat farther-flung than those emanating from any of the towns of the Repartimiento of Otavalo. While 71 percent of the absentees of Otavalo's towns migrated within their home province, only 55 percent of Guaca's migration was an intra-corregimiento movement (table 11). Another 21 percent migrated south to nearby Otavalo, while smaller but significant percentages moved on to Popayán, Quito, and unknown locations.[18]

Surprisingly only 18 percent of Guaca's total population was resident in the Spanish sphere in 1650, while that of Otavalo totaled 37 percent for the same period (table 12). Although the retention of large numbers of migrants in the Indian sphere could easily be interpreted as an indicator of a healthy native economy, it will be shown later that this was, sadly, not the case. A last difference is that a considerably higher percentage of Guaca's absentees had migrated alone: 18 percent as opposed to Otavalo's 7 percent (table 13).

What can account for these puzzling variations? Most of these disparities can readily be explained by the political and economic conditions that prevailed in the region and that shaped the migratory choices of Guaca's inhabitants. Ibarra's relative remoteness from colonial power centers and its labor-intensive and dangerous economic activities—sugar and minerals—combined to create an atmosphere of gross exploitation and intolerable abuses. It is certain that dreaded labor in the "hot lands" and in the mines goes a long way toward explaining the high incidence of "loner" migration, the wider geographic range of the movement, and the lower percentage of Andeans resident in the Spanish sphere.

Considering the trends that have been culled from the census, it would appear that the town's migration was, at least in part, the spontaneous flight of desperate tributaries—many alone, eager to leave the area, and reluctant to incorporate themselves into exploitative Spanish enterprises. Judging from other characteristics of Guaca's demographic profile, these migratory patterns and styles served to accentuate an already adverse situation. Higher

Table 11: Migratory Flows of Indigenous Population of Town of Guaca
(Corregimiento of Ibarra), 1650 (percentages in parentheses)

Place of Origin by Ayllu	Place of Residence by Corregimiento					
	IBARRA	OTAVALO	POPAYÁN	QUITO	OTHER	UNKNOWN
Pu-Guachan	38 (78)	5 (10)	1 (2)	1 (2)	1 (2)	3 (6)
Puentestar	16 (57)	8 (29)	2 (7)	2 (7)		
Chuquín-Chuquín	4 (100)					
Chuquín-Chalacam	12 (29)	21 (51)	2 (5)	5 (12)		1 (3)
Ytul	8 (29)	10 (35)	2 (7)			8 (29)
Quatinpas		5 (100)				
Chuquín-Tulcanasa	16 (44)	2 (6)	1 (3)	14 (39)	1 (3)	2 (6)
Guecaran	31 (94)			1 (3)		1 (3)
Pu-Chalacam	22 (58)	8 (21)	7 (18)			1 (3)
Camcam	25 (49)	7 (14)	7 (14)	1 (2)	11 (21)	
Town Totals:	172 (55)	66 (21)	23 (7)	24 (8)	13 (4)	16 (5)

Source: AN/Q, Indígenas 5, 20-VII-1650.

female-to-male sex ratios, greater incidence of single and widowed people, pathetically depleted ayllus, and an age pyramid indicating that most generations were just barely reproducing themselves all combine to portray Guaca as a community in the process of destructuration.[19] Although Guaca did not, in fact, disappear—it was listed in tribute records in 1730 as having 166 tributaries—it never recovered from its enfeebled demographic state

Table 12: Location Categories of Absentees from Town of Guaca, 1650
(Corregimiento of Ibarra) (percentages in parentheses)

	Place of Residence				
	Spanish Sphere			Indian Sphere	
Ayllu of Origin	URBAN CENTER	HACIENDA	TOTAL	COMMUNITIES	TOTAL ABSENT
Pu-Guachan	5	19	24	22	46
% of absentees	(11)[a]	(41)	(52)	(48)	
% of total pop.	(4)[b]	(14)	(18)	(16)	
Puentestar	8	14	22	6	28
% of absentees	(29)	(50)	(79)	(21)	
% of total pop.	(14)	(25)	(39)	(11)	
Chuquín-Chuquín				4	4
% of absentees				(100)	
% of total pop.				(15)	
Chuquín-Chalacam	6	4	10	34	44
% of absentees	(14)	(9)	(23)	(77)	
% of total pop.	(5)	(3)	(8)	(28)	
Ytul	2	6	8	12	20
% of absentees	(10)	(30)	(40)	(60)	
% of total pop.	(3)	(9)	(12)	(18)	
Quatinpas		2	2	3	5
% of absentees		(40)	(40)	(60)	
% of total pop.		(7)	(7)	(10)	
Chuquín-Tulcanasa	12	18	30	6	36
% of absentees	(33)	(50)	(83)	(17)	
% of total pop.	(9)	(13)	(22)	(2)	
Guecaran	1	11	12	12	24
% of absentees	(4)	(46)	(50)	(50)	
% of total pop.	(1)	(14)	(15)	(15)	
Pu-Chalacam	1	18	19	11	30
% of absentees	(3)	(60)	(63)	(37)	
% of total pop.	(2)	(29)	(31)	(18)	
Camcam	3	12	15	28	43
% of absentees	(7)	(28)	(35)	(65)	
% of total pop.	(3)	(13)	(16)	(30)	
Town Totals	38	104	142	138	280
% of absentees	(14)	(37)	(51)	(49)	
% of total pop.	(5)	(13)	(18)	(18)	

Source: AN/Q, Indígenas:5, 20-VII-1650
Note: Although the total absent population of the town totaled 322 (table 10), the above total of 280 represents all absent Indians for whom locations were listed in the census.
[a] The first set of figures in parentheses is the percentage of all absentees for each town who are in the Spanish and Indian spheres.
[b] The second set of figures in parentheses is the percentage of the total population for each town that is in the Spanish and Indian spheres.

Table 13: Migratory Styles from Town of Guaca, 1650 (Corregimiento of Ibarra) (number of kin groups in parentheses; percent in brackets)

Lone Individuals	Kin Groups (2–5)	Kin Groups (6–9)	Kin Groups (10 or more)	Total
57	148	87	30	322
	(51)	(12)	(2)	
[18]	[46]	[27]	[9]	

Source: AN/Q, Indígenas: 5, 20-VII-1650.

Table 14: Andean Absenteeism in Town of Calpi, 1663 (Corregimiento of Riobamba)

Ayllu	Total Population	Absent Population	%	Economically Active Population	Absent Active Population	%
Calpi	516	92	(18)	237	58	(24)
Ñacchucay	325	60	(18)	150	37	(25)
Balelbut	383	43	(11)	166	23	(14)
Bacsi	276	46	(17)	116	25	(21)
Town Totals:	1,500	241	(16)	669	143	(21)

Source: AN/Q, Cacicazgos 9, 1749-V-21, "Visita y numeración de los yndios del pueblo de Calpi (Corregimiento de Riobamba) y encomienda del Duque de Lerma y Useda, 1663," presented as evidence in "Autos de Don Melchor Albares, yndio, contra los indios cujis sobre la acumulación a su parcialidad de Bagsi, 1749," ff. 62–247.

and continued on a steady, downward spiral for the rest of the colonial period.[20]

In contrast the migration patterns of the town of Calpi in the Corregimiento of Riobamba suggest a very different set of demographic and economic conditions for that region from those of either Guaca or Otavalo. Of the fifteen hundred Andeans registered in the census of 1663, only 16 percent were reported as absent (table 14). Of these, sixteen Indians were camayos who resided in the town of Pelileo (Ambato) on community business; therefore the true absentee rate was only 15 percent.

Calpi's migration range was wider than that of the previous two regions (table 15). The absent group was more evenly distributed over a larger area, with the Corregimiento of Quito rivaling that of the home Corregimiento of Riobamba as the preferred destination. In addition the proportion of absentees whom the cacique could not locate far exceeds that of Otavalo and Guaca, while the number of people who migrated alone is the highest of the three studies (tables 16 and 17).

Table 15: Migratory Flows of Indigenous Population of Town of Calpi, 1663 (Corregimiento of Riobamba) (percentages in parentheses)

Place of Origin, by Ayllu	Place of Residence by Corregimiento					
	RIOBAMBA	CHIMBO	QUITO	AMBATO	CUENCA	UNKNOWN
Calpi	43		30			19
	(47)		(32)			(21)
Ñacchucay	23		7	16	3	11
	(38)		(12)	(27)	(5)	(18)
Balelbut	6	8	5		2	22
	(14)	(19)	(12)		(5)	(51)
Bacsi	2	19	10			14
	(4)	(42)	(22)			(31)
Town Totals:	74	27	52	16	5	68
	(31)	(11)	(21)	(7)	(2)	(28)

Source: AN/Q, Cacicazgos 9, 1749-V-21, "Visita y numeración de los yndios del pueblo de Calpi (Corregimiento de Riobamba) y encomienda del Duque de Lerma y Useda, 1663," presented as evidence in "Autos de Don Melchor Albares, yndio, contra los indios cujis sobre la acumulación a su parcialidad de Bagsi, 1749," ff. 62–247.

Table 16: Location Categories of Absentees from Town of Calpi, 1663
(Corregimiento of Riobamba) (percentages in parentheses)

| Ayllu of Origin | Place of Residence | | | | TOTAL ABSENT |
| | Spanish Sphere | | | Indian Sphere Communities | |
	URBAN CENTER	HACIENDA	TOTAL		
Calpi	41	28	69	4	73
% of absentees	(56)[a]	(38)	(95)	(5)	
% of total pop.	(8)[b]	(5)	(13)	(1)	
Ñacchucay	7	15	22	23	45
% of absentees	(16)	(33)	(49)	(51)	
% of total pop.	(2)	(5)	(7)	(7)	
Balelbut	4	4	8	6	14
% of absentees	(29)	(29)	(57)	(43)	
% of total pop.	(1)	(1)	(2)	(2)	
Bacsi	10		10	22	32
% of absentees	(31)		(31)	(69)	
% of total pop.	(4)		(4)	(8)	
Town Totals:	62	47	109	55	164
% of absentees	(38)	(29)	(66)	(34)	
% of total pop.	(4)	(3)	(7)	(4)	

Source: AN/Q, Cacicazgos 9, 1749-V-21, "Visita y numeración de los indios de Calpi (Corregimiento de Riobamba) y encomienda del Duque de Lerma y Useda, 1663," ff. 62–247.
[a]The first set of figures in parentheses is the percentage of all absentees for each town who are in the Spanish and Indian spheres.
[b]The second set of figures in parentheses is the percentage of the total population for each town that is in the Spanish and Indian spheres.

Calculation of the number of absentees resident in the Spanish sphere was somewhat problematic, since data for this variable were not as consistently available in the census as they were in those of Otavalo and Guaca. Locations were often noted as general toponyms, such as Quito or Cuenca, without urban or rural designations. Specific locations were listed for only 164 of the 241 absent Andeans. Of these it can be ascertained that at least 7 percent of the total population was resident in the Spanish sphere in 1663

Table 17: Migratory Styles from Town of Calpi, 1663 (Corregimiento of Riobamba) (number of kin groups in parentheses)

Ayllu	Lone Individuals	Kin Groups 2–5	Kin Groups 6–-9	Kin Groups 10 or more	Total Absent
Calpi	11	38	25	18	92
		(12)	(3)	(1)	
Ñacchucay	7	29	7	16	60
		(8)	(1)	(1)	
Balelbut	17	19	7		43
		(6)	(1)		
Bacsi	10	27	9		46
		(9)	(1)		
Town Totals:	45	113	48	34	241
		(35)	(6)	(2)	
Percentages:	19	47	20	14	

Source: AN/Q, Cacicazgos 9, 1749-V-21, "Visita y numeración de los indios de Calpi (Corregimiento de Riobamba) y encomienda del Duque de Terma y Useda, 1663," ff. 62–247.

(table 16). Even assuming that the missing 77 cases had all migrated to Spanish cities or haciendas, the proportion would only rise to 12 percent. This is a paltry figure when compared with Otavalo's minimal estimate of 37 percent eighteen years earlier.

What do the above figures signify, and how can some of the contradictory results of the census analysis be explained? First Calpi's low incidence of absenteeism may indicate that the community was able to maintain sufficient resources to support itself and to fulfill its financial obligations to the Spanish state. If the latter was not possible, there were numerous obrajes in the vicinity, to which Calpi's caciques may have sent their subjects to earn tributes. Also land encroachment, while certainly prevalent throughout the period, was not as extensive in Riobamba as in Otavalo, presumably owing to its distance from Quito's major urban markets. Indeed both a slower rate of resource divestment and the proliferation of a rural textile industry functioned to preserve intact the area's Indian sphere until the catastrophes of the 1690s.

Neither is there other evidence of destructuration in Calpi. Sex ratios were nearly equivalent; there was no excess of single or widowed people;

and the community's age pyramid, while deficient in two generations, owing to an earlier epidemic, showed signs of demographic recovery in the others.[21] In addition there is evidence that Calpi was able to retain, over a period of 130 years of Spanish colonization, both the material and human resources necessary to conserve some elements of pre-Hispanic organization. Remnants of its economic archipelago are a prime example. Besides the sixteen camayos stationed in Pelileo, it is also likely that many of the absentees resident in Chimbo were there in the capacity of camayos.[22] Clearly Calpi was still a viable, cohesive community in 1663.

Nevertheless the census analysis produced a few negative indicators that threatened Calpi's continued demographic integrity. Although the town's general absentee rate was low, the migration that did take place appears to have been spontaneous and to have represented a complete break with the community on the parts of many. The high incidence of "loner" migration, the tendency of some Andeans to wander far from home, and the caciques' ignorance of the absentees' whereabouts in 28 percent of the cases all indicate that a substantial part of this movement was not planned or monitored in any way; although it was a small movement in 1663, its patterns and styles contained a potentially destructive seed.

Perhaps indicative of what lay ahead, a list of absentees from the neighboring town of Yaruquís indicates a migration rate nearly double that of Calpi only three years later (1666). There 155 tributary Andeans out of 529, or nearly 30 percent, were reported to have fled the town.[23] One possible explanation is that the Corregimiento of Riobamba had a more varied experience than other regions because it was dominated by private encomiendas. The personal styles of encomenderos and their administrators may have caused demographic differentiation within the corregimiento.

In short an analysis of selected census materials indicates that Otavalo, Guaca, and Calpi were fairly representative cases along a continuum of midcentury migration patterns ranging from the minimal movements of Calpi on one end, to the compact migrations of Otavalo at midpoint, to the more destabilizing movements of Guaca at the other end. It has also been possible to measure, to some extent, the effects on the Indian sphere of the somewhat diverse migratory flows and styles exhibited by these three indigenous groups. The Otavaleño migrants' limited geographic range helped to preserve cultural cohesion, but their propensity to migrate to the Spanish sphere implied a marked shift toward a Spanish-dominated economy. The somewhat wider scope of Guaca's movement and the higher incidence of loner migration are patterns that surely contributed to the town's progressive destructuration. Finally the comparatively small size of Calpi's migration reflects the town's apparent ability to maintain its material and human resources and hence to preserve intact not only its demographic integrity but also some of its pre-Hispanic forms.

Late-Seventeenth-Century Migration

The variations in midcentury migration patterns described above all but disappeared in the 1690s, as certain audiencia-wide conditions arose that were uniformly detrimental to the maintenance of the Indian sphere. During this decade and subsequent ones, the decline of the textile industry, the epidemics and *composiciones* (regularization of land titles) of the 1690s, and the earthquake of 1698 all functioned to push indigenous peoples onto Spanish haciendas in large numbers.[24] The migratory variations so evident at midcentury were rapidly flattened out by this conjuncture of events, leaving the native towns half-empty and the Spanish sphere newly inflated. This sudden acceleration of a process already underway became generalized throughout the highlands and stimulated a flood of official complaints and judicial proceedings concerning land-grabbing, tribute arrears, extensive absenteeism, and the disappearance of whole communities.

For a better understanding of both the quantitative and qualitative differences between the midcentury and late-century movements, a second group of census materials has been selected for analysis. Optimal research conditions would have dictated a late-century study of the same towns presented above, but unfortunately the extant record does not permit this. What makes a comparison possible, however, is that the qualitative data for the turn of the century present a consistent picture of accelerated intersphere migration for all regions. Considering this homogeneity, a demographic analysis of just about any town in the audiencia serves as a representative example.

The available data are not as dense as those for the midseventeenth century; they consist of perfunctory lists of absent tributary Indians. As a result the demographic analysis is less deep; family reconstruction and determination of the kin composition of migrant groups, for example, cannot be extracted from the data. Nevertheless these records do contain the most essential categories of the midcentury analysis and will divulge comparative information on the rates of absenteeism and general migration flows characteristic of turn-of-the-century Andean populations.

The problem of Andean absenteeism became especially acute in the second half of the seventeenth century, with the result that the ubiquitous *memoria de ausentes* came to dominate the demographic record. These were nominal lists of tributaries, arranged by town, that usually recorded two simple facts: the presence or absence of all tributaries and, in the case of absence, their places of residence, if known.

The proliferation of these absentee lists reflected a number of late-seventeenth-century trends, the most noted of which were the critical demographic state of the reducciones, the breakdown of the colonial tribute and labor systems, and the deterioration of Andean chiefly authority. The main issue at hand is the first.[25]

The following analysis will center on the absentee lists of seven major Andean communities in the central highlands. They are Licto, San Andrés, Chambo, Ylapo, and the *vagamundos* (vagabonds) of Riobamba, all in the Corregimiento of Riobamba; the town of Patate in the Corregimiento of Ambato; and the town of Mulahaló in the Corregimiento of Latacunga. The lists were composed between the years 1685 and 1708, although most were recorded in the 1690s. This was a time of crisis for the entire audiencia, but especially for the central sierra, where the natural and economic disasters of the period had a decidedly hard impact. For this reason the incidence of absenteeism may be slightly higher in Riobamba, Ambato, and Latacunga than in other corregimientos, but not so much higher as to make it atypical; data from other areas show surprisingly uniform trends.

If we examine the statistical field for the five communities of Riobamba, the salient characteristic is that nearly every town had an absentee rate of more than 50 percent, the low point being that of Licto (42 percent) and the high point that of Ylapo (59 percent) (table 18).[26]

What is so stunning about these figures, however, is that the Corregimiento of Riobamba had exhibited the densest and most stable indigenous population of the entire audiencia only a few years before. Indeed Tyrer and Alchon report dramatic increases of tributary population for Riobamba between the 1590s and the 1660s and 1670s (table 4). Such a demographic explosion, even if largely a growth on paper, as posited in chapter 1, precludes a steady out-migration of the type that might have resulted in a 50-percent absentee rate by the 1690s; on the contrary the population increase of the first half of the seventeenth century was, in part, the result of in-migration.[27]

Unlike those of Quito, Otavalo, and Ibarra, the native population of the Corregimiento of Riobamba was characterized up to this point as more stable than that of any other province. That suddenly in the 1690s five of its major communities should exhibit a combined absentee rate of 52 percent can only attest to the centrifugal force generated by the catastrophes of the

Table 18: Andean Absenteeism in Corregimiento of Riobamba, 1690–1698
(partial totals)

Town or Unit	Tributary Population	Absent Tributary Population	Absentee Percentage
Licto	451	189	42
San Andrés	348	191	55
Chambo	409	233	57
Ylapo	225	134	59
Vagamundos of Riobamba	168	84	51
Totals:	1,601	831	52

Sources: AN/Q, Indígenas 18, 1690-7-II, analyzed in Christiana Borchart de Moreno, "Camayos, forasteros, y vagamundos: Algunos datos sobre la migración en la región de Riobamba en el siglo XVII." Paper presented at the Fifth Encuentro de Historia y Realidad Económica y Social del Ecuador, Cuenca, 17–21 November 1986; AN/Q, Tributos 4, 12-IX-1695; AN/Q, Indígenas 21, 1695-IX-7; AN/Q, Religiosos 7, 1698-II-7; AN/Q, Presidencia de Quito: 14, ff. 194–203. Discrepancies in source data reflect inconsistencies in the cataloging practices at the national archive in Quito. *Note:* The towns and units listed above represent approximately one-third of the major towns in the Corregimiento of Riobamba.

period. The degree of absenteeism in Riobamba had caught up to that of the Corregimientos of Otavalo and Ibarra, measured previously.[28] The destructurating trends of the 1690s had the effect of diluting the migratory variations of the midseventeenth century and homogenizing the demographic experience of highland communities.

More importantly, however, this absenteeism was qualitatively different from that of earlier periods in a number of ways. The purpose of the memorias de ausentes was precisely to bring to the attention of the authorities the staggering number of Andeans who had left their communities and had reneged on their tribute and labor obligations to the Spanish state. Hence the Andeans recorded as being absent were truly "gone"; for the most part, they were not the casual fieldhands of midcentury Otavalo who worked on local Spanish haciendas, wandered in and out of town at will, may have paid their tributes, and may even have participated in community festivals. While it is true that the labor of these Andeans was lost to their communities and that they were paralleled by a smaller group of "true deserters," midcentury movements simply do not appear as disruptive as those now under analysis.

Table 19: Migratory Flows of Tributary Population of Corregimiento of Riobamba, 1690–1698 (percentages in parentheses)

Places of Residence by Corregimiento	LICTO	SAN ANDRÉS	CHAMBO	YLAPO	VAGAMUNDOS	TOTAL
			Town or Unit of Origin			
Riobamba	50	19	15	80		164
	(26)	(10)	(6)	(60)		(20)
Ambato	5	5	10	16	7	43
	(3)	(3)	(4)	(12)	(8)	(5)
Chimbo	17	18	13	9	20	77
	(9)	(9)	(6)	(7)	(24)	(9)
Cuenca	40	41	55	4	21	161
	(21)	(21)	(24)	(3)	(25)	(19)
Loja	1	1			2	4
	(1)	(1)			(2)	(.5)
Guayaquil	2	13	3		8	26
	(1)	(7)	(1)		(10)	(3)
Latacunga	4	5	9	11	5	34
	(2)	(3)	(4)	(8)	(6)	(4)
Quito	39	37	32	13	8	129
	(21)	(19)	(14)	(10)	(10)	(15)
Otavalo		11			2	13
		(6)			(2)	(2)
Ibarra		6			2	8
		(3)			(2)	(1)
Lima	2					2
	(1)					(.5)
Other			5		3	8
			(2)		(4)	(1)
Unknown	29	35	91	1	6	162
	(15)	(18)	(39)	——	(7)	(20)
Totals:	189	191	233	134	84	831

Sources: AN/Q, Indígenas 18, 1690-7-II; AN/Q, Tributos 4; AN/Q, Indígenas 21; AN/Q, Religiosos 7, 1698-II-7; AN/Q, Presidencia de Quito:14, ff. 194–203. Discrepancies in source data reflect inconsistencies in the cataloging practices at the national archive in Quito.

The Andeans recorded in the absentee lists of the turn of the century are the subject of a texturally distinct phenomenon. If we examine the migration flows of the five Riobamba communities, it is immediately apparent that the geographic range of the movement is quite extensive (table 19). The region's peoples migrated throughout the audiencia and, although they clustered occasionally in certain corregimientos, there was no single predominant destination. Ylapo was the only town that experienced a significant intra-corregimiento movement, with 60 percent of its migrants remaining in Riobamba. The rest of the communities' movements, however, exhibited a rather dispersed configuration, with a slight preference for the Corregimientos of Quito and Cuenca.[29]

Bringing into the analysis the towns of Patate and Mulahaló, it becomes evident that the trends prevalent in Riobamba also obtained in other parts of the central sierra. Patate, in the Corregimiento of Ambato, suffered an official absentee rate of 54 percent, while 96 percent of the population was described as living outside the town (table 20). One assumes that the official and de facto absentees were distinguished by tribute payment; nevertheless an important point to keep in mind is that none of these Andeans was available to the community's economy. Patate also exhibited the same dispersed migration pattern as the towns of Riobamba, but with significant clusters in Quito and Otavalo (table 21).

Places of residence were not listed for Mulahaló's truant population; therefore it was not possible to measure migratory flows. Nevertheless the town exhibited an absentee rate of 58 percent.[30] This figure, in combination with qualitative data that will be discussed later, places the Corregimiento of Latacunga squarely inside the central-sierran migration patterns of the turn of the century.

What also makes late-seventeenth-century migration patterns distinctive from earlier trends is the leap in the number of absentees about whom the cacique claims he has no knowledge of residence. While tables 19 and

Table 20: Andean Absenteeism in Town of Patate, 1685
(Corregimiento of Ambato) (percentages in parentheses)

Tributary Population	Absentees	Official Absentees
254	243 (96)	138 (54)

Source: AN/Q, Tributos 4, "Padroncillo de los indios tributarios del pueblo de Patate, 1685."

Table 21: Migratory Flows from Town of Patate, 1685
(**Corregimiento of Ambato**) (percentages in parentheses)

Corregimiento of Destination	Number of Migrants
Quito	27 (20)
Otavalo	16 (12)
Cuenca	8 (6)
Latacunga	2 (1)
Popayán	1 (1)
Unknown location	81 (59)

Source: AN/Q, Tributos 4, "Padroncillo de los indios tributarios del pueblo de Patate, 1685."

21 show a wide range of percentages for the category of "unknown locations," most of the figures serve as a striking contrast to those of the 1645 census of Otavalo, where only 5 percent of the absent population could not be located.

Throughout the audiencia, native leaders complained persistently that their administrations were plagued by the "unlocatable absentee." Of course, as will be delineated in chapter 5, both caciques and local Spanish officials frequently attempted to manipulate this phenomenon in the interests of tribute extortion. While there can be no denying this practice, the very success of the strategy must lie in its believability; that is, in the real increase in the numbers of unlocatable absentees. Even if only one-half of Mulahaló's elusive population, for example, had truly disappeared, the detachment of these individuals from the community would still be highly significant.

In addition the growth of this category of absentees signifies important changes in the political climate of the indigenous world.[31] Indeed the rise in numbers of unlocatable absentees, combined with the wider geographic range described previously, gives these central-sierran movements a certain air of spontaneous abandon. They were most certainly not planned from above; rather, in most cases they appear to be unrestrained or to have run out of control.

Perhaps the quantitative and qualitative differences between late-century and earlier movements can best be demonstrated through a comparative analysis of census materials for the town of Chambo, in the Corregimiento of Riobamba. Chambo is the only Indian town in the audiencia for which a time series can be constructed. The town's seven ayllus, as recorded in the

Table 22: Comparative Andean Absenteeism, 1603 and 1695
in Town of Chambo (Corregimiento of Riobamba)

Ayllu	1603			1695		
	Trib. Pop.[a]	Absent Trib. Pop.	Unloc.[b] Absent Pop.	Trib. Pop.	Absent Trib. Pop.	Unloc. Absent Pop.
Hasatus	94	28	4	104	58	31
Picollan	58	27	1	51	33	13
Llucut	77	27	2	59	25	11
Cugtus	99	32	1	112	65	5
Guayacondos	71	29	3	44	26	13
Ymango	36	16	0	14	12	8
Zizibies	38	25	0	25	14	10
Totals:	473	184	11	409	233	92
Percentages:		40	6		57	39

Sources: AGI, Cámara 919A, "Visita y numeración de los indios del pueblo de
Achambo, hecha por Joan de Munoa Ronquillo, jues de comisión y escribano mayor,
1603," ff. 1–460; AN/Q, Tributos 4, 12-IX-1695, "Padroncillo de los indios tributarios
del pueblo de Chambo, encomienda del señor Conde de Castrillo, 1695"; AN/Q,
Indígenas 21, 1695-IX-7, "Padroncillo de los indios tributarios del pueblo de
Chambo de la encomienda del señor Conde de Castrillo, 1695."
[a]Tributary population
[b]Unlocatable

absentee list of 1695, are also included in the household census of the
encomienda of Achambo, carried out in 1603. The comparable variables
for these two dates are rates of absenteeism, migration flows, and unlocatable
absentees.

The tributary population did not decline as significantly as one would
have anticipated in these ninety-two years (table 22). This might be confirmation of the demographic stability previously posited for the
corregimiento, but it may also be the artificial statistical creation of a colonial administration reluctant to lower tribute and labor quotas. More significant for this study, however, is that the town's tributary absentee rate
increased during the period from 39 percent to 57 percent; likewise tributary absentees who could not be located rose from 6 percent to 39 percent.

It is also notable that during this period the definition of "absenteeism"
appears to have changed. In 1603 there were 184 tributaries living apart
from their ayllus, yet it is quite clear that they were considered bona fide
members of the community and were still in the charge of their caciques.
This should not be surprising, considering the traditional extraterritorial

residence of substantial numbers of Andean peoples so characteristic of pre-Hispanic economies.

In the text of the census, those who resided outside the town were described as "ausente," but in the official summary of each ayllu, only absentees for whom the cacique had no residential information were listed under this rubric. In addition it is clear from the text that the cacique knew exactly where all the others were residing and the activities in which they were occupied. The implication is that only unlocatable absentees were considered to have detached themselves from the community.

A more detailed analysis of the whereabouts of one ayllu's absentees will be instructive. The Cugtus ayllu had ninety-nine tributaries, thirty-two of whom were living out of the polity; the cacique knew the location and the specific occupation of all except one, who was listed as an official "ausente." Of these thirty-one, eleven were members of a colony permanently resident in the city of Quito. This group was composed of artisans and domestic servants who resided there under the supervision of an Andean official from the community.[32] Seven more of the absentees were shepherds on nearby estates of Spaniards and native lords; seven others were in the city of Riobamba, either performing some form of mita duty or working in the obraje of the encomendero, Lorenzo de Cepeda; two were working in the community obraje; three more were in Pelileo (Ambato) in the capacity of camayos; and one was in the neighboring town of Penipe with his wife, who was a native of that town. Although at first glance it seems that a fairly significant number of tributary members were absent from the community, they were not really absent in the late-seventeenth-century sense of the word; they were outside the community on "legitimate" business.

That the texture of absenteeism changed significantly during the remainder of the seventeenth century is witnessed by the purpose and format of the absentee list compiled for the town of Chambo in 1695. First the list was put together for the express purpose of either locating truant tributaries or having them subtracted from the tribute rolls. It is clear that even the subjects for whom the cacique had residential information had detached themselves from the community and from the fate of their fellow ayllu members through noncompliance with the town's obligations; otherwise why would their names have appeared on the list? It is true that desperate caciques would frequently hunt them down in an attempt to collect tributes, but even the wording of the documentation on this subject implies violence and coercion, certainly not reflective of the earlier pattern in which absentees willingly maintained bonds with their towns of origin. Hence by the late seventeenth century, the term *ausente* implied not just physical absence but a severance of ties with the community.

The absentees' places of residence reveal certain distinguishing trends between the two dates. In 1603 the only members who ventured outside the immediate area of the town were those who resided in the Quito colony and those who worked as camayos in Pelileo (Corregimiento of Ambato), a somewhat scattered but controlled settlement pattern. In 1695, in contrast, there was a highly diffused migration pattern, with significant clusters in Cuenca and Quito (see table 19). The higher rates of migration and of unlocatable absentees, the qualitative change in the concept of absenteeism, and the dispersed configuration of the town's migrants characterize the 1695 movement as uncontrolled and may reflect a partial breakdown not only of community, but also of chiefly authority.

The last and perhaps most important variable of late-seventeenth-century movements is sectoral destination; that is, movement toward the Spanish or the Indian sphere. Unfortunately the absentee lists of the period rarely distinguish places of residence in this fashion. This precludes the kind of analysis that is possible with midcentury documents. Nevertheless there is considerable qualitative data pointing to an exodus to the Spanish sphere at the turn of the century.

In the case of the central sierra, it is evident that most, if not all of the absentees were working on Spanish haciendas. Annotations made on the list for the town of Ylapo (1698) indicate that all one hundred absentees from the ayllu of camayos were resident on local haciendas.[33] Indeed in her work on land transfer in the Corregimiento of Riobamba, Borchart de Moreno characterizes the late seventeenth century as a period of hacienda consolidation. During this time the indigenous population experienced divestment and the appropriation of much of its labor by the large estates.[34] Consequently Andeans who remained within the corregimiento were undoubtedly incorporated into the evolving hacienda complex.

There is scant data on the Corregimiento of Ambato, but one surviving record, the absentee list for the town of Patate (1685), records specific locations for 57 of the 138 absentees, all of them Spanish cities or areas dominated by Spanish haciendas.[35] Quito, Cuenca, Guayaquil, and Popayán were the urban destinations, while Perucho, Nono, Punapi, Tontapi, Guayllabamba, and San Antonio de Pomasque, all on the outskirts of the city of Quito, were farming areas well integrated into the urban market.

In Latacunga, data pointing to hacienda absorption of the indigenous population abounds. Fortunately a protracted dispute between parish priests and *hacendados* (Spanish landowners) provides important information about migration trends in that province. The Franciscans claimed that hacendados were hiding large numbers of their Andean parishioners on the estates and refusing to allow the friars to administer to them.[36] Specifically the priest of the town of Mulahaló lamented that the parish had 785 tributaries in 1672 but only 253 in 1706, 243 of whom were on the haciendas of the vicinity.[37] Lastly considerable out-migration took place from Latacunga to haciendas in other areas. The Otavalo census of 1720, for example, recorded substantial numbers of Latacungans residing on the haciendas of that corregimiento (table 23).[38]

The accelerated move to the Spanish sphere at the end of the seventeenth century, most especially to the hacienda complex, was not restricted to the Andean peoples of the central sierra, but had its counterparts in other areas as well. According to Galo Ramón, over 78 percent of the native population of Cayambe (Corregimiento of Otavalo) had moved onto the haciendas by 1685.[39] There is no reason to believe that the rest of Otavalo had a different experience, considering that this trend was well under way by the time of the 1645 census.

In addition the consolidated hacienda complex of Otavalo, vitalized by the decline of the central sierra and the rise of new markets in Nueva Granada, became, as already suggested by the Latacungan data, a migratory magnet for large numbers of Andeans. The census of 1720 records significant migrations to Otavalo from both the northern and central highlands (see table 23). The movement from the north, that is, from the Corregimiento of Ibarra and the Gobernación of Popayán, infused the expanding hacienda complex of Otavalo with the labor of numerous tributaries and their dependents. The overwhelming majority of these migrants were reported as working on the haciendas; sixty-four of the ninety-one Indians of Tulcán (Corregimiento of Ibarra), for example, were living on the Mercedarian hacienda of Pezillo near Cayambe, while the remaining twenty-seven were divided between the hacienda of Zuleta, near the town of San Pablo, and other Spanish properties.[40]

From the central sierra (that is, the Corregimientos of Riobamba, Ambato, and Latacunga) a fairly respectable contingent of Andeans descended upon Otavalo in search of relief from the instability of their homeland. In addition the census recorded large numbers of vagabonds, for whom the provenance was unknown or at least unrecorded. Together these "outsiders" represented a tributary population of 1,517 and a total population of 6,862. If we consider that the native tributary population of the Corregimiento of Otavalo was reportedly 2,665 during the years 1721–26, then the total tributary population resident in the province at the time was 4,182, of whom 36 percent were forasteros. In short a great deal of movement took place from north and center toward Otavalo at the turn of the century, as did movement from many other unidentified places.

Other movements, especially those to and from the corregimientos of

Table 23: Forasteros Resident in Corregimiento of Otavalo, 1720

Provenance	Tributary Population	Total Population
Ibarra	336	1,565
Popayán	447	2,040
Latacunga	259	1,158
Ambato and Riobamba	63	244
Vagamundos	412	1,855
Totals:	1,517	6,862

Source: AN/Q, Indígenas 37, 1720-VIII-15, "Quadernos de los yndios pertenecientes al corregimiento de la Villa de Ybarra que residen en este de Otavalo . . . , 1720"; "Quadernos de los indios pertenecientes al corregimiento de Riobamba y al asiento de Ambato que residen en Otavalo . . . , 1720."

Quito and Cuenca, are not as well delineated in the documents. Data for Cuenca is too scant to venture much more than a guess about population movements. Since it was a preferred destination for substantial numbers of Riobamba's peoples, and its own inhabitants rarely appeared in northern and central documents at this time, we must assume that Cuenca was demographically stable and offered attractive employment to new arrivals.

In relation to the Corregimiento of Quito, one must consider that this region, owing to its proximity to urban markets, underwent land divestment and the consolidation of a Spanish agricultural economy at a much earlier date. Consequently both local peoples and in-migrants might already have been absorbed into the hacienda complex of that region. In support of a hypothesis of generalized movement to the Spanish sphere at the turn of the century, however, suffice it to say that the censuses of the 1710s and 1720s were beginning to be arranged by haciendas rather than by Andean communities in many areas of the audiencia. By the second half of the eighteenth century, this shift had progressed considerably.

Andean Demography and the Spanish Economy

What were the historical conditions that provoked this massive movement of people, labor, and resources from the Indian to the Spanish republic? Although the movement's push factors were similar to those of the sixteenth century—abuse, dangerous working conditions, epidemics, land divestment, and natural disasters—its pull factors were unique to the sev-

enteenth century. Their delineation requires examination of the Spanish
colonial economy (most especially the obraje/hacienda complex) and of
the evolution of the region's labor systems.

Throughout the seventeenth century, indigenous peoples migrated to
all sectors of the Spanish economy; but the textile industry, and later the
hacienda complex, drew the largest numbers away from their communities. Unfortunately the data do not permit a differentiated sectoral study of
the impact of demographic movements on each. Even taking as a unit of
analysis the obraje (the region's primary industry for the first half of the
seventeenth century) the linkage between the quantitative and qualitative
data is at best obscure. In addition the illicit nature of one sector of the
industry precludes a quantitative assessment of labor flows; part of Quito's
textile boom was predicated upon the proliferation of informal workshops
operated with forastero labor, whose owners counted upon escaping bureaucratic notice.

Despite the lack of correlative quantitative data, however, there is abundant qualitative data that point to a symbiotic relationship among the obraje
complex, Indian migration, and the formation of a free-labor market. The
steady migratory outflow from the Indian sphere during the sixteenth and
early seventeenth centuries, while of limited proportions, did constitute an
incipient "free" work force. During the seventeenth century, this group was
greatly inflated by the increasing number of new arrivals in the Spanish
sphere. But more importantly, the availability of this growing forastero labor supply lent dynamism to the region's economy at a propitious moment. Between the 1580s and the 1660s, the silver mines at Potosí served as
a growth pole and generated an integrated and far-flung colonial economy.
Each region specialized in one or two products for export to the mines and
associated urban centers. Quito participated in this economic network by
providing textiles to Potosí, Lima, and to a lesser extent, Nueva Granada.

According to Tyrer's study of the obraje complex, cloth export to the
cities and mining centers of the viceroyalty was a perfect economic activity
for Quito's colonists. It was the only way that a relatively unendowed, peripheral Spanish population could earn enough specie to participate as con-
sumers in the trans-Atlantic trade.[41] In addition textile production was
highly suited to the region for a variety of reasons. The extensive páramos
of the central Ecuadorean sierra were superb grazing lands for the huge
flocks of sheep necessary for wool production, making possible vertically
integrated enterprises that were more profitable.[42]

In addition cloth production was labor-intensive, and the central and
north-central sierra had a dense indigenous population with a long weav-

ing tradition.[43] Quito was also able to solve the problem of distance from lucrative markets by producing cloth, a product that was non-perishable, light, compact, and hence relatively easy to transport.

The crucial element in the success of Quito's textile industry, however, was the availability of forastero labor. The proliferation of small and medium-sized mills worked by the absentees functioned to meet local demand, while the large obrajes, worked by mitayos, supplied exports for external markets. It was the mass migration of indigenous peoples away from their communities of origin that stretched the textile labor supply far beyond that provided by the state-sponsored mita. Although Alchon and Tyrer posit that this expanding native work force derived from a dramatic population increase, the study of Quito's migration patterns proves otherwise. Indeed the seventeenth century saw a continual swelling of labor available to the Spanish economy, but at the expense of that of the Indian republic. The expansion reflected an interspheric shuffling of people, not a demographic recovery.[44]

The chain of events looks like this: the mines of Charcas generated both primary and secondary commercial opportunities, which, when combined with the economic needs of a growing Spanish population in Quito, motivated further divestment of native resources and accelerated abuses of the forced-labor system. Many Amerindians responded by fleeing to the Spanish sphere, both to escape tribute and the mita and in search of subsistence. The migration of dispossessed and abused Andeans created an alternative labor force, which generated new enterprises. These new enterprises created more employment opportunities and spurred more migration and more new enterprises. The cycle was played out repeatedly, until a dialectic was formed between Andean migration and the partial composition of a free-labor market. The result was the expansion of both the textile industry and of native population movements toward the Spanish sphere.

As production at the Potosí silver mines fell off during the second half of the seventeenth century, so did that of Quito's textile industry—an industry that depended heavily on demand generated by the "red mountain."[45] Parallel to this downswing, the end of the seventeenth century also saw extensive expropriation of native lands, severe epidemics with high mortality, and a major earthquake that devastated the central highlands. In the face of a newly disarticulated textile economy, agriculture assumed added importance, spurring waves of land-grabbing and the formation of the "classical" hacienda. This phenomenon was facilitated by the vacant tracts resulting from native depopulation and by the havoc that always characterizes the aftermath of a natural disaster.

A widely accepted view is that this was a period of great uncertainty, during which indigenous peoples took refuge on landed estates. This impression, while not categorically untrue, does require some qualification. The word *refuge* suggests medieval hordes of peasants fleeing to the security and protection of the feudal lords in times of crisis. The native population movement toward the haciendas at the end of the seventeenth century, while voluntary and spontaneous in some regions of the audiencia, was orchestrated by land-hungry Spaniards in others. Migration was accompanied by wholesale dispossession and extreme violence; hardly a matter of seeking "refuge," but rather one of being in "checkmate." Regardless of differences in the recruitment methods of hacendados or the personal motives of Andeans, however, a large proportion of the native population was resident on Spanish haciendas by the turn of the eighteenth century. Indeed the movements of indigenous peoples—spontaneous, planned, or coerced—ended in the near collapse of the Toledan reducciones.

Conclusion

The major distinction between sixteenth- and seventeenth-century population movements in the Audiencia of Quito centered on migratory flows. Most earlier movements took place within the Indian sphere and, while disruptive to native society, they at least ensured its demographic integrity. In contrast seventeenth-century migrations were increasingly channeled toward the Spanish republic, with the effect that by the turn of the century, more than 50 percent of Andean people were no longer residing in their communities of origin.

During the first half of the seventeenth century, there was significant regional differentiation of Quito's migration patterns. The movements' absentee rates, geographic ranges, migratory styles (groups or individuals), and the number of unlocateable migrants all varied according to the preexisting wealth (land and labor) of individual ayllus, levels of Spanish resource divestment, labor conditions, political climate, and the personal style of private encomenderos.

The result was a continuum of migration patterns whose consequences ranged from progressive destructuration to considerable reproduction of Andean society. The perils of mining and sugar production and the distance from colonial power centers informed the disintegrative movements of the town of Guaca in the Corregimiento of Ibarra. In contrast royal protection, the proximity of the large crown obraje, and the milder labor conditions of the textile industry engendered compact, kin-based migration patterns in Otavalo. Evidently controlled by the native leadership, these movements were disruptive to the Andean economy, but were at least conducive to the social reproduction of the area's ayllus. At variance with both these regions is Calpi (Corregimiento of Riobamba), where migration was so minimal that the town was able to reproduce part of its pre-Hispanic economic archipelago. There distance from urban markets limited rates of land divestment, and employment in local obrajes helped to keep the town intact.

In the late seventeenth century, these variations were flattened out, as pan-audiencia conditions painted nearly all Andean communities across regions with the same demographic brush: widespread absenteeism owing to increased migration to the Spanish sphere. In the 1690s the decline of textile production, systematic composiciones, severe epidemics, and the earthquake of 1698 combined to cause massive flight to the landed estates. Higher migration rates, more dispersed configurations, a greater incidence of unlocatable absentees, and a qualitative change in the concept of absenteeism reflect more pervasive levels of destructuration for late-seventeenth-century movements. In addition the rise of the classical hacienda was accompanied by extensive land expropriations and labor appropriations, often resulting in the rapid disappearance of many native communities. Indeed at the turn of the century the Indian republic was nearing demographic collapse.

Considering the historically unstable population conditions described above, it is puzzling to ponder the cultural cohesiveness exhibited by contemporary ethnic groups in highland Ecuador, most notably those of Imbabura (Otavalo) and Chimborazo (Riobamba). This study hints at some possible explanations. In areas where short-range migrations were prevalent and where groups of families from the same ayllu migrated to the same destination, social organization was most likely reconstituted in a new location. This is not surprising, since pre-Hispanic settlement patterns resembled more closely this seventeenth-century dispersion than the concentrated distribution of the late sixteenth-century reducciones. Close physical proximity, that is, was never a prerequisite of cultural cohesion among highland ethnic groups.

3

Colonial State Formation and the Politics of Andean Demography

When Columbus first tread on New World soil, he could not have foreseen that the eventual administration of its vast territories and their peoples would involve a much more arduous struggle than his transatlantic voyage. The consolidation of Spain's power in America was plagued by alternating advances and setbacks, resulting in a perilously fragile institutional structure.

The route to state formation was everywhere strewn with formidable obstacles of both New and Old World origins—Amerindian rebellions, Spanish civil wars, incoherent policies, epidemics, and distance from the metropolis, to mention a few. Nevertheless a workable government was finally established throughout the colonies, although the length and nature of the process varied regionally. Some differentiating factors were the level of cultural complexity and political organization of indigenous groups, topographic and climatic conditions, and the temperament of Spanish colonists.

Despite a multiplicity of regional variations, the evolution of the Spanish colonial state in the sixteenth and seventeenth centuries was characterized in the main by three major stages: (1) the imposition of state apparatus on a colonized indigenous population; (2) the crown's power struggle with colonial elites and temporary consolidation of rule; and (3) the breakdown of royal authority and the creolization of government. This chapter will focus on the roles of Andean demography and human agency in shaping the process and outcome of each of these three stages.

The relationship between Andean demography and the successful imposition of a colonial regime is quite straightforward: the establishment of a viable colony based on the extraction of revenue and labor from subjugated peoples would depend, in part, on the administration's ability to achieve an accurate population count. This causal relationship was not lost on the indigenous peoples. Hence the quest for demographic accuracy in Quito, as elsewhere, was an uphill battle and would eventually become the subject of an ambitious, multitiered state project. Bringing the indigenous

population under statistical control was a long, laborious process, with caciques retaining significant de facto autonomy until the early seventeenth
century. What follows, then, is an analysis of the strategies and
counterstrategies employed by Andeans and Spaniards in the struggle for
and against "demographic accuracy."

Demographic Control and the Imposition of State Apparatus

Although the periphery-to-center migrations of the second half of the
sixteenth century resulted in an expansion of the population in the central
and north-central sierra, the newcomers or return migrants continued, for
some time, to lack demographic representation in official records. There
were also many *originarios* (Andeans residing in their communities of origin), called *ocultos* ("hidden"), who had been hidden by their caciques and
were not included in Spanish counts. Throughout the colonial period, but
most especially in the sixteenth and early seventeenth centuries, both caciques and ordinary Andeans engaged in a vast array of strategies to deceive
census takers and obfuscate their true numbers. In addition the intrasierran
population exchanges, generated by land divestment and excessive labor
demands, proceeded unabated, causing administrative confusion and con-
tributing to the proliferation of the "hidden" population.

As migration and subterfuge enabled increasing numbers of Andeans to
"fall through the cracks" of the system, colonial officials were forced to match
wits with the colonized peoples. Eventually they countered with equally
clever strategies to incorporate elusive Andeans into the tributary base. The
late sixteenth and seventeenth centuries, then, would witness a tenacious
tug-of-war between the Spanish state and the ethnic peoples of Quito over
demographic accountability.

Though difficult to quantify, it is certain that the "hidden" population of
the late sixteenth century was considerable and that native strategies to cam-
ouflage its true size took many ingenious forms. Since the caciques played a
central role in the official inspections of the period, they enjoyed an advantageous position for undercounting the tributary population and often concealed large numbers of people as their retainers.

Many Andeans, particularly forasteros, entered a cacique's service in return for access to subsistence lands and exemption from state obligations.
This practice was widespread in the Audiencia of Quito and produced quite
beneficial results for many native leaders, as well as for the communities
they ruled. Another foil was the reporting of false deaths and the sale of

fraudulent death certificates, both of which impeded an accurate assessment of the population during many an official census.

Inflation of the yana population was also a favorite method of tax evasion in Quito. Yana were Andeans who, dating from Incaic times and perhaps even from the pre-Incaic period, were detached from their ayllus.
Exempt from community and state obligations, they devoted themselves
exclusively to the service of a cacique or other noble person. According to
Salomon's analysis of the 1559 inspection of Francisco Ruiz's encomienda,
caciques in the Chillos Valley commanded yana groups that often reached
10 percent of the total subject population; this was in sharp contrast to
other areas of the Inca empire, where yana composed only 2–3 percent.[1] If
the peoples of Quito took to using the tactics of their Cañari compatriots,
then how such an inflation may have occurred will be clear. Numerous
Cañaris lived in the Yucay Valley outside Cuzco, having been placed there
by the Inca. When informed in 1572 by the visitador, Gutiérrez Flores, that
yana could consider themselves exempt from tribute and mita, all the inhabitants of the Valley declared themselves yana. The status of yana became
a refuge.[2]

An examination of specific cases of subterfuge should provide a better
understanding of precisely how these strategies enabled an entire segment
of the Andean population to remain elusive for relatively long periods of
time. The case of Don Francisco Hati, cacique of San Miguel, in the Corregimiento of Latacunga, is especially instructive.

In 1582 and again in 1592, royal officials visited the town of San Miguel,
in order to count the native population. An analysis of these two censuses
yields considerable data about chiefly strategies aimed at demographic subterfuge and also about Don Francisco's efforts to create a labor reserve. In
1582 Don Francisco reported six camayos, five of whom were in Tunguragua,
presumably tending coca fields, and one of whom was working in the salt
mines of Tomavela. He also reported in the same visita two servants. Combined with the six camayos, this amounted to a total of eight Andeans who
were exempt from tribute and mita.[3] Later in 1614 he requested that he be
permitted to keep in his service precisely eight workers who were not on
the tribute rolls, but rather were his *concertados* (contract laborers).[4] This
sounds suspiciously like an attempted conversion of camayos (former economic colonists) to the status of yana, or personal servants, who were exempt from tribute and mita obligations; one of the eight even bears the
same name as a camayo reported in the census of 1582.[5]

Another strategy that comes to light upon analysis of the 1582 census is
the attempt to hide a percentage of the tributary population from the cen-

sus taker—a common strategy of the period, but one especially illuminated in the documentation on San Miguel. The census of Zorrilla in 1592 was based on Ortegón's count of 1582 and appears to represent an effort both to incorporate new tributaries and to redress inaccuracies of the previous record. The latter attempt is especially revealing, since it affords an opportunity to assess the demographic frauds of an earlier period.

In 1592 it became readily apparent that Don Francisco had engaged in various forms of subterfuge with regard to the count of 1582. These included false absences, fraudulent deaths, and failure to report some entering tributaries. For example, when the visita of Zorrilla was about to close with 100 tributary Andeans, the visitador must have investigated further, prompting Don Francisco to declare seven more of his subjects; four were males whom he had reported dead in 1582, two of whom were only ten and fifteen years old at the time, reflecting subterfuge with an eye to the future. Suddenly, however, as the visita was about to close for a second time, he declared three more, evidently outsmarted once again by the visitador.[6] These 10 Andeans plus the 6 camayos and 2 servants totaled 18 tributaries out of 110, or 16 percent of the community's male labor supply. Clearly Don Francisco Hati had attempted to create a private, tax-exempt work force by engaging several of the most frequently used demographic tricks of the time.

Although the case of San Miguel is important for what it reveals about specific strategies for creating and maintaining demographic reserves, this cacicazgo's (chiefdomship) small size does not make it an appropriate example for demonstrating the magnitude of the "hidden" population. Fortunately, however, there are numerous examples of subterfuge in larger polities that point to an "unofficial" native population of considerable size. As early as 1559, when Juan Mosquera and Gaspar de San Martín visited the encomienda of Francisco Ruiz, they suspected that the caciques of Chillos (Corregimiento of Quito) were hiding part of the subject population, but could not prove it.[7]

One of the most startling incidents of demographic fraud, however, occurred in the Corregimiento of Riobamba. Between the visitas of Cárdenas (1571) and Ortegón (1582), Don Sancho Lema, cacique of the town of Guano, concealed 431 men, or 41 percent of the tributary population.[8]

In the Corregimiento of Ambato, irregularities were also reported for the Toledan visita of 1575. Don Diego Pindumba, cacique of the town of Guambahaló, was accused by his encomendero, Alonso de Bastidas, of hiding a great number of his subjects from the visitador.[9] Encomenderos always had an ulterior motive for claiming undercounts, but considering the many similar reports for this visita, it would be remiss not to take Bastidas's complaints seriously.

Likewise in the northern town of Otavalo (Corregimiento of Otavalo), similar strategies were in evidence. In 1600 the president of the audiencia, Licenciado Miguel de Ybarra, dispatched two royal officials to investigate charges that the town's caciques had failed to report a large number of potential tributaries. They returned having discovered more than 660 tributary Andeans whom the previous inspector had "missed."[10] In 1591, Otavalo was reported to have had a tributary population of 2,011; if 660 Andeans were hidden from the visitador, then the real tributary population of that year must have been approximately 2,671.[11] In this case the unreported tributary population of Otavalo in 1591 would have represented 25 percent of the total. Similar complaints about the visita of the 1590s also obtain for the Corregimiento of Chimbo, where the *corregidor* (royal magistrate) reported in 1600 that the caciques had concealed many people in remote places, especially in the montaña regions and the hotlands.[12]

In light of the tactics described above, it is not difficult to comprehend how numerous Andeans remained hidden to the view of sixteenth-century census takers. Furthermore it is important to note that while the visita method of counting subject peoples may have missed some segments of the populations of Andean communities, it completely ignored, for most of the sixteenth century, the many thousands of detached vagabonds who hid themselves in the cities or wandered in the sierra.[13] Together these omissions must have encompassed a significant number of unreported Andeans. Clearly the data confirm that both native migrations and the caciques' subversion of Spanish census-taking efforts were generalized and effective survival strategies in the Audiencia of Quito. As the sixteenth century drew to a close, Andean agency was still a vital force in destabilizing Spanish plans for demographic accountability.

The documentation of the turn of the seventeenth century describes a colony plagued by demographic chaos and fiscal collapse, both of which were attributed to the caciques' subterfuge and the physical movements of indigenous peoples. In some areas, most notably Quito and Otavalo, migration away from communities of origin had reached epidemic proportions by the year 1600. Priests complained that half their parishioners had taken up residence in other towns, and treasury officials became alarmed at the amount of back tributes the migrants left in their wake. In 1619, for example, a single *parcialidad* (administrative unit of Andeans) of the Corregimiento of Otavalo owed 100,000 pesos in tribute arrears, which officials attributed to the out-migration of its inhabitants.[14]

Indeed the cunning of the native leadership was, during this period, still unrivaled. Not only had the caciques succeeded in concealing part of the population, but they had also learned to manipulate the migratory process. Numerous were the official complaints of the late sixteenth and early seventeenth centuries regarding caciques who purportedly knew the whereabouts of the absent population and secretly collected their tributes for their own or their communities' coffers.[15]

The blame for the critical state of the Spanish administration in Quito was assigned squarely to the clandestine population—both hidden originarios and runaway forasteros. The threat of colonial disintegration prompted a barrage of royal demands for a stricter approach to census taking, general reducciones, and measures to curb migration and forasterismo.[16] Officials of the Audiencia of Quito were always realistic about the possible outcome of these measures; one audiencia president explained to the Council of the Indies that expectations should not be too high, because "the Indians, after all, were prendas con pies" ("possessions with feet"). Nevertheless the audiencia went about creating and enforcing its own, somewhat unorthodox guidelines for achieving demographic accountability.[17]

In the absence of significant mines or other lucrative enterprises, the Andeans were the audiencia's most important resource. By the year 1600, Quito had gained a reputation for the easy availability of Andean labor. This was apparently an incentive for movement toward the region, as witnessed by the explosive growth of the Spanish population during the years 1574 to 1630. Clearly the indigenous peoples were the mines, and if Quito were to maintain its viability as a colony, the cunning of the native leadership would have to be challenged and truant Andeans would have to be brought into line. The seventeenth century, then, witnessed an intense Spanish struggle both to coopt the caciques' strategies and to incorporate as many stray people as possible into the tributary base.

Although the most effective strategies were not developed until the seventeenth century, the Spanish effort to harness the unofficial native population had its beginnings in the second half of the sixteenth century. From the 1560s on, Quito's officials made numerous attempts to integrate the invisible population into the colonial system. In 1565 Santillán, in one of his first acts as president of the audiencia, ordered an investigation of Spanish landowners to uncover the manner in which they procured Andean labor. He was said to have improved fiscal matters substantially, by discovering many potential tributaries in the employ of hacendados.[18]

This period also witnessed the initiation of cooptative strategies, that is, efforts to "buy off" both the native leadership and ordinary Andeans in the interests of accurate counts. In 1570 the visita instructions forwarded to the Audiencia of Quito by Viceroy Francisco de Toledo stated that any Indian, whether cacique or commoner, who exposed unreported tributaries would be rewarded by being appointed the leader of those he declared.[19]

Also in response to the Toledan instructions, the yanaconas of the city of Quito were converted to tributaries in 1576, and in 1578 two Amerindian towns were established on either side of the city for yanaconas and vagabonds. The latter were then placed under the rule of a governor and taxed in accordance with a regularized rate.[20] These sixteenth-century efforts were, however, scattered, experimental, and of limited effectiveness.

In contrast the early seventeenth century would see the consolidation of a systematic and efficient program to account for the hidden population of Quito. The administrative style of this period was characterized by a vast array of both official and highly unorthodox methods for incorporating delinquents into the colonial system. These measures included the *manifestación,* which rewarded Spaniards and Andeans alike for exposing truant tributaries; the appointment of special agents to round up vagamundos and aggregate them into artificial ayllus, which were then attached to the crown; and an attempt to channel migratory flows toward crown parcialidades, by offering stray Andeans advantageous terms.

Andean Migration and the Consolidation of Royal Power

As the sixteenth century progressed, the New Laws of the 1540s, which called for the gradual transfer of Amerindians from private encomiendas to royal jurisdiction, began to be implemented. These transfers were accompanied by the aggregation of vagamundos into crown parcialidades.[21] Although the formation of these new units got underway in the 1560s, they first appeared in fiscal records in 1593 and grew rapidly in size and number throughout the entire seventeenth century.[22] Their proliferation can be squarely attributed to royal incentives, such as a tribute rate only one-third or one-fourth that of encomienda Indians and exemption from the mita.[23] These enticements gave rise to migrations toward crown jurisdictions, whether composed of originarios or forasteros, from the 1590s on.[24] If the units were composed of forasteros, incorporation was quite simple: one claimed to be a native of a distant location or not to know one's origins at all. When dealing with crown parcialidades of originarios, however, attachment was even more unorthodox, as officials often integrated Andeans of different ethnic backgrounds into the ayllus of the originarios. A poignant example of the success of this official strategy was the case of Otavalo, where the crown parcialidad grew by nearly fourteen thousand new members in the twenty years between 1592 and 1612.[25]

That the crown was able to manipulate the migratory process in its own interests is abundantly clear, but what needs further analysis is what exactly those interests were. How did the strategy of channeling migratory flows toward royal jurisdictions benefit the crown? One possibility is that it might have been a way of breaking the power of the encomenderos without having to make a frontal assault on the encomienda system.

This unobtrusive method may have been particularly desirable in a colonial backwater like Quito, where in the absence of mines and other lucrative enterprises, encomiendas constituted the only source of wealth and prestige. Apropos of this, Santillán, president of the audiencia, appealed to the king in 1564 to slow the pace of crown incorporation of encomiendas and to allow him to continue to grant small encomiendas to worthwhile citizens. He claimed that in the absence of encomiendas or other rewards, anybody who was somebody was leaving the region, while the audiencia was being overrun with "riffraff," who engaged in riots and altercations daily.[26] What better way to stem the flow than to keep awarding encomiendas and then lure Andeans toward the crown with offers of a better deal.

Indeed the encomenderos of the period complained persistently that their Indians were migrating to crown parcialidades, where royal officials registered them without further ado. In 1626 one encomendero charged bitterly that any Indian who wished to be exempt from normal tribute and mita obligations had only to say that he was from Cuzco or some other distant province; he would then be summarily attached to the crown at the expense of his encomendero.[27]

A somewhat less speculative benefit of the incorporation of migrant Andeans into crown parcialidades was that it served the fiscal interests of the royal administration. This was especially so in the case of parcialidades of crown forasteros or vagamundos, who not only enjoyed the lower tribute rate assigned to all crown Indians, but also were exempt from the mita. Although these parcialidades did not yield significant revenues at first (the royal account books of the 1590s recorded infinitesimal amounts of tribute for the early aggregations[28]), as time wore on crown forasteros reportedly gained a reputation for paying their tributes punctually and in full. This was probably due to their employment as artisans and in private obrajes, where they frequently earned wages double those of mitayos.[29]

The special importance for the royal coffers of crown Indians in general and of crown forasteros in particular is borne out in the following analysis

Table 24: Tribute Records of Corregimiento of Latacunga, 1672–1674

Administrative Unit	Tributaries	Tribute Rate
Vagamundos de la Corona	540	2 pesos
Encomienda de Cuzubamba	128	2.4 pesos
Encomienda de Mulahaló	785	2.4 pesos
Encomienda de Calzada	2,798	NA[a]
Encomienda de Sandoval y Silva (vaco por muerte, Corona real)[b]	3,532	2.8 pesos
Encomienda de Angamarca	877	2.4 pesos
Encomienda de Hatunsichos	2,177	NA
Encomienda de Collanas	2,015	NA
Total:	12,853	

Source: AN/Q, Indígenas 11, "Cartas Cuentas de Latacunga, 1672–74."
[a] Not available.
[b] Vacant due to the encomendero's death and in temporary possession of the crown.

of payment rates in the Corregimiento of Latacunga. An examination of tribute records for the years 1672 to 1674 reveals that there were 12,853 tributaries in the corregimiento, only 540 of whom were crown forasteros (table 24). Nevertheless the nine parcialidades of vagamundos, or forasteros, paid 2,017 pesos of the 13,906 pesos collected during these years (table 25). In short the crown forasteros of Latacunga represented only 4.2 percent of the tributary population but paid 14.5 percent of all tributes collected in the district. In addition when the tributes paid to private encomenderos (the "dos tercios" category) are deleted, the amount actually delivered to the crown was 11,450 pesos, of which the vagamundos paid 2,017 pesos, or 18 percent.

The example of the encomienda of Don Juan Sandoval y Silva will illuminate further the significance of the crown vagamundos. In November of 1672, the encomienda was left vacant by the death of Sandoval y Silva and was given over to the crown. Its 3,532 tributaries were responsible for payment of two of the tribute categories listed in table 25 (Corona Real and Año del vacante), and their tributes amounted to 7,037 pesos.

The Andeans of this encomienda represented 27.5 percent of the tributary population of Latacunga and paid nearly 51 percent of all tributes collected and 61 percent of all royal tributes collected. Indeed the recent

Table 25: Summary of Royal and Private Tributes of
Corregimiento of Latacunga, 1672–1674

Royal Tribute	Amount
Vagamundos	2,017 pesos 5 reales
Un tercio de encomiendas	2,396 pesos 2 reales
Corona Real	2,395 pesos 1 real
Del Año de vacante[a]	4,642 pesos 5 reales
Private Tributes	
Dos tercios de encomiendas	2,456 pesos 4 reales
Total	13,906 pesos

Source: AN/Q, Indígenas 11, "Cartas Cuentas de Latacunga,
1672–74."
[a] Income from vacant encomienda that usually accrues to
the crown.

incorporation of this encomienda translated into a windfall for the crown,
revealing that before Sandoval y Silva's death, the percentage of royal tributes paid by the vagamundos was significantly higher than during 1672–74.
Some simple calculations will be instructive.

In the Audiencia of Quito, one-third of each private encomienda was
shared with the crown during this period. Hence Sandoval y Silva delivered
2,322 pesos of the 7,037 pesos of his encomienda's tributes to the royal coffers. This figure, when added to the one-third share ("un tercio" category
of table 25) of the remaining private encomiendas and the tributes of the
crown vagamundos, yielded royal tributes totaling 6,735 pesos, 2,322 pesos
(30 percent) of which were paid by the crown vagamundos.

Note that the encomienda of Sandoval y Silva passed to the crown only
for a very brief period, since it was reportedly redistributed to the Condesa
de Lemus sometime in the 1670s.[30] This means that both immediately prior
to and subsequent to the years of these tribute records (1672–74), the crown
forasteros, representing only 4.2 percent of the tributary population, paid
30 percent of all royal tributes collected in Latacunga. In short the
vagamundos were significant well beyond their demographic import.

Why and how did such disparity develop in the payment rates of crown
forasteros and private-encomienda Indians? As mentioned previously one
of the incentives for migrating to crown jurisdictions was a lower tribute

rate than that paid by Indians in encomienda. If one examines the tribute
rates presented in table 24, however, it is evident that the vagamundos paid
less tribute individually than the average encomienda Indians (the former
paid 2 pesos annually, while the latter were assigned a rate between 2.4 and
2.8 pesos), but not substantially less. Clearly other factors must have loomed
larger in the differential ability to pay, the crown forasteros' exemption from
the mita certainly being of prime importance.

Although the standard exemption had become a beleaguered privilege
in other regions, the forasteros of Latacunga succeeded in obtaining a royal
provision in 1652 confirming their exemption from the mita.[31] That this
privilege remained steadfast in the district is witnessed by the conspicuous
absence of Latacungan forasteros in the frequent judicial battles that took
place elsewhere over this exemption.[32] With their dispensation from the
mita secured, the crown vagamundos of Latacunga enjoyed an enormous
economic advantage over encomienda Indians, in that they worked in the
corregimiento's obrajes, haciendas, and even in the royal gunpowder factory for higher wages than those of their nonexempt cohorts.

The case of Latacunga is a poignant example of the potential importance of vagamundos to the royal treasury and goes far in explaining why
Andeans received incentives to migrate to crown jurisdictions. If Tyrer is
correct in his assessment that the crown did not monopolize encomiendas
in the Audiencia of Quito as it did in other parts of the viceroyalty, then the
privileged status of crown forasteros and their greater ability to pay may
have served as a counterbalance to the large number of Andeans who continued to be held in private encomiendas. In the absence of similarly detailed tribute records for other corregimientos, however, it is unclear whether
the hefty subsidy forwarded by the crown forasteros of Latacunga was part
of a general trend or was owing to the specific historical conditions of the
region.

The royal strategy, if indeed it can be termed a coherent strategy, did not
operate without impediments and alterations, as witnessed by the responses
of other colonial actors. Traditional elites (encomenderos, large obrajeros,
and prominent landowners) attempted to check the migratory flow toward
the Spanish sphere in general and toward crown parcialidades in particular. Because they depended on tribute and forced labor, which in turn depended on the continued integrity of the Indian republic, traditional elites
pushed the audiencia to pass legislation that would define the juridical position and treatment of forasteros in a way that was favorable to them. The
audiencia periodically ceded to this pressure and issued decrees ordering
forasteros, even those belonging to the crown, to perform the mita in their

places of residence; this in spite of the fact that it had no authority to do so.[33] These half-hearted efforts were successfully blocked by competing local interest groups (small landowners, unlicensed obrajeros, and corrupt officials), who benefited from the alternative labor force supplied by the forasteros.[34]

In 1618 and 1631, the crown requested reports on the feasibility of a general reducción of forasteros. Quito's officials insisted that such a project would be exceedingly difficult, if not impossible, owing to the near institutionalization of forasterismo in the region's economy. They then suggested that the problem be resolved by ordering that forasteros throughout the viceroyalty have mita obligations wherever they resided and admitted to having taken it upon themselves to pass local decrees to that effect on several occasions.[35] Evidently the Audiencia of Quito was well ahead of the Viceroy duque de la Palata, who attempted to put this general reform into effect in the 1680s. In relation to the audiencia's independence of action, Palata himself would complain fifty years later that Quito had represented the biggest problem of his administration, owing to the frequent insubordination of its officials.[36]

The audiencia's sporadic attempts to convert forasteros to mitayos met with varying degrees of success. Once again the Andean population countered with carefully devised strategies of its own. Documentation indicates that on occasion forasteros were forced to participate in the mita, but more often than not they are depicted as indefatigable litigants, who succeeded in obtaining royal provisions confirming their exempt status. Furthermore they almost always framed their arguments in terms that pitted local elite interests against those of the crown. For example the crown forasteros of Cuenca, in a petition of 1666 against their assignment as agricultural mitayos, threatened that if made to do the mita, they would only flee again and the crown would lose its tributes. They also insinuated in a frankly worded statement that they should be rewarded for staying put and paying their royal tributes promptly.[37] This playoff between forced labor for private citizens and tribute for the crown appears time and again in Andean petitions; the implication is always that they were mutually exclusive obligations.

Thus in spite of occasional audiencia decrees ordering Andeans to perform forced labor in their communities of residence, traditional elites did not have much success imposing the mita on the forastero population. Failing this, however, they frequently attempted to circumvent royal provisions by pushing for local ordinances that would change or restrict the definition of "forastero." By midseventeenth century, a forastero was described only as an Andean who had migrated outside his corregimiento of origin and who was repeatedly resistant to being "reduced" to his community of birth. All Andeans who migrated within their corregimientos were subject to tribute and mita in their original pueblos. In addition any forastero who resided in a town for more than ten years or for reasons of marriage was automatically considered an originario, with all the obligations and privileges of that status.[38] It proved impossible, however, to put these ordinances into practice. Caciques and corregidores were often remiss in searching their districts for short-distance migrants, and long-distance migrants frequently picked up and moved to another town before the ten-year limit.

The royal strategy of rounding up stray Andeans, aggregating them into crown parcialidades, and offering them a low tribute rate and exemption from the mita motivated migrations toward crown-controlled jurisdictions. These crown parcialidades of forasteros or vagamundos came to exist in every urban center and in nearly every Andean community of the colony. Evidently the peoples of Quito preferred to avoid the excessive exactions of their communities by aggregating themselves to the crown rather than retiring to remote areas where life was precarious. Numerous sixteenth- and seventeenth-century observers reported that the desirable conditions offered by the crown created a situation in which large numbers of Andeans tried to declare themselves vagamundos. The general tenor of these reports is: "now they all want to be crown vagamundos."[39]

Quito's peoples also challenged the colonial system by making an industry out of manipulating the audiencia's differentiated tribute system. In 1694 the *fiscal* (attorney to the audiencia), Antonio de Ron, cited the lack of uniformity in tribute rates as a major push/pull factor of internal migrations. Andeans migrated from communities with heavy tribute and labor obligations to those that were less burdened and frequently bribed Spanish officials to enumerate them in the rolls of the latter.[40] They deliberately searched for the least-onerous situation, and incorporation into the crown was the best possibility of all.

The advantages of being incorporated into crown parcialidades are evident in the abundance of suits that occurred over jurisdiction; Andean migrants were often counted twice, once in their communities of origin and again in crown jurisdictions, a situation that resulted in many legal battles concerning the parcialidad to which they truly belonged. The documentation is replete both with the bitter charges of encomenderos that their Indians had been wrongfully enumerated in crown parcialidades and with the persistent rebuttals of Andeans, who did everything within their power to hold on to their status as crown Indians.

An especially representative example of this conflict is the case of Don Juan Vásquez, an encomendero of Chimbo, who claimed that several of his Indians were living in Cuenca, where they had been attached to the crown; the Andeans in question, however, denied any such affiliation, in spite of imprisonment in the public jail and a protracted battle between the corregidores of both jurisdictions. Vásquez charged further that they fled to Cuenca to avoid paying the enormous amount of back tributes they owed in Chimbo; one was the *alcalde* (mayor) of the encomienda and was responsible for collecting tributes. Vásquez's representatives insisted that this kind of subterfuge should not be allowed to continue, because it had already become a general trend in the audiencia; all Andeans who owed tribute arrears tried to get themselves incorporated into the crown.[41]

The abundance and complexity of these suits often gives one the impression that migration patterns in the Audiencia of Quito were akin to an oversized game of musical chairs, with the crown parcialidades as the most-coveted seats. More often than not, litigation ended in victory for the crown Indians, frequently in spite of convincing evidence to the contrary; the effectiveness of the survival strategy founded upon movements to crown parcialidades was thus enhanced and subsequent migrations encouraged. Also enhanced by this movement, however, was the crown's consolidation of colonial power.

While Andean commoners manipulated crown parcialidades for individual survival and personal gain, caciques attempted to coopt and even institutionalize them for a broader politicoeconomic agenda. Indeed the advantages enjoyed by crown Indians made them both candidates for making willing contributions to their original communities' coffers and targets of chiefly extortion. Through incorporation into the crown, migrants acquired a protected legal status that permitted them to remain safely in areas where there were higher-paying jobs; that is, their position as crown forasteros afforded them some security against being shipped back home by the *buscadores*.[42] In addition they were not subject to the rigors of the mita and were less prone to flee than other Andeans. Eventually these circumstances imbued crown forasteros with residential stability and higher earning potential, both of which made them a dependable financial alternative for their original caciques. The latter frequently hunted them down and collected tributes either for personal enrichment or community survival.[43]

Some migrations to crown jurisdictions were orchestrated by the caciques themselves; migrations composed of family groups and even whole parcialidades are especially suspect. In this case a cacique's subjects constituted a type of economic colony, not unlike those of pre-Hispanic times, and their tributes might be considered "remittances back home."[44]

Through cooptative measures such as the Toledan instructions of 1570, the manifestación system, and the formation of crown parcialidades of forasteros, the Spanish state was able to render ineffectual many of the demographic survival strategies of the Andean population and to stymie the subversive tactics of the native leadership. The colonized peoples did create mechanisms to limit their incorporation into the colonial system, but it is clear that by the 1620s the crown had succeeded in imposing a more effective state apparatus on its Andean subjects.

Andean Demography and the Political Ascent of Local Interest Groups

The efforts of the early seventeenth century succeeded in temporarily integrating the Andeans' demographic reserve into the fiscal system, if not into the mita. Operating from a position of strength, the colonial administration now moved from cooptation to coercion. The 1620s would see the beginning of a new type of visita, one based on more precise methods. For the rest of the seventeenth century, colonial officials would engage in all manner of unauthorized actions and procedures in order to obtain from Andean communities not a true count, but an overcount of the population whenever possible. Since this period coincided with the increasing financial desperation of the Spanish crown and the apogee of Quito's textile economy, the new bureaucratic rigor appears to have been initiated in the interests of maximizing both royal revenues and the labor force.

The first new-style visita was that of the *oidor* (judge) Matías de Peralta, who made a general inspection of the audiencia between the years 1614 and 1626. As demonstrated above, the Toledan visita of the 1570s was conducted in a rather lax manner and did not achieve for Quito the administrative efficiency that it purportedly achieved for other areas of the viceroyalty. The audiencia would have to wait for Matías de Peralta in order to get its house in order; for this reason the latter figure is known among Ecuadorean historians as the Toledo of Quito.[45]

It was the famous visita of Matías de Peralta that succeeded in establishing fixed tribute rates, based on the economic and human resources of each community, and that drew up official guidelines for the operation of the audiencia's obrajes. More importantly for this study, it also instituted measures to eliminate the loopholes through which the native leadership had manipulated the census-taking process. It was this visita of the 1620s that

would be used as a baseline for all subsequent colonial visitas and which
would set the stage for both harsh statistical control and the indiscriminate
use of irregular practices in the interests of demographic "accuracy."

The Matías de Peralta visita represents the Spanish bureaucracy's most
definitive effort both to incorporate the "hidden" population into the tributary base and to streamline the administration of the colonized peoples.
The attempt to integrate forasteros and other marginal elements into the
official mainstream took many and varied forms, some official and others
highly unorthodox. One such measure was the granting of a lifetime exemption from tribute and mita to any Andean who reported four potential
tributaries to the census takers.[46] Another was the intensification of the
manifestación system, in which native leaders, royal officials, and private
Spaniards exposed ocultos and vagamundos, in return for their labor.

The most productive method of the visita, however, and that which devi-
ated most from conventional norms, was the incorporation of forasteros into
the ayllus of their places of residence. According to various seventeenth-century
documents, Matías de Peralta was reported to have systematically included
all stray Andeans in the tributary base of the communities where they were
living.

Aside from bureaucratic reports, an anthroponymic analysis of subsequent seventeenth-century censuses shows that "outsiders" had been summarily registered on the rolls of originarios at an earlier point. One example
is the 1663 census of the town of Calpi, in the Corregimiento of Riobamba.
Since the Inca had dispatched numerous mitimaes there, the presence of
Quechua names was quite common, but another 5 percent of the population carried non-Quechua surnames clearly not indigenous to the region
of Riobamba. The latter names originated in other areas of aboriginal Quito
and reflected population shifts during the Spanish colonial period.

Most aboriginal personal names are linguistically distinct and correspond
to discrete localities of the Audiencia of Quito; consequently by tracing the
movements of names, one can trace the movements of people, although
the exact time of migration cannot always be determined. For example the
record for Calpi reveals that an in-migration from the north took place
probably up to two generations earlier, which would put the original incorporation of the migrants at the time of the Matías de Peralta census. Names
such as Quilago, Farinango, and Pasto are common Otavalo and Ibarra
names that appear in the Calpi census of 1663.[47]

In addition the formula for all seventeenth-century enumerations of
Quito's indigenous population includes a record of how each Andean was
reported—that is, whether counted in person, by virtue of inclusion in the

last visita, or by declaration of a cacique or relative. Thus it is also possible to discern the period in which migrants were incorporated into the ayllus of the town, if not the approximate moment of their arrival. For example it is evident that the Otavaleños had been in Calpi since at least 1647, since they were reported as having been registered there in the last visita. It is also probable that they were not newly arrived in Riobamba in 1647, since forasteros often spent long periods of time unnoticed before being officially recognized and counted. Furthermore an audiencia decree ordered that forasteros be resident in the same town for ten years before they could be legally enumerated and taxed there, although this time period was often flagrantly disregarded. Thus it is most likely that Calpi's Otavaleños had arrived quite a bit earlier than 1647 and more than likely that they had been incorporated into the ayllus of the originarios during the Matías de Peralta visita in 1620. Indeed complaints regarding the systematic incorporation of forasteros into the fiscal jurisdictions of their places of residence were most forthcoming from the Corregimiento of Riobamba.

The dual approach of the Matías de Peralta visita—that is, the use of incentives to uncover the hidden population along with the unorthodox integration of marginal groups into the colonial system—resulted in a statistical inflation of the heartland population of the audiencia. This means that Tyrer's and Alchon's projection of explosive demographic growth between 1590 and 1660–70 was the result not only of the periphery-to-center movements described in chapter 1, but of the increasing administrative efficiency of the Spanish regime and its rigorous efforts toward demographic accountability.[48] In short the Spanish state had caught up with the forasteros and with the "hidden" population in general.

Administrative efficiency, another objective of the Matías de Peralta visita, was also achieved through a variety of methods, some of them diametrically opposed to both viceregal law and Andean norms. These included the unilateral removal of "incompetent" leaders, the forced retirement of elderly caciques, and the promotion of one of several equally ranked leaders to the position of *cacique principal* (paramount lord).[49] The second half of the seventeenth century witnessed the proliferation of lawsuits over cacicazgos in which the native leadership complained bitterly about the irregularities that had taken place during the Matías de Peralta visita. Their most common charge was that the regime's earlier efforts toward administrative efficiency and political centralization had eroded the power of many hereditary leaders and had caused serious rifts in their communities.[50]

The corruption of native polities and the gross overcounts of their populations were informed not only by administrative objectives but also by the most blatant colonial-style nepotism. Matías de Peralta was accused by both native leaders and private Spanish citizens of having inflated the population statistics of the encomiendas of his friends and relatives, as well as having taxed those encomiendas at higher rates.

Don Diego de Sandoval, a prominent encomendero of Latacunga, charged in 1617 that during the visita of 1615, Matías de Peralta had assigned tribute rates varying between three and four pesos to his encomienda, while he assigned a single rate of four pesos to that of Don Christóval de Bonilla, the husband of the visitador's niece. According to Sandoval there was no justification for this discrepancy, since the two encomiendas were in the same town and enjoyed equivalent lands and resources.[51] Evidently the lack of uniformity in tribute rates cited earlier was not owing solely to differences in the economic resources of native groups, but was also informed by the concept of "government as booty." Considering that the taxes established by Matías de Peralta became the baseline for all subsequent levies, this practice had very concrete and long-term consequences.

Sandoval also claimed that Bonilla, the visitador's relative, had received an excessive number of mitayos in comparison to the other Spaniards of Latacunga, an inequity of which numerous parties complained after every seventeenth-century visita. In addition it was reported that Matías de Peralta had forced the indigenous peoples to pay ten thousand pesos for documents proving ownership of lands to which they already had title and also collected from Spaniards eight thousand pesos in fines and two thousand pesos for titles proving their rights to mitayos; this to swell the coffers of the official scribe, who was none other than Juan de Vera, another in-law.[52]

Sandoval declared that the visitador and his relatives were able to escape with these fraudulent practices by threatening the Spaniards that if they appealed, they would not assign them mitayos for their haciendas. Likewise they threatened the Andeans that if they issued official complaints, they would "visit" them again.[53] Clearly an interlocking web of familial relationships and economic interests had already begun to leave a mark on bureaucratic processes as determinant as the enumeration of the colonized peoples. Nepotism and the needs of particular interest groups would henceforth color all population counts of the colonial administration.

Overcounts and other abuses intended to maximize the fiscal and labor obligations of the indigenous population became the order of the day for seventeenth-century visitas. The native response to this new administrative rigor was one of renewed flight, that both subverted bureaucratic objectives aimed at demographic accuracy and made nepotic projects counterproductive. In predictable fashion migrations intensified after each and every

census, as Andeans attempted to escape excessive labor quotas and the status of "eternal mitayo." Caciques were quick to point out that the
heavy-handed style of the "new" visita was to blame for accentuating the
problem of absenteeism and related tribute deficits. Indeed the contradictions inherent in the "improved" system can be clearly seen in the reports
of native leaders, who claimed consistently that great numbers of their subjects had fled "after the last enumeration."

These claims were numerous for the visita of Matías de Peralta, but they
became even more common in association with later inspections.[54] In 1666,
for example, the cacique of Yaruquís (Corregimiento of Riobamba) reported
that 26 of 155 absentees (17 percent) had fled immediately after the visita
made by Don Pedro de Viteri in 1665.[55]

Borchart de Moreno, in her study of seventeenth-century migration in
Riobamba, also notes that visitas and censuses were often in themselves
causes of flight.[56] This chain of events—enumeration, flight, the need for
subsequent enumeration—would repeat itself throughout the rest of the
period. In short the new-style administration of the seventeenth century,
while it had some short-lived successes, ended by causing even more demographic instability. The ensuing turmoil would eventually contribute to
the crown's losing its newly attained but slippery grasp on the Quito colony.

The general weakening of royal authority, so prominent in administrative studies of the late-seventeenth-century Viceroyalty of Peru, was reflected
in the turn of demographic events in the Audiencia of Quito.[57] As the seventeenth century proceeded and the crown's economic and political position in Europe became increasingly debased, financial measures intended
to underwrite a recovery resulted in a concurrent debasement of royal power
in the colonies. The increasing sale of public offices and the escalating practice of composición (the legalization of ill-gotten Andean lands through
the payment of a fee) became important components of a desperate program to pull the Spanish crown out of the abyss.

Ironically these provisional measures both prompted population movements that were injurious to royal interests and facilitated new forms of
subterfuge; they resulted in the movement of Andean tributes away from
royal coffers and into the pockets of increasingly corrupt Spanish and native officials. As will be seen shortly, the excesses of those who had purchased their offices, in combination with the dispossession of the indigenous
peoples, gave rise to accelerated migration rates and a considerable expansion of the absent population. In turn, the new "independence" of the
corregidores and other local officials created a free-for-all atmosphere that
enabled the latter to form highly productive alliances with some segments

of the native leadership. The central objective of these partnerships was to manipulate two statistical categories: the "ausentes" (absentees) and the "rezagos" (back tributes).

The absent population that resulted from out-migration had traditionally presented caciques and corregidores with myriad opportunities for fraud. Nevertheless, as described in chapter 2, migration toward the Spanish sphere caused the number of absentees to surpass that of the resident population in many Andean communities. These movements, accompanied by diminishing royal control of the colonial bureaucracy, generated conditions under which it became possible to create a large-scale industry out of the manipulation of both demographic and fiscal statistics.

In the Audiencia of Quito, the corregidores were permitted, for unknown reasons, to enter the unpaid tributes of absent Andeans in the royal accounts as rezagos, for which they were not held personally responsible. While this privilege had always facilitated lucrative deals between caciques and corregidores concerning the population counts of individual towns, the removal of the traditional system of checks and balances that resulted from the sale of public offices and the creolization of the audiencia's bureaucracy paved the way for unimpeded and comprehensive demographic fraud.[58]

The typical scam of the late seventeenth and early eighteenth centuries, and one which appears to have become generalized to the entire audiencia, involved the statistical manipulation of ausentes and rezagos. Absent Andeans became the centerpiece of a form of subterfuge in which the corregidores of their towns of origin listed them on the tribute rolls as ausentes and recorded their delinquent tributes as rezagos, while the corregidores in their places of residence omitted them from fiscal records because they were forasteros. In this way large numbers of Andeans disappeared from official records as accountable individuals and were lost to the royal tribute system. They had not, however, disappeared for the corregidores, their lieutenants, the collectors, and the caciques, who made a veritable business out of searching the audiencia for absentees, extracting their tributes, and pocketing them.

It is evident from the documentation that the native leadership, although it participated in the fraudulent practices of the period, no longer enjoyed parity with Spanish officials in the proceeds. One incensed royal official claimed that the frauds committed by the audiencia's caciques were of little impact when compared to those of their Spanish counterparts, because when caciques engaged in embezzlement they were content with less.[59] Indeed in a desperate letter to the king in 1677, a group of apparently disenfranchised caciques of Quito stated: "there are no vagamundos because even the Indians who flee their communities end up paying tribute [ostensibly] to the crown, the proceeds of which are pocketed by the corregidores and their collectors."[60]

That tribute frauds based on the absent population were both lucrative and widespread was borne out by the number of cases brought to the attention of audiencia officials during the late seventeenth and early eighteenth centuries. The first documented case appears in 1677 and involves both the caciques and Spanish officials of Chimbo. Don Juan Guerrero Salazar, an official scribe of Chimbo, was granted a commission to investigate reports of tribute frauds in his district. In the course of the investigation, the corregidor's assistants threatened his life; evidently an indication of both the veracity of the reports and of the financial import of local operations.[61] Indeed Guerrero eventually uncovered several cases of graft. In 1677 he became aware of the great number of Andeans who appeared on the original tribute rolls and whom local officials had since declared dead or absent, their tributes being reported as rezagos. After a fair amount of probing, he uncovered receipts in the tributaries' possession that proved categorically that Spanish officials of Chimbo were collecting tributes on a regular basis from 288 absentees resident in Guayaquil and 50 absentees resident in the city of Quito.[62] In addition, Chimbo authorities were reported to have had absentees in Cuenca, Riobamba, Ambato, Quito, Latacunga, and Ibarra from whom they collected tributes and even back tributes at times. In one instance the corregidor's tribute collector, Antonio de Mora, and his son, Marcelo de Mora, collected 2,000 pesos over a two-year period from Andeans who lived in Guayaquil, but left them unreported.[63]

In another case reported in 1694, Guerrero Salazar came upon clear-cut evidence for the withholding of funds. By comparing the Andeans' receipts with fiscal records that the corregidor had presented to the royal treasury, he discovered a large discrepancy in one community; the receipts of 188 tributaries amounted to 3,973 pesos, while the money the corregidor had delivered to the royal coffers totaled only 1,749.[64] He charged that Spanish and native officials had conspired to retain two-thirds of the tributes by reporting two-thirds of the population as dead or absent and their tributes as rezagos.[65] Indeed he claimed that the statistical manipulation of absent Andeans and their "unpaid" tributes was a prevalent strategy among local bureaucrats throughout the length and breadth of the land. That this scam had become, by the late seventeenth century, a generalized phenomenon in the Audiencia of Quito is clear from the geographic dispersion of the data. Examples have surfaced as far north as the city of Pasto, where caciques and corregidores received a provisional decree in 1688 from the protector of the

Indians, Don Ignacio de Aybar, freeing them of all responsibility for the tributes of the absent population.[66]

In 1690 the crown countered with a decree reversing this exemption and reprimanded the audiencia for overstepping its authority. In the course of the communication, it was revealed that local officials of Pasto were using this provision to hide large numbers of Andeans as ausentes. This practice succeeded in creating an unofficial population that then migrated freely to the obrajes of the city and to those of Ibarra, leaving enormous gaps in the royal tribute system. Tellingly the official who facilitated the provision was himself an obraje owner.[67]

The most impressive scandal of all, however, took place in the Corregimiento of Quito, seat of the Audiencia. The existence of widespread demographic fraud in a region so close to the reins of power is significant for what it says about the audiencia's lack of authority or, perhaps, its partial acquiescence. In 1691 the oidor, Don Matías de Lagúnez, reported that there were 150,000 tributaries, both originarios and forasteros, in the Corregimiento of Quito, who should deliver 300,000 pesos annually to the royal coffers, if tribute were collected properly. He claimed that under the present system, only 15,000 Andeans appeared on the tribute rolls of the corregimiento and only 13,000 pesos were collected per year.[68] With regard to the city proper, he charged that there were 40,000 Andeans resident within its confines, but that the corregidores had enumerated only 1,200 on the tribute rolls.[69] This vast discrepancy between potential and real tributaries in both the city and the corregimiento was attributed to the huge number of absentees in the audiencia, many of whom worked in the city's obrajes and whose caciques came from as far away as forty or fifty leagues to collect their tributes surreptitiously.[70]

Lagúnez reported that the audiencia's bureaucracy was organized as follows: 13 corregidores, each of whom had 3 lieutenants who assisted with the collection of tributes; each lieutenant had, in turn, 6 collectors; in addition there were 300 caciques who searched for the absentees during the collection.[71] With a flare for the dramatic, he pointed out that there were 563 Spanish and native officials in the Audiencia of Quito, all of whom made their living from the manipulation of the ausentes and many of whom had gone from rags to riches through tribute frauds.[72]

In contrast the fiscal of the audiencia, Antonio de Ron, responded to these charges in 1694, insisting that while fraud existed on some level, Lagúnez had exaggerated its magnitude. He claimed that the crux of the problem lay with the corregidores, who retained the Andeans' tributes during the tenure of their offices in order to invest them in their own enterprises, but who had no intention of keeping the funds indefinitely.[73]

Interestingly he reversed his position in 1695 and admitted that the manipulation of ausentes and rezagos on the part of the corregidores and their assistants had grown out of control.[74] Evidently there was some truth to Lagúnez's reports. Even if only a quarter of all Spanish and native officials participated in this scam, royal divestment would have been considerable. Indeed additional documentation indicates that the tribute frauds of the audiencia's corregidores had reached startling dimensions by the early eighteenth century.[75]

Far from the overcounts so prevalent earlier in the seventeenth century, some areas of the audiencia reported gross undercounts for this period—a reversal that reflects a loss of crown control and a transition of labor systems.[76] Escalating royal crises gave way to a creolization of colonial bureaucracy that if not always consonant with the provenance of officials (some continued to be peninsular Spaniards), coincided frequently with local objectives.

The crown's tenuous grasp on its colonies facilitated the statistical manipulation of the native population for the benefit of both creoles and resident peninsulars. Considering that the majority of large encomiendas in the audiencia continued to be granted as pensions to royal courtiers, the underreporting of the native population was not prejudicial to local elites. Conversely for those involved in government, population undercounts and the embezzlement of Andean tributes allegedly represented quite a bonanza.

In addition increased migration to the Spanish sphere in the late seventeenth century undermined the mita and caused the ascendance of free wage labor as the predominant labor system. Consequently overcounting the population for the purposes of assigning excessive numbers of mitayos was no longer a viable demographic tactic. Now that the majority of Andeans had been incorporated into the obraje/hacienda complex, undercounts became highly desirable. After all, how many creoles cared to be responsible for the royal tributes of their native workers?

In short undercounts and the tribute frauds that accompanied them became the centerpiece of strategies for autonomy and self-determination on the part of local elites. According to the assessment of the oidor, Don Matías Lagúnez, local officials were, by 1680, already draining the majority of the audiencia's tributes out through a huge crack in the system.[77] It should not be surprising, when one considers the southern parallels; this is, after all, the period during which extraordinary amounts of silver were being diverted from Potosí to Buenos Aires, a contraband route, the flow of which was undoubtedly facilitated by the creolization of the region's bureaucracy. Since the indigenous peoples were the mines in the Audiencia of Quito, it is only logical that the trend toward crown divestment should take the form of extensive tribute fraud.

Conclusion

The tug-of-war between the Spanish state and the Andean population over demographic accountability followed a tortuous route and had a rather surprising outcome. During the sixteenth century, the subterfuge practiced by the native leadership and the physical movements of ordinary Andeans created a substantial "hidden" population, which gave the colonized peoples a decisive edge in the struggle.

The years 1590 to 1666, however, saw a concerted Spanish effort to tighten up administration and account for the unreported population. During this period various strategies were utilized to integrate marginal groups into the fiscal and labor systems of the colony. These included the manifestación, the formation of crown parcialidades of vagabonds, and the incorporation of forasteros into the ayllus of originarios. Native peoples struggled to maintain some autonomous space within this increasingly efficient colonial system. But by the 1630s, the Spanish state, representing the interests of the crown and traditional elites, had not only wrested control of population statistics from the caciques, but had committed excesses (overcounts and inflation of mita quotas) in its quest for demographic accountability.

The late seventeenth and early eighteenth centuries, however, witnessed a reversal of this trend, as the weakening of royal authority, combined with the growing movement of Andeans to obrajes and haciendas, facilitated an alliance between Spanish officials and a segment of the native leadership. This alliance had as its major objective the statistical manipulation of the absentees and their tribute arrears for the purposes of embezzlement.

The new demographic frauds of the period reflected the increasing autonomy of local elites at the expense of both the crown and the majority of Andeans. The crown's position deteriorated, as its loss of control was translated into significant financial divestment. The indigenous position was also further undermined, because royal desperation led to extensive divestment of Andean lands through composiciones. This loss generated more migration to the Spanish sphere, which solved the resource shortage but ended in the almost complete forfeiture of native autonomy. In addition movement no longer provided escape from tributes, since local officials, though eager to underreport the native population, now harassed the absentees to pay them on a systematic basis.

In short during the sixteenth and seventeenth centuries, manipulation of demographic statistics passed from Andean control to that of the state; nevertheless the texture of control changed once again in the second half of the seventeenth century, from that of a colonial state operating in the interests of the crown to a creolized state that functioned under the auspices of local elites. The concept of demographic accountability also changed, in accordance with the needs of whatever group was dominant.

Lastly it is important to note that the transformation of the state was not solely Spanish-generated, but was also informed by Andean actions. The decision to migrate, for example, to crown jurisdictions in the early seventeenth century helped to undermine the position of local encomenderos and secure royal control of the colony. Conversely the accelerated movements from the Indian to the Spanish sphere in the late seventeenth century contributed to the decay of crown authority and helped to place the reins of state apparatus in the hands of local elites.

4
Migration and the Reproduction
of the Cacicazgo

If Andean migration was a compelling force in the state formation of the Spanish colony, it was pivotal in the ethnogenesis of Quito's indigenous societies. As previous chapters have shown, migration away from communities of origin was an Andean survival strategy, an individual and collective response to the pressures of the colonial regime. It was not, however, a static response, but one that changed forever the social and political framework within which native individuals rose to leadership, as well as the power base upon which they established and maintained authority. I will argue that these interior changes in indigenous sociopolitical structures were often the key to community reproduction in the Audiencia of Quito until the late seventeenth century.

The consequences of migration and forasterismo for Andean society were many and far-reaching. In the next two chapters, however, I will limit my analysis to one institution—the cacicazgo (chiefdom)—since the trajectory of the caciques' historical experience mirrored, in important ways, the general evolution of indigenous society under the early colony. This correlation had its origins in Andean concepts of rule that typically created a confluence of chiefly and community interests.

Although Quito's cacicazgos were pre-Incaic polities adulterated early on by Spanish practices, their members continued to have more than political expectations of leaders. The cacique, owing to his role as administrator of his subjects' labor and resources, was not just a political figure, but the guardian of the community's socioeconomic system as well. Furthermore his legitimacy rested on the efficiency with which he carried out his administrative and redistributive obligations and on his ability to practice "institutionalized generosity." The community reciprocated by providing its leader with labor. Although the reciprocal relationship between rulers and ruled weakened considerably during the early colonial period, its partial continuation ensured that the reproduction of the cacicazgo, even if narrowly defined as the successful retention of the cacique's personal power, often translated into the reproduction of the community. Thus the strategies by which leaders maintained their position merit more probing examination.

Documentation of the fate of early Quiteño caciques is highly contradictory. Evidence for the frequent dispossession of cacicazgos by dissatisfied Spanish officials is juxtaposed with an abundant record of prestigious awards and offices granted members of the indigenous elite. Administrative reports and royal decrees of the 1550s and 1560s are replete with futile complaints from failed caciques, whose descent from power was early and swift and whose names disappeared from the archival record without a trace.[1] Alongside the fallen, however, are the ubiquitous Hachos, Zámbizas, Puentos, Angos, and Hatis, to mention a few, whose families' illustrious activities fill hundreds of documents over the span of three centuries.[2] Obviously some of Quito's caciques learned to maneuver within the new colonial system from an early date and some did not. What distinguished those who survived the colonization process from those who vanished?

A great part of the answer lies in a cacique's personal ability to resolve the leadership dilemma of the period. The successful colonial cacique legitimized his authority in both the Spanish and Indian spheres by simultaneously satisfying two sets of criteria. A cacique's power rested on his ability to fulfill contracts with both the colonial regime and the community by promptly provisioning tribute and labor, on the one hand, and by efficiently administering his people's work and resources and ensuring their good treatment, on the other. His subjects depended on him not only to prevent their exploitation but to show them great generosity, which in turn depended on his accumulating and maintaining wealth.[3]

Naturally the dilemma arose from the competing needs of each sphere for the same resources and the frequency with which requisites of the two contracts came into gross conflict. In the sixteenth century, a period characterized by native depopulation and a fledgling colonial state incapable of mediating the excessive demands of the colonists, the pressure point of this dilemma was labor; later in the seventeenth century, land also became a serious point of contention between the two contracts.

Resolving such conflicts tended to depend upon a chief's adeptness at accruing additional wealth and labor to himself and his community. Ironically migration, which has been posited in other studies as a catalyst for the destructuration of indigenous society, contained the seeds of resolution for the early caciques of the Audiencia of Quito.[4] What follows is an exposition of how successful caciques of the sixteenth and early seventeenth centuries developed adaptive strategies based on migration, forasterismo, and other related demographic phenomena, which enabled them both to maintain personal power and to reproduce Andean society. These successful indigenous authorities will be referred to as early colonial caciques. While their ranks included both hereditary and non-hereditary rulers, they shared a common leadership style in that they strove to straddle the fence between the Spanish and Indian spheres and to fulfill the contracts of both; that is, they did not entirely forsake their Andean responsibilities in an attempt to appease the colonial regime.

The Composition of Private Work Forces

It is known from previous studies, both in Quito and elsewhere in the Andes, that many of these leaders became enormously wealthy in the sixteenth century, through their participation in the European market economy.[5] But how did they manage to fulfill the excessive labor demands of the Spanish state and still retain enough labor to operate their own and their communities' enterprises?[6]

Abundant evidence corroborates that during the sixteenth and early seventeenth centuries, Quito's caciques resolved the Spanish/Andean conflict over human resources through the unilateral formation of labor reserves. These extraofficial reserves consisted of Andeans who were not formally subject to the obligations of the colonial state and were put together in a variety of ways through the autonomous actions of indigenous rulers. As demonstrated in chapter 3, an inefficient Spanish bureaucracy, combined with an astute native leadership, produced a large, elusive demographic element throughout the sixteenth century; that is, caciques traditionally hid a percentage of the population from census takers, in an attempt to create private workforces. Nevertheless this strategy was effective only for as long as the Spanish regime remained incompetent. As the colonial administration became progressively tighter, the numbers of Andeans who could be hidden from view diminished considerably; by the census of Matías de Peralta (1614–26), Spanish officials were aware of most forms of demographic subterfuge.

Another well-documented strategy was privatization of the labor resources of the Inca state; that is, the cooptation of camayos. After the collapse of the Inca empire, many Andeans who had formerly been designated as workers on state projects (coca cultivation, public works, and communications, for example) were summarily incorporated into the labor reserves of local caciques. Far from the semiprivileged outlier workers of pre-Hispanic times, camayos of the late sixteenth century appeared, at least to Spanish eyes, as a captive labor force, described by one ecclesiastic as "slaves" of the caciques.[7]

The effectiveness of these strategies, however, pales in significance when compared to the extraofficial potential of large numbers of forasteros. The aggregation of hundreds of vagabonds and the deliberate enticement of Andeans from other communities became the strategy par excellence for composing private work forces. That the conscientious recruitment of forasteros became a generalized solution for the caciques' labor dilemma is abundantly clear from the record. Sixteenth- and early-seventeenth-century examples abound for nearly every major region of the intermontane corridor and for some lowland areas as well.[8]

This survival strategy has been analyzed for three regionally specific cases: (1) The Valley of Chillos and the town of Chillogallo, in the Corregimiento of Quito; (2) the town of Tontaquí, in the Corregimiento of Otavalo; and (3) several towns in the Corregimiento of Latacunga. These illustrations point to a marked forastero presence in the indigenous sphere and to the prominent role these outsiders played in underwriting the caciques' ability to meet the demands of two mutually exclusive contracts.

The first illustration, that of the Corregimiento of Quito, centers on the importance of forasteros in key sectors of the native economy and most especially in the production of cotton textiles. As demonstrated by the work of Chantal Caillavet, cotton-textile production was an important pre-Hispanic industry in Quito, Otavalo, and the eastern lowlands. These areas not only provided cloth for local subsistence, but produced a surplus that was exported throughout the region and even transported by sea to Peru. With the imposition of the Spanish regime, a large part of the production was diverted to the colonial market through tributes to encomenderos, private contracts with Spanish individuals, public contracts with the colonial state, and the new entrepreneurial efforts of the caciques themselves.[9] Yet while the Spanish economy placed inordinately heavy demands on the industry, the native export economy did not disappear. The volume of cotton textiles destined for native commerce declined, causing a serious contraction of the geographic scope of the industry's pre-Hispanic trade patterns; nevertheless production for the Andean economy was sustained, though at substantially reduced levels.[10]

How was it possible to achieve this balancing act between the excessive demands of the Spanish economy and the requirements, albeit constricted, of the Andean economy? Obviously the new strain necessitated the accelerated production of both raw materials and finished textiles; this must have implied intensification of cotton cultivation in the hotlands and of spin-

ning and weaving activities everywhere, both of which required amplifica-
tion of the work force during a period punctuated by severe epidemics and
high mortality. That the production rate was very high in spite of these
depopulating events is evident both from Spanish reports of large profits
made in cotton textiles and from official and ecclesiastical complaints about
the near monopolization of native labor in textile production.[11] How were
such high production rates sustained throughout the sixteenth and early
seventeenth centuries?

The competing needs of the Spanish and Indian spheres were resolved
by supplementing the labor force with forasteros. Abundant evidence points
to widespread recruitment of "foreign" Andeans both by caciques and even
by native commoners, in a desperate attempt to satisfy the requirements of
the colonial regime while maintaining their own economies.

Dire dependence on the labor of these recruits is reflected in the sizable
remuneration the latter often received for their spinning and weaving skills.
A letter written by Quito's bishop, Fray Luis López de Solís, is especially
illuminating. While describing his inspection of an unnamed repartimiento,
he made the following observation in 1598:

> While making an inspection of my bishopric, I passed through one
> repartimiento where the corregidor's wife undertook every morn-
> ing to assemble all the Indian women of the town in a corral . . . to
> spin cotton for the corregidor . . . all the corregidores monopolize
> the Indians' labor to such an extreme that they do not have time to
> produce clothing for themselves or their families, nor to pay their
> tributes, nor to cultivate their fields . . . with the result that they
> must hire foreign Indians at excessive prices in order to make the
> cloth for their tributes.[12]

In contrast to the mass of forasteros whom sixteenth- and early-
seventeenth-century observers described as the "slaves of Quito's caciques,"
these foreign spinners and weavers apparently received adequate compen-
sation for their labor.[13]

The Valley of Chillos in the Corregimiento of Quito was an area where
cotton-textile production predominated and which traditionally harbored
large numbers of forasteros. Already in the visita of 1559, forasteros represented 7 percent of the population of the six towns inspected, while one of
those towns, Anan Chillo, reported a forastero population of nearly 14 percent.[14] These "foreign" Andeans were said to have been in Chillos since 1544
by permission of the local caciques, and, as will be seen subsequently, their
true numbers may have been much greater than those officially recorded.

The proliferation of forasteros in Chillos comes to light again in 1596, when the Cabildo of Quito investigated reports that the indigenous population of Uyumbicho had, for many years, been clearing the city's timberlands to plant corn. Both Spanish and Andean testimony revealed that part of the community's land squeeze could be attributed to the large numbers of forasteros who had gravitated toward or been recruited to the town and who, in the absence of land, cultivated crops on the previously forested slopes in flagrant violation of city ordinances.[15]

That Chillos was an especially productive cotton-textile region is evident from data presented in the *residencia* (official review) of the corregidor, Licenciado Juan de Salazar Villasante, in 1564–66. In testimony presented for this official review, it comes to light that the cotton-textile economy of Chillos experienced all the usual pressures of the period. Francisco Ruiz, the encomendero, was reported to have monopolized the labor of Andean women in cotton spinning to the detriment of their families and communities; the corregidor was accused of dealing in textiles for his own account and collecting tributes (presumably in cloth) in excess of the official rate; and the caciques allegedly followed the example of the encomendero and the corregidor, setting up private enterprises based on the unremunerated labor of their subjects. It is claimed that this abuse of the textile-producing abilities of the Chillos peoples had caused many of them to migrate out of the region.[16]

Nevertheless these communities, far from disintegrating, not only remained intact, but experienced explosive demographic growth between 1559 and 1591, as demonstrated in chapter 1. Evidently Andean leaders succeeded in devising strategies not only to fulfill the requisites of the official colonial contract and to absorb its unofficial abuses, but also to siphon off enough of the proceeds to reproduce the community and retain power.

Closer examination of the documentation on Chillos reveals that forasteros played a significant role in underwriting the community's reproduction. According to the census of 1559, there were a number of forasteros resident in the towns of this region from an early date. Though difficult to quantify, their numbers grew steadily, as witnessed by testimony of 1596 that the area had become a magnet for foreign Andeans.[17]

That these forasteros formed part of the caciques' labor reserve can be deduced from an accusation made in the official review of 1566. Witnesses testified that "the encomendero coerces the caciques to work the Indians harder by threatening to report to the audiencia that they have excessive numbers of Indian servants who do not pay tributes."[18] Many of these Andeans who "do not pay tributes" were undoubtedly forasteros and other

retainers who belonged to the private work forces of the region's caciques—
work forces that the encomendero threatened to have the state confiscate if
the caciques did not comply with his demands. Considering the strain placed
on the cotton-textile industry of Chillos, it is logical that the caciques' labor reserves would have been closely tied to this important economic sector.

The employment of forasteros in the production of cotton textiles comes
to light later, in the payment records of a state contract. In 1617 the viceroy,
the príncipe de Esquilache, cognizant of the cotton-textile tradition of
Quiteño peoples, commissioned the twenty-four native communities of the
Corregimiento of Quito and the seven Andean parishes of the city of Quito
to spin cotton for the canvas and ropes necessary to equip the crown's ar-
mada. The spinners were paid one real per pound of cleaned and spun cotton and received their pay as individuals.[19]

Payment records for the towns of Amaguaña and Chillogallo reveal that
all payments were made to Andean women, but of more interest for the
discussion at hand is that many of these women were forasteras.[20] In
Chillogallo, sixteen out of fifty-five women (or 29 percent) listed in the
payment record belonged to an ayllu of forasteros, while a few of the names
of women listed in other ayllus were readily identifiable as foreign to the
area. Names such as Quilago and Payatanga, of Otavalo and Chimbo origins, indicate that some forasteros had already been incorporated into the
ayllus of originarios either through marriage or official error.[21]

Conversely while most of the names recorded for forasteros were clearly
of foreign extraction, a few were local, such as Sinaylen and Locnango—
surnames that also appeared in the ayllus of the originarios.[22] This contradiction suggests a number of possible trends: (1) That these women were,
perhaps, originarias married to forasteros, indicating that by the early seventeenth century, forasteros were well integrated into the community;[23] (2)
that some migration was fairly localized and may have been the result of
enticement of Andeans from nearby towns; and (3) that caciques may have
formed labor reserves from the members of their own communities by des-
ignating them as forasteros, who would consequently be exempt from the
mita.

In Amaguaña the record does not list an ayllu of forasteros, nor are the
names especially foreign to the area; nevertheless prior to the payments,
Spanish officials demanded that all Andeans who had spun cotton for the
crown, whether originarios or forasteros, be present at the transaction.[24]
Since Amaguaña, previously called Anan Chillo, supported the largest
forastero population of the 1559 census (151 Andeans), it is not surprising

that officials should assume that some of the task had been done by
forasteros.[25]

The labor of forasteros is evident in other sectors of Amaguaña's economy
as well. In a suit of 1626 over lands, Miguel Chicaiza of Sigchos testified
that he and several other forasteros worked for the Tomaico people of
Amaguaña; the latter were described as tributary Andeans who paid
forasteros to cultivate their fields.[26] Evidently they had more lucrative or
pressing business and so, reproduced their community's subsistence
economy with the labor of foreign Andeans.

That the Valley of Chillos and its environs was, in the sixteenth century,
a focal point of in-migration is demonstrated by documentation available
for Chillogallo, Amaguaña, and Uyumbicho, three of the region's largest
communities. Whether the caciques and commoners of this area had benefited serendipitously from population displacements in other regions or
had deliberately recruited these Andeans from other communities remains
unclear. What is clear, however, is that the forasteros that these migrations
produced were used to supplement the work force in key sectors of the
economy at crucial times, thereby underwriting the successful reproduction of the region's indigenous society.

In contrast to the Corregimiento of Quito, where forasteros were incorporated almost imperceptibly into indigenous economic activities, the case
of Tontaquí, in the Corregimiento of Otavalo, is a straightforward example
of how caciques utilized the forasteros' labor in direct fulfillment of the
community's obligations to the Spanish state. As demonstrated in chapter
1, Otavalo experienced a continuous influx of migrants from the region of
Pasto who were reported to have been lured south by Otavaleño caciques.
Tontaquí, one of the corregimiento's largest Andean towns, absorbed a substantial number of its wandering northern neighbors. Not surprisingly legal problems surfaced in the eighteenth century that bring to light the terms
of the original agreement between the town's authorities and the ancestors
of forasteros from Pasto.

A suit of 1701 between Don Marcos Camuento, leader of the Camuento
ayllu, and twenty families of Pastuzos resident in Tontaquí, reveals that the
ancestors of these forasteros had contracted with Don Marcos's grandfather to exchange their labor for access to land. Don Marcos accused the
forasteros of trying to gain legal possession of lands that he said were assigned to them by him, and by his father and grandfather before him, in
exchange for their labor. He then described the specific terms of the contract: in return for access to lands left vacant by absent ayllu members, the
forasteros were obliged to work in the repair of the community obraje, the

houses of the cabildo, the monasteries, and the public jail of the *asiento* (Spanish urban center) of Otavalo, as well as to perform many other tasks of the Indian republic.[27] In other words these forasteros were unofficially incorporated into the *mita de obras* (labor draft for public works) of Otavalo.

Much can be extrapolated from this suit about the adaptive strategies that caciques derived from Andean migration and associated phenomena. Although movement from Pasto to Otavalo began soon after the Spanish conquest, these forasteros claimed that their ancestors arrived in Tontaquí eighty years before the date of the suit, or around 1621. This period was marked by a precipitous increase in the Spanish population and the apogee of the obraje economy—two factors that may explain the very specific terms of the original forasteros' contract with one of Tontaquí's leaders. According to the testimony of their descendants, they were contracted to work in the transport of timber to the asiento of Otavalo and in the repair of the town's buildings. The defendants stipulated further that they and their ancestors had always performed this labor, because it had traditionally been the job of all forasteros who settled in the Corregimiento of Otavalo. They then went on to explain that the region's originarios worked only in the crown obrajes and were not assigned to do any other kind of labor.[28]

Several trends in the formation and purpose of labor reserves can be discerned from this testimony for the early seventeenth century. First a growing Spanish population transformed the asiento of Otavalo into a flourishing urban center that required a progressively larger mita de obras—an obligation that Otavaleño caciques were apparently able to meet by utilizing forastero labor.[29] Second by assigning forasteros to the mita de obras, the caciques could dedicate the originario work force exclusively to the *mita de obrajes* (labor draft for the textile industry), thereby maximizing woolen-textile production at a time when the demands of the Potosí market were at their highest. The forasteros may also have taken up the slack in other spheres, enabling local leaders to retain more workers for their own and their communities' enterprises.

The forasteros' participation in the mita, however, gives rise to a puzzling question and one that the suit addresses only obliquely: since Andeans were always reported to have fled their communities to escape the mita, why did the Pastuzos migrate to Otavalo and agree to perform mita duties? Judging from two of the six Pasto names that appear in the suit, Nicolás Potosí and Francisco Potosí (Potosí being the name of a small mining center near Pasto), it would seem that at least some of these Pastuzos fled to escape mining work. In the Pasto region, mining was reportedly performed as personal service, that is, without benefit of even the little remuneration that usually accompanied the mita.[30] Undoubtedly repairing buildings in Otavalo in return for land was more attractive than forced labor in the mines of Pasto. The relatively benign nature of the mita de obras in comparison to labor conditions in Pasto may be the reason why Otavalo represents an aberration in the contractual agreements generally found to exist between caciques and forasteros in other areas. For most forasteros of this period, exemption from the mita was highly coveted and became the crux of numerous suits.

The litigation of 1701 also reveals that the original forasteros were given access to the lands of the ausentes of the Camuento ayllu. This indicates that Tontaquí had experienced its own out-migration and sought to resolve the resultant problems of labor shortages and vacant lands by filling both vacuums with forasteros.[31] As will be seen subsequently, "land for labor" was the constant refrain of agreements between indigenous leaders and forasteros throughout the audiencia and indeed throughout the Andean region.[32]

It is also evident that the ancestors of the Pasto forasteros constituted part of a chiefly labor reserve, unknown to and uncontrolled by the Spanish regime. An examination of the Pasto names appearing in the suit of 1701 and the names listed in the census of the Camuento ayllu in 1646 reveals that of the six Pastuzos whose names appear in the suit, only one is listed in the 1646 census; since his name, Lorenzo Morales, is a common Spanish name, it could have belonged to someone else. Of the distinctly Pasto personal and place-names borne by these men—Tangualpaz, Caltarín, Potosí, and Pasto—none appears in the census.[33] Although there is a possibility that their family names may have changed across generations, there are so few out-of-area names in the enumeration of this ayllu that it is almost certain that the Pasto forasteros eluded the census taker. Considering the almost absolute anthroponymic homogeneity of the census and the absence of an ayllu of forasteros, it seems unlikely that the ancestors of these defendants were incorporated into the official count of the community's tributaries; rather they were part of a truly private work force, subject only to the dictates of the indigenous leadership.

In short the caciques of Otavalo succeeded in keeping abreast of the ever-increasing demands of the Spanish regime by composing an alternative labor supply from the Pastuzo refugees and their descendants. The case of Tontaquí may represent only the tip of the iceberg with regard to the pivotal role played by forasteros in the reproduction of Otavalo's indigenous society. As demonstrated in chapter 1, one of the more substantial and identifiable migratory flows of the period was that from Pasto to Otavalo; forasteros from Pasto were a generalized phenomenon in Otavalo, and judging from the defendants' assertion that performing the mita de obras was the traditional role of the region's forasteros, it is certain that the leaders of Tontaquí were not the only ones to formulate adaptive strategies on the basis of this alternative labor supply.

The third and last case, that of the Corregimiento of Latacunga, while not as reflective of the specific economic role of the forasteros, is the most developed example of the precise mechanisms by which caciques composed private work forces and of the methods by which the Spanish state eventually coopted their efforts. Latacunga is also the region for which there is the most aggregate data on forasteros, which may indicate either that they had an especially important function in these cacicazgos or simply that this is a fluke of historical preservation.

The abundance of material culled from lawsuits, wills, and other sources points to a strong and continuous forastero presence in the region. Furthermore the acumen which Latacungan caciques displayed in attracting these outsiders to their communities indicates that they were highly sought after and must have been assigned a significant role in the indigenous sphere of the area, whatever that role might have been. The attention the Spanish state diverted toward Latacunga's forasteros and the eagerness with which it sought to account for them is also highly instructive.

In 1633 Andrés de Sevilla, the chief scribe of royal inspections, was given a commission by the audiencia to enumerate all the "vagabond" Indians of the Corregimiento of Latacunga. He enlisted the aid of one of the regime's most favored Andean allies, the Hati family, giving Don Guillermo Hati Zanipatín authorization to round up all stray Andeans of the region in July of that year.[34] Within a startlingly short period of time, Don Guillermo produced two hundred potential tributaries and their families, seventy of whom were residing in his own town of San Miguel.[35] Andrés de Sevilla then registered these vagamundos on the rolls of San Sebastián, Saquisilí, Alaques, Mulahaló, and San Miguel, being careful to stipulate that they were to pay a lower tribute than the originarios, owing to their poverty and lack of land. He also emphasized that they were totally exempt from the mita and from any other form of forced labor or personal service.[36]

Almost immediately, however, Sevilla issued a decree (in November of 1633) revealing that the newly enrolled vagamundos of these towns had been and continued to be grossly mistreated by local caciques, hacendados, and royal officials. It is implied that these unfortunate outsiders had become over time an underclass who functioned as slaves and forced laborers for Andeans and Spaniards alike. He recommended that for their own protection they be aggregated under the rule of a single native governor, who could streamline tribute collection and ensure their status as free laborers.[37] In January of 1634, the governorship of all vagamundos of the Corregimiento of Latacunga, regardless of their towns of residence, was bestowed upon none other than Don Guillermo Hati Zanipatín. On that occasion Sevilla issued a strong warning that no other Andean or Spanish official should impinge on Don Guillermo's rule in any way, nor should they have anything at all to do with the administration of the vagamundos.[38]

Much can be extrapolated from the events of 1633–34 about the role of migration in the maintenance of chiefly power and community survival. That Don Guillermo and Andrés de Sevilla could have rounded up and officially enumerated two hundred vagamundos within a couple of months indicates that these Andeans, far from being ensconced in remote hideouts, were already in place as retainers of the caciques in the towns of the corregimiento.[39] Furthermore their utilization as a labor reserve was probably an established modus operandi in these cacicazgos, long before it came to the attention of the Spanish state.

It seems that in the years prior to 1633, the following chain of events took place. The caciques of Latacunga had made a prolonged and concerted effort to lure forasteros to settle in their towns by offering them access to land. There are a variety of reasons why the availability of land should have functioned as a pull factor in Latacunga. According to Carrera Colín, Latacunga had probably served as an agricultural colony for the Inca state. The Inca had confiscated or put under new cultivation vast expanses in this area for the production of maize, legumes, and tubers; hence the thousands of mitimaes resident in many of the corregimiento's towns.[40] When the Spanish conquest decapitated the Inca state, it appears that many Latacungan caciques privatized these lands. In addition out-migration and absenteeism, so prevalent by the turn of the seventeenth century, must have created even more vacant tracts, while Spanish encroachment, though significant in Latacunga by this period, had not yet caused widespread Andean losses. In contrast the Andeans of the neighboring Corregimiento of Quito were divested of their lands quite early, owing to their proximity to the Spanish city of Quito, seat of the audiencia and axis of the regional economy. Land shortage in Quito, then, functioned as a significant push factor for migration to Latacunga, where lands were still available.[41]

Latacungan caciques offered land as a powerful incentive for attracting forasteros to their communities and in exchange utilized the latter's services as a source of alternative labor; hence the accusations in 1633 of abuses and of the imposition of personal service obligations. Undoubtedly some forasteros migrated to Latacunga spontaneously, due to poor conditions in their communities of origin, but there is also evidence for a history of deliberate recruitment by local caciques. In 1580, for example, Doña Francisca Sinagsichi, wife of the famous Don Sancho Hacho, mentioned in her will that she had in her service many Andeans called Angoroes whom she "acquired" and brought from Cotocollao by promising them subsistence lands from among her private properties.[42] The proximity of Cotocollao to the city of Quito would dictate an early dispossession of these Andeans, making quite plausible their willingness to move to Latacunga. Nevertheless there is also an element of coercion in Doña Francisca's story, as she then recounted that they fled from her community to Ambato, where she pursued them and finally bent them to her will.[43]

Other examples of land incentives abound for Latacunga. A case of special interest is migration from the eastern montaña region of Quijos; poor treatment by encomenderos there induced indigenous peoples to migrate to the sierra, where they were said to have become "slaves" of highland caciques in return for land.[44] Considering the traditionally intimate relationship between Latacungan caciques and the Quijos, one can assume that a substantial part of this migratory flow was directed toward Latacunga. In the eighteenth century, tellingly, forasteros appear in the corregimiento's litigation records whose ancestors had migrated from Quijos a century before.[45]

Though impossible to quantify, it would appear from the abundance of qualitative data that the "land-for-labor" arrangement offered by the caciques attracted quite a large forastero population to Latacunga. The distribution of this population—clusters dispersed among several of the corregimiento's towns—reveals that deliberate aggregation of "foreign" retainers was a generalized strategy in the region.

The audiencia, however, must have been alerted to this growing number of vagamundos over whom Andean leaders had absolute power and who paid no tribute to the Spanish state. As shown in chapter 3, it became official policy to expand and tighten Spanish administration over this marginal population—marginal, that is, to Spanish control. In short Andrés de Sevilla's commission to count the "vagabond" Indians of Latacunga represents part of a wider attempt by the Spanish regime to usurp the aggregative efforts and reorganizational achievements of the audiencia's caciques.[46] Thus Andean leaders did the work of recruiting and coordinating the vagabond mass, and then Spanish officials moved in and took over their hard-won labor reserve.[47]

In Latacunga the state's usurpation of this indigenous project was accomplished by coopting one Andean leader. The audiencia offered a commission to Don Guillermo Hati Zanipatín to undertake an official roundup of the vagamundos and evidently promised him the governorship of all those he declared. By manipulating the sociopolitical ambitions of the indigenous leadership, the audiencia was able to concentrate the forasteros under the central administration of a single Indian official and then to incorporate them to the crown. This most certainly caused an erosion of power for many of the region's caciques, by depriving them of their tribute and mita-exempt work forces, while Don Guillermo Hati expanded his power tremendously at the expense of his cohorts.

The importance of forasteros to the Latacungan caciques, however, is disclosed by their reaction to the events of 1633–34. Indigenous leaders responded to the state's cooptation by accelerating recruitment efforts and struggling to recover political control of their "stolen" retainers. By 1655 the reported forastero population of Latacunga had jumped from 200 to 400 and by 1672 to 539; the number who remained unreported or who had been incorporated into the ayllus of originarios is a matter for conjecture. In addition they were eventually divided among nine towns, each contingent with its own governor.[48] Apparently the undermined caciques of 1633 had waged a battle to gain gubernatorial nominations of the new parcialidades that had been formed with their forastero recruits. A compromise with the colonial system was preferable to losing the forasteros altogether. It is evident, then, that audiencia officials had used the ambitions of Don Guillermo Hati to force the remaining Andean leaders to capitulate to colonial objectives—the incorporation of forasteros into the tributary base. The latter were, however, still exempt from the mita, an exemption that allowed caciques to continue their former strategy of utilizing forasteros in their own and community enterprises and perhaps even to continue operating as labor brokers to influential local Spaniards.

As in other areas of the Andes, the exchange of land for labor was the principal mechanism by which the caciques of most areas of the audiencia composed private work forces from the forastero mass. This strategy enabled them to retain power in the face of epidemics and out-migration, facilitating their ability to provide labor to the Spanish regime at the same time that they retained enough workers to operate both the community's and their own enterprises. The forasteros' occupation of the land also served, at least temporarily, to protect it from Spanish encroachment.

As seen in the works of Glave, Saignes, Sánchez-Albornoz, and Wightman, hiding Indians and making arrangements with forasteros were prevalent strategies among caciques in the southern Andes as well.[49] What is different about the north, however, is that there caciques actively recruited numerous forasteros not only from the vagabond mass, but also from among the subjects of other caciques. Since Saignes also found some recruitment among the caciques of Alto Perú, this may be a difference of degree rather than kind. Nevertheless it is reported so widely for the northern Andes that it takes on the air of an institutionalized practice. This difference may be related to two pre-Hispanic structures that distinguished the northern from the southern Andes: a more fluid political organization and long-distance merchants called *mindalaes*.

With regard to the first, it is important to consider that the caciques' deliberate recruitment of outsiders was very likely an integral element of the pre-Hispanic politics of north Andean chiefdoms. The works of Ramírez, Ramón, and Salomon point to more fluid political arrangements for the north Peruvian coast and the Ecuadorean highlands. Ramírez has found that "foreign" Andeans on the north coast were often attracted to prosperous communities and joined the ranks of successful caciques either by marrying into the group or by exchanging their labor for protection and assistance.[50] That Andeans in Quito utilized both these and other mechanisms to attach themselves to wealthy caciques and communities is abundantly clear.[51]

In addition Ramón reports similarly fluid pre-Hispanic patterns for the northern Ecuadorean sierra. In his study of the cacicazgo of Cayambe, he suggests that "land-for-labor" contracts between Andeans and hacendados of the area had their roots in similar pre-Hispanic arrangements between caciques and their Andean servants.[52] Whether these Andeans were recruited from within or from outside the community is unclear; nevertheless this practice may have established a pre-Hispanic precedent upon which similar agreements could be based between highland caciques and forasteros during the early colonial period.

The recruitment of outsiders was a mechanism by which caciques sought to enhance the importance and productivity of their communities, while attachment to a prosperous group was a mechanism by which commoners sought to improve the quality of their lives. Once there they were integrated into north Andean polities with more ease than appears to have been the case in the south. In Quito the frequent integration into town censuses of out-of-area surnames, in combination with qualitative data gleaned from land litigation, leaves an impression of high rates of intermarriage between originarios and forasteros and little or no assignment of low status to "outsiders," as had been found in the southern Andes.[53] Incorporation could also have been facilitated by the pre-Hispanic use of exogamy and child-loan to cement interzonal exchange arrangements in the Ecuadorean highlands.[54]

With regard to mindalaes (long-distance merchants), there is some evidence that points to their eventual use as migration agents or labor recruiters. In pre-Hispanic times one of the most important resources for a cacique's maintenance of power was exotic goods that he could distribute both inside and outside his community for political purposes. These were acquired by mindalaes working in his service. Under the Spanish regime, as labor became the most important requirement for continued rule, it appears that mindalaes used their skills and networks to acquire new subjects for their lords. Salomon, for example, reports that a cacique in Tusa used the services of a mindalá in 1563 to entice the Andeans of a neighboring community to join his ranks by offering them exotic goods.[55] In addition the geographic range where I have found most evidence for the caciques' recruitment of outsiders parallels the area that Salomon found to have the most mindalá activity—from Quito northward (although I would include Latacunga as well).

It would seem, then, that Quiteño peoples did not invent migration and forasterismo in reaction to the Spanish regime; rather these phenomena had their roots in aboriginal structures. While the incorporation of forasteros into community life may have been an old phenomenon, however, it undoubtedly took on substantially new forms and objectives during the early colonial period. The gross displacements occasioned by the Spanish conquest and by abuses of the new regime stimulated migrations that robbed communities of their original populations at the same time that they created a much larger pool of forasteros from which caciques could recruit new followers. In addition the enormous strain placed on the Indian sphere by colonial demands made recruitment efforts more urgent and more desirable than before, owing to the forasteros' exemption from state obligations. Thus intercommunity migration, once a casual mechanism for mutual enrichment, was escalated to a survival strategy, as caciques made a desperate attempt to fulfill the requisites of both Spanish and Andean contracts—that is, to appease the Spanish regime and maintain power, at the same time that they ensured the ongoing integrity of their communities. Clearly forasterismo is a perfect example of how pre-Hispanic sociopolitical structures were adapted and, in this case, accentuated to fit new colonial imperatives. In Sahlinsian terms, its cultural meaning was revalued by history. And in the light of Roseberry's model, that history was informed by political economy, more specifically, by Spanish colonialism.

The formation of chiefly labor reserves from the forastero mass was especially successful during the sixteenth century, but by the early seventeenth century this indigenous project had become more and more adulterated by Spanish aims. As the colonial state grew progressively stronger, its efforts toward demographic accountability and increased royal revenues (the systematic enumeration of forasteros and their incorporation into the tributary base) seriously undermined the effectiveness of this reproductive adaptation. A strategy that had once produced a tribute-exempt, private work force under the exclusive control of the indigenous leadership now yielded diminishing returns, as caciques were forced to compromise with the Spanish regime (that is, to declare the forasteros) in order to maintain at least nominal control over their recruits.

Another by-product of the burgeoning colonial bureaucracy and its increasingly prominent role in Andean life was that the Spanish judicial system offered an alternative to the forasteros themselves. Many descendants of the original migrants began to resort to litigation, in order to escape the bonds of former agreements. As time wore on, they refused to honor the contracts that their ancestors had made with the caciques and even attempted on occasion to gain legal possession of the lands that had been assigned to them in exchange for their labor.[56]

Lastly as demonstrated in chapter 2, the early seventeenth century saw a pronounced growth of Spanish population and of economic opportunities occasioned by the demands of Potosí. The latter stimulated a marked transition from a predominantly Andean economy to a predominantly Spanish economy and had serious repercussions on indigenous society. As the means of production passed from Andean to Spanish hands, migration was increasingly redirected toward the Spanish sphere, leaving the caciques with an ever-shrinking forastero mass from which to compose their private work forces. As the colony matured, both politically and economically, the survival strategy based on chiefly labor reserves began to break down.

According to the works of Glave and Saignes, when this trend occurred somewhat later in the southern Andes, some caciques continued to reproduce their communities by using the pre-Hispanic structure of the archipelago to orchestrate collective migrations to Spanish enterprises.[57] There allyu members extracted a new resource, wages, which subsidized the community's tributes and other expenses. In addition Andean officials frequently attempted to have these economic migrants subtracted from the tribute rolls, by claiming that they had fled. As discussed in chapter 3, this type of organized migration was reported for the central Ecuadorean highlands (corregimientos of Chimbo and Riobamba) but was less common for the northern region of the audiencia.[58] Tellingly the central sierra is precisely the region where Salomon found the most developed pre-Hispanic

archipelago.[59] Since this area was under Inca rule longer than northern Ecuador, it is logical that it manifested reproductive strategies based on southern Andean structures. In the north, however, where caciques depended on
the labor recruitment of forasteros, the increasing domination of the Spanish economy and the shift of migration toward the Spanish sphere served to
undermine the position of native leaders by the 1640s.[60] As will be demonstrated in chapter 5, the remainder of the seventeenth century witnessed
the spread of this disintegrative trend to the entire audiencia.

Land-Rental Strategies

As the seventeenth century progressed, out-migration accelerated, tribute arrears mounted, and caciques all over the Andes looked to a new pana-
cea, that of land rentals.[61] The ausentes may have fled their communities,
making their labor unavailable and leaving the burden of state obligations
to their cohorts, but they left behind one important resource—the land
that had been assigned to them. By renting the lands of absentees to Spaniards and Andean forasteros, caciques managed, at least for a while, to stave
off the inevitable. The labor of the ausentes was lost to the community, but
the vacant tracts they left in their wake could be used both to raise money
for tribute payments and to underwrite chiefly wealth and community inputs. During the seventeenth century, then, land replaced labor as the predominant component of indigenous survival strategies.

In Quito the strategy was an ingenious one, since it enabled caciques to
play off one Spanish objective against another; that is, land divestment and
the integrity of the forced-labor system became mutually exclusive aims.
By casting all vacant tracts as the land of ausentes who might someday return, the caciques were able to argue, at least temporarily, that it was imperative not to alienate community resources. Their logic was that if these
vacant tracts were designated as surplus lands and sold at public auction,
all hope would be lost of convincing the ausentes and their progeny to return to their towns of origin and fulfill their responsibilities to the Spanish
regime. This argument made the community's retention of the absentees'
lands synonymous with the state's hoped-for rehabilitation of the embattled
mita. The strategy, while fairly productive for some communities, was also
a double-edged sword, however, in that retention of the ausentes' lands
implied continuing to declare them as community members and paying
their tributes, a contradiction that became more acute as the number of
absentees grew.

Recent historiography assigns a prominent role to land-rental strategies in the transition from Andean to western property rights.[62] Spalding claims that rentals in Huarochirí, for example, were an important step in the transformation of Andean concepts of land. Land as a source of income broke the Andean relationship between land and labor and was a catalyst for the socioeconomic differentiation of indigenous communities.[63] While land rentals in the northern Andes represented the beginning of changing concepts of land, they also served to perpetuate old concepts. The following case study is instructive. Quito's seventeenth-century land battles reflect both the intensity of the struggle for community survival and the variation of interior meaning that land-rental strategies could embody across the Andean culture area.

Communities from every part of the audiencia used land rentals to resolve the "ausentes/rezagos" problem. The proceeds were applied to the current tributes of absent community members as well as to the arrears that inevitably accumulated, owing to depopulation through disease and migration.[64] Though employed uniformly as a survival strategy, land rentals were often based on differentiated pre-Hispanic structures and sought to reproduce a variety of agrarian arrangements.

Despite variation, however, land rentals constituted, at least for a time, an especially productive strategy, as witnessed by the intercommunity and even intracommunity strife that they generated. Although seventeenth-century land conflicts between indigenous groups appear, at first glance, to be the result of a land shortage, it becomes evident upon closer examination that some communities struggled for land not because resident ayllu members needed it, but because renting it out was such a lucrative venture. The cases of Tusa and Urcuquí in the northern sierra are especially instructive.

In eighteenth-century litigation between the towns of Tusa and Puntal in the Corregimiento of Ibarra, Tusa was described by both Andean and Spanish witnesses as an exceedingly wealthy community. A copy of the composición that Tusa's leaders obtained in 1647 was inserted into the suit and demonstrates that in that year the town already possessed 326 caballerías of land (3,677 hectares) and 1,695 head of cattle.[65] What makes this case unusual is that Tusa had also experienced severe depopulation throughout the entire colonial period, as had most of the Andean towns in this northernmost corregimiento, being as it was a focal point for out-migration to the south. In 1623 the caciques of Tusa, Puntal, and Angel complained that the population of the three towns had dwindled from 900 to 600 tributaries since the early 1590s.[66] According to demographic data presented in the composición of 1647, Tusa's tributary population had plummeted by that year to a mere 171 Andeans, scattered throughout fifteen depleted ayllus; this number, however, did not include the ausentes.[67] The paltry number of people present in the town compared to Tusa's enormous resources translates into 21.5 hectares of land and nearly a hundred head of cattle per resident tributary. How did such an incongruous situation come about?

It is charged in the suit of 1791 that Tusa had amassed huge tracts by usurping the communal lands of its neighbor, Puntal, and legalizing them during the composición of 1647. The caciques of Tusa argued that they needed this land in order to pay tributes, presumably those of absentees. Since the town's only productive economic activity was livestock raising, extensive pastures were imperative. Puntal's leaders claimed, however, that Tusa rented and sold these lands to Spaniards when need be, and that was why the town never accumulated tribute arrears. Conversely they complained that the people of Puntal were forced to risk their lives working in the "hot lands" or attach themselves to Tusa's families as retainers in order to pay their tributes.[68] Central to this intercommunity conflict, then, was a desperate and enduring struggle for survival.

Considering the continual population drain experienced by the area, the retention of land became the sine qua non of communal reproduction. The caciques of Tusa had evidently perceived early on that land, even if it had to be stolen from a neighboring town, was the only way to prevent community disintegration. By amassing lands at the expense of Puntal, Tusa was able to keep up with tribute demands and maintain its material wealth through rentals, sales, and participation in an apparently lucrative cattle trade.

Clearly the geographic location and economic possibilities of the community informed the effectiveness of the land strategy. Tusa was on the Camino Real, along the route of the cattle drive that proceeded regularly from Popayán to the capital city of Quito; such a fortuitous location obviously enabled the town to reap handsome profits from its livestock industry. In addition, since cattle raising is not labor-intensive, Tusa's depopulated state was irrelevant; all that was needed was land, and that requisite it was able to fill by usurping the resources of its neighbor, Puntal. It should also be noted that the cacique of Tusa was accused of "stealing" the Andeans of a neighboring community, most probably Puntal, in the sixteenth century and was now charged with having usurped the lands of that community in the seventeenth century—a perfect reflection of changing strategies to fit changing colonial conditions.[69]

This long-standing intercommunity conflict between Tusa and Puntal, then, illustrates well the importance that land assumed in the seventeenth-century struggle for survival. Tusa's success also points to how caciques were able to use land to compensate for the human deficit occasioned by migration; depopulation did not cause Tusa to disappear, nor did its leaders fall from power, because land replaced labor as the dominant means of production. Tusa's survival depended on the commodification of land and the community's thorough integration into the market economy. Hence it is a poignant example of the transition toward western concepts of property cited by other Andeanists.

In contrast the land-rental strategies of Urcuquí, in the Corregimiento of Otavalo, reflect an intensive effort to survive as a community by reproducing pre-Hispanic agrarian patterns. Several seventeenth-century episodes reveal the trajectory by which the town acquired, utilized, and lost lands in its attempt to weather the colonial storm.

In the years prior to 1647, migration and absenteeism had caused serious fiscal and economic problems, which the community sought to resolve through land invasions. What makes Urcuquí's strategy especially poignant, however, is that the lands upon which the town intruded belonged to one of its own ayllus.[70] As reported by the leader of the Yacelga ayllu, the leader of the Urcuquiango ayllu, who was also the governor of the town, had engineered a ruthless invasion of Yacelga's lands, in an attempt to amass resources for sale and rental.

The urgency with which the town's leadership sought to accomplish this adaptation is borne out by the violence and bloodshed that accompanied the episode. Yacelga's leader claimed that his subjects had been removed from their lands by force and had since migrated to other towns in search of subsistence.[71] The veracity of his story is partly confirmed by the 1647 census, which shows the Yacelga ayllu dispersed in four different towns of the repartimiento of Otavalo, as well as in out-of-area places.[72] The purpose of the invasion was to force one group out of the town, thereby freeing up prime resources that could produce rental income. Apparently the community's plight was desperate enough to necessitate the dispossession and subsequent atomization of one whole ayllu.

During the composición of 1647, the governor, Don Sebastián Cabezas Urcuquiango, legalized many of the town's lands, including those stolen from Yacelga. These lands were reportedly located in various ecological niches in both temperate and subtropical zones, indicating that the leader's strategy had succeeded both in preserving the community's microvertical economy and in composing rental properties that would yield significant monetary benefit.[73]

That the strategy worked remarkably well is more than evident in testimony given in a suit of 1666 between Don Sebastián and two local Spaniards. Juan Gonzáles de Escobedo and Diego Paes Altamirano charged that the people of Urcuquí had extended beyond their own lands and were now renting out lands that belonged to the complainants.[74] While this is not proven in the suit, what does come to light is that Urcuquí had, for many years, been renting lands to Spaniards and Andeans alike, in order to meet tribute demands and prevent expropriation. It was claimed repeatedly that migration had caused the near disintegration of the town and that the lands of the ausentes reverted to the caciques and Andean governors, who kept themselves and the community afloat by renting them out.

Thus far there is nothing unusual about Urcuquí's scenario. Agrarian conflicts between ayllus had been a fact of Andean life since "time immemorial." In addition communities all over the Andes were using land-rental strategies with the same motive and result—community solvency. What is perhaps unique about this case are the pre-Hispanic structures underlying the strategy and their particular revaluation of meaning.

In the panoply of economic exchange mechanisms that Salomon found for pre-Hispanic Ecuador, the region where Urcuquí's lowland possessions were located was characterized by ethnically mixed colonies, usually dominated by one particular group. In return for access to lowland resources, their members compensated the group to which the lands belonged through a variety of arrangements, including sharecropping.[75] Through invasion and subsequent rental of these lands, Urcuquí may very well have attempted to reproduce this pre-Hispanic pattern. The following analysis, while not conclusive, suggests that this was the case.

In Urcuquí witnesses claimed in 1666 that there were only seven Spanish renters and that the Andean forastero renters were so numerous that they could not be named.[76] It was also clear that the Urcuquiangos greatly preferred forastero renters to Spanish renters. Interestingly the forasteros to whom they rented lands were not unattached Andeans, but the subjects of other local caciques and governors (of Cotacache and Tumbaviro). Since some of the lands that Urcuquí had usurped and then "composed" in 1647 were prime cotton and coca lands, it is probable that the forasteros were not renters in the Spanish sense of the word, but rather members of mixed colonies who had a variety of arrangements with Urcuquí's leaders.[77]

Judging from the works of Susan Ramírez on the north coast of Peru, Spanish officials often mistook Andean "resource sharing" for European rental.[78] That this was so in Urcuquí is further borne out by the town's fiscal history. Simple rent from uprooted Andeans would not have produced the kind of income that is reported below for Urcuquí. Now supported in its legal possession of the lands by the Spanish judicial system, Urcuquí would surely not have been satisfied with a flat fee.

Considering the huge profits that could be made on the colonial market from lowland products like cotton and coca, Urcuquí probably reproduced pre-Hispanic patterns by demanding a part of the crop. Or since Ecuador was distinguished by the only market system known to exist in the Andes, the town's leaders may have controlled the marketing of these products through their mindalaes, as groups located in transitional zones (lowland to highland) did in the pre-Hispanic *tianguez* (market) system. By stealing lands from the Yacelga ayllu, then, the Urcuquiango ayllu was able to extend its pool of desirable resources and to use them not only to produce rental monies from Spaniards, but also to reap increased benefits from pre-Hispanic arrangements with neighboring communities, predicated upon the need for interzonal exchange.

Whatever the form of remuneration, these lands yielded more than enough to keep the community solvent. In 1647 Don Sebastián insisted that the rising number of absentees had caused such an accumulation of tribute arrears that the town was on the verge of fiscal collapse; he argued at that time that a refusal to grant a composición of the town's lands would be to the detriment of the royal coffers.[79] In 1667, however, he claimed that the town had no tribute arrears at all and always met its fiscal responsibilities punctually.[80] This is all the more puzzling when one considers that in spite of repeated complaints about continued migration and absenteeism, the tributary population of the town remained statistically constant, and even increased a bit, between the censuses of 1647 and 1665; in 1647 the town's tributary population was 196, while in 1665 it was registered as 229.[81] Evidently Don Sebastián and the Andeans of Urcuquí preferred to devise strategies to pay the tributes of the ausentes rather than to have the latter subtracted from the town's rolls and risk losing their lands through official designation as *realengas* (crown lands).

In addition the suit of 1666 demonstrates that the rents were used not only to underwrite the community's fiscal obligations to the state, but also to bolster Don Sebastián's prestige and position as a leader. A list of expenditures from 1654 was presented as evidence and revealed that a great part of the proceeds from land rentals was devoted to decorating the town's church and financing religious festivities. The exquisite nature of many of the items on the list attests to the renewed prosperity of the community and points to a much more lucrative "rental" strategy than one based solely on collecting rents. Furthermore the church sacristan testified that the items were gifts from Don Sebastián Cabezas Urcuquiango.[82] Whether these objects were personal donations or contributions he made on behalf of the community is unclear. Nevertheless it is certain that his generosity, whether personal or institutional, served to enhance his position both in relation to the community and to the colonial regime. Lavish donations to the church were a vehicle for achieving and maintaining status in Spanish society, while Spalding has pointed out the importance of religious leadership as a requisite for prestige in Andean society.[83] Furthermore this income may also have given him the wherewithal to continue fulfilling his reciprocal obligations to the community, as witnessed by the religious festivities he financed and his payment of tribute for sick members. Clearly land rentals underwrote both Don Sebastián's maintenance of power and Urcuquí's survival as a community.

Once again the location of the town and the nature of the area's resources were important factors in determining the strategy's effectiveness. Urcuquí possessed lands in a number of ecological niches, devoted to livestock, grains, fruit, *ají,* coca, and cotton; the last four products were grown only in the hot lands, lands to which access was limited and which were, therefore, highly attractive as rental properties.[84]

Unfortunately for Urcuquí and for many other communities of the audiencia, this strategy fell victim to Spanish land hunger and royal destitution during the latter part of the seventeenth century. In the case of Urcuquí, local Spaniards convinced the audiencia, in 1667, that the community's lands were really surplus resources no longer needed by a shrinking population. They insisted that nearly all the town's seventy caballerías were being usurped by the caciques at the expense of the royal coffers and recommended that the proceeds from those lands be directed toward the crown, either in the form of rentals or sales. Urcuquí's survival strategy was then coopted and inserted, almost without modification, into the regime's bureaucratic structure. The audiencia redistributed lands to the community based on its resident population, dispossessed the Andean forasteros, and assumed direct administration of the town's former rental lands.[85] They were subsequently rented to the same local Spaniards, for annual sums that were to be forwarded to the administrator of the crown obraje in Otavalo. Since the town of Urcuquí had not been fiscally delinquent for many years, this money was to be applied to the tribute arrears of the entire corregimiento.[86]

Just as in the case of the caciques' private work forces, a reproductive strategy developed and directed by the indigenous leadership was usurped once again by the Spanish state and made to coalesce with Spanish aims.

Beneath the surface, however, and more importantly, the actions of the colonial regime replaced the forastero "renters" with Spanish renters (in the European sense of the word), thereby destroying not only the community's microvertical economy, but also an exchange mechanism that, though adapted to external colonial conditions, was pre-Hispanic in its structural origins. Had northern Ecuador exhibited the pre-Hispanic archipelago pattern of the southern Andes, Don Sebastián might have attempted to salvage at least a part of the structure by sending mitimaes to work on the estates of the new Spanish renters in return for wages or, better still, part of the crop. That this did not happen is also owing to historical circumstances; rates of depopulation and out-migration in relation to small community size had, by the second half of the seventeenth century, left many Quiteño caciques without the human resources to engage in such strategies.

The second half of the seventeenth century saw the obliteration of the land-retention strategy as official policies, designed to rescue the Spanish crown from dire financial straits at the expense of the colony's native peoples, were formulated and rigorously enforced. Accentuated by the decline of the obraje economy and the inclination of the local Spanish populace to revert to agriculture, general composiciones and periodic local auctions cut back community resources to the bare minimum in many areas.[87] The 1640s, the 1660s, and 1690s were periods of extensive land divestment. Litigation records and administrative reports are replete with the arduous but futile attempts of the caciques to cling desperately to the last resource that would enable them to fulfill their fiscal responsibilities to the colonial regime and still maintain some semblance of community cohesion.[88] Furthermore subsequent land shortages motivated new migrations and obstructed the longed-for return of the ausentes.[89] The depletion of resources made impossible both the demographic recuperation of the community and the future reconstruction of Andean society. With the loss of land came a loss of hope; things would never again be as they were.

Conclusion

Migration and forasterismo caused an initial dislocation of Andean society that was successfully bridged in the sixteenth and early seventeenth centuries by the reorganizational efforts of the indigenous leadership. Some caciques succeeded both in maintaining personal power and in salvaging the integrity of their communities, by turning the debits of the situation into assets; that is, by creating survival strategies out of the problem itself.

These strategies were rooted in preexisting structures whose meanings were revalued to fit the conditions of a colonial political economy.

Migration caused communities to lose labor but gave rise to forasteros, who provided labor under more advantageous conditions than the original population. Since forasteros were exempt from tribute and the mita, it was preferable for a cacique to have a contingent of outsiders living in his community than to have a homogeneous originario population, all of whom were subject to the Spanish labor system. In this sense demographic instability may actually have served to improve labor and living conditions for some communities during this early period.

Migration also produced vacant lands, which at first glance appears to have been detrimental to the Indian sphere. It is probable that depopulation initially created labor shortages that prejudiced microvertical economies, giving rise to a less varied diet and a lower standard of living. In addition idle tracts were certain to have invited Spanish encroachment. Some caciques, however, were able to resolve this problem as well by offering land to forasteros in exchange for their labor. Through this arrangement they succeeded in occupying the lands and perhaps in putting them under cultivation, thereby preserving at some level both the pre-Hispanic economy and their people's quality of life.

During the seventeenth century, caciques developed yet another strategy based on land that, while not as productive, since it yielded money but not labor, succeeded in tempering destructuration. As depopulation progressed owing to epidemics and out-migration, land reverted to Andean leaders, who rented it out to Spaniards and forasteros. Land rental gave caciques an easily obtained, disposable income, since it did not require labor or capital inputs. They used the proceeds both to reproduce the community and to legitimize their authority vis-à-vis Spanish and Andean societies.

Ironically migration and forasterismo provided astute, resourceful caciques with a reserve of land and labor that they could manipulate in their own and their communities' interests. This enabled them to retain power without deviating radically from Andean norms and may even have created conditions conducive to the temporary strengthening of their cacicazgos. Throughout the seventeenth century, the Spanish state made a concerted effort to wrest control from the indigenous leadership over these officially unharnessed resources. As the labor of forasteros and the land of ausentes passed progressively into Spanish hands, adaptive strategies broke down, causing the demise of many early colonial leaders and the rise of intruder caciques, a subject to be explored in chapter 5.[90]

5

Decline of the Cacicazgo
and the Reconstitution of Andean Society

During the late seventeenth and early eighteenth centuries, Quito's cacicazgos were exposed to an unrelenting wave of intrusions by outsiders. These intrusions were facilitated by the pervasive social, political, and economic changes that had evolved in the Indian sphere over the course of a century and a half. Intruder caciques were typically forasteros or dissident ayllu members who had migrated to the Spanish sphere, acquired wealth and prestige, and risen to positions of leadership through influential connections. They differed from early colonial caciques in that they ruled as purely collusive agents of the Spanish regime and without regard for Andean ways. Although predominant in the eighteenth century, the intruders and their new politics were a long time in the making and were just as much a product of demographic movements as of other colonial processes.

While migration and forasterismo constituted important components of early strategies for the reproduction of indigenous society, they also served as major catalysts for its subsequent transformation. Although the sixteenth and early seventeenth centuries were characterized by a substantial retention of pre-Hispanic organization, the adaptive strategies that secured this continuity were paralleled by erosive trends. Native population movements, while initially manipulated by Andean leaders in the interests of community survival, eventually led to the fragmentation of indigenous polities and the loss of chiefly legitimacy. Throughout the seventeenth century, the constant depletion of human and material resources caused by population movements toward the Spanish sphere undermined Andean communities and the power base of the early colonial caciques.

This chapter will trace the demographic and administrative developments that caused the institutional weakening of the north Andean cacicazgo and made the turn-of-the-century intrusions possible. The analysis will focus on the role of demography and human agency in: (1) the atomization of indigenous political organization; (2) the emergence of new norms for acquiring and maintaining social prestige and political hegemony; and (3) the debacle of many established leaders and their replacement by intruder caciques.

The Spanish Reorganization of Indigenous Polities

Although the conquest resulted in the political fragmentation of indigenous society everywhere in Spanish America, there was a great deal of regional variation on the disintegrative process.[1] Even within a single culture
area, such as the Andes, the colonial trajectory of the cacicazgo was differentiated by preexisting conditions specific to each area and ethnic group.
Clearly the experiences of the peoples of Ecuador cannot be gauged by those
of Peru or Bolivia, both well-integrated core areas of the Inca empire, characterized by dense populations, large political units with central authority
figures, and the economic archipelago system. The uniqueness of Quito's
geography and microvertical economies, its late incorporation into the Inca
empire, and the small size of its aboriginal polities translate into a different
political evolution under Spanish rule with a distinctive outcome.

A detailed examination of Quito's political fragmentation from the conquest to approximately 1650 will illuminate the unique process by which
the "new indigenous politics" eventually came into being. Upon the arrival
of the Spaniards, the Inca were still consolidating vast areas of the region
later to be known as the Audiencia of Quito, and had not yet conquered
Pasto, located in its northernmost reaches. Nevertheless they had already
imposed an administrative superstructure over the majority of the local
population and most groups south of Quito (the later Spanish
corregimiento) had been fairly well integrated into the political and economic structures of the Incaic state. Consequently when the Spanish conquest decapitated the Inca empire, the result was an instantaneous
polarization of indigenous society, as the former political organization split
into two distinct parts: (1) Aboriginal leaders and the local populace; and
(2) Incaic leaders and the mitimaes.[2]

Polarization then gave way to atomization, as local leaders took advantage of the shift in power either to create or to recover autonomy. As the
Incaic veneer was removed, a multiplicity of small polities was exposed anew,
many of whose leaders claimed to be subject to no higher authority. Although it is not always clear whether the local lords' clamor for self-rule
was a manifestation of the desire to recuperate power lost under the Inca or
merely to seize an opportunity for social advancement, most scholars would
agree that the pre-Incaic political organization of the area tended toward
small groups whose leaders owed no formal allegiance to a superior, central
authority.[3]

This suggests a major difference between the political evolution of colonial Quito's indigenous societies and that of many groups to the south. The

acute decentralization of much of the region's Indian sphere required centralization in the interests of effective Spanish government. It was precisely Spanish-imposed centralization that became the point of conflict in many a sixteenth-century suit, as leaders were forced to submit to the dictates of former peers, raised from their midst by Spanish authority. The colonial regime, considering many Quiteño polities to be too small for efficient administration and too dispersed for lucrative encomiendas, often set about forming larger polities through the creation of caciques principales who had never existed before.[4]

Although some groups were larger and more politically concentrated and thus were less subjected to Spanish interference, others fell victim to

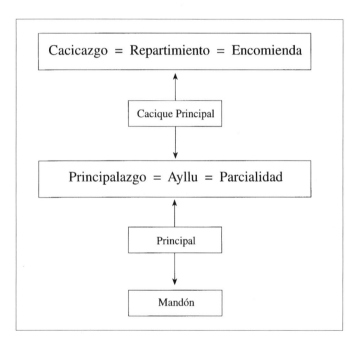

Figure 2. Administrative Organization of Indigenous Society Under Spanish Rule.

Note: The repartimiento was the largest administrative division of Andeans and was usually consonant with the cacicazgo, theoretically a pre-Hispanic grouping of indigenous people under the same supreme leader. The repartimiento could be designated as an encomienda or as a crown jurisdiction. In addition, the terms principalazgo, ayllu, and parcialidad are used interchangeably in the documentation as a sub-unit of the cacicazgo/ repartimiento.

the administrative inventions of early colonial bureaucrats. Even more-centralized polities, such as Otavalo, did not escape the reach of the colony's reorganizational tentacles. Although the audiencia did not tinker much with the superstructure of the unit (the rather large Spanish repartimiento of Otavalo may in fact reflect pre-Hispanic organization), it did eventually seek to reorganize its component parts. As reported by Caillavet, a royal decree was directed to the Corregimiento of Otavalo in 1580 ordering that all *principalazgos* (subunits of cacicazgos) with few members be eliminated and merged, in order to form groups of one hundred tributary subjects per *principal* (secondary leader), to avoid the administrative confusion of having so many local lords in one town (see figure 2).[5] According to Caillavet the decree was not systematically enforced, as witnessed by the number of groups that appeared in the cotton-distribution records of 1582 with fewer than one hundred tributaries.[6] Other areas of the audiencia, however, did not elude as easily the reorganizational efforts of the Spanish regime and in fact became targets for extensive political reconstruction. Ironically reconstruction contributed to political destructuration. Two cases in Riobamba are especially illustrative.

A suit of 1683 over the cacicazgo of Guano provides a rich body of documentation for the years 1575 to 1600 that brings to light the divisive effects of earlier Spanish policies of centralization. Various sixteenth-century petitions, royal provisions, and suits were presented as evidence that provide both a comprehensive overview of local resistance to centralized authority and a blow-by-blow account of the nasty and enduring tug-of-war that took place between the Spanish-appointed cacique principal and the town's "secondary" authorities.[7]

During the Toledan visita of 1572, Don Sancho Lema, the cacique of Ñacchucay, a single parcialidad in the town of Guano, was appointed cacique principal of Juan de Galarza's encomienda. This encomienda included all the parcialidades of the town of Guano, as well as some in the towns of Calpi and Ylapo. Undoubtedly an attempt at administrative efficiency, this move set off a pitched battle between Don Sancho and the principales of the encomienda's numerous political units.[8]

In addition several of the named polities appeared as pueblos in the early record but as parcialidades of the pueblo of Guano in later documentation. In the visita of 1539, for example, the toponyms Olti and Suichi, appeared as distinct pueblos, each with an autonomous cacique; in the record of the 1570s, they often still appeared as pueblos, but were subject to the cacique principal of Guano, and finally in 1620, they were listed as parcialidades of the town of Guano.[9] The progression indicates strongly that a Spanish reducción, accompanied by a concurrent concentration of power, had taken place, probably in the 1570s.[10] The intractable struggle between Don Sancho Lema and his new underlings, then, was definitely the consequence of this colonial centralization process.

That the administrative measures imposed by the Spaniards were not exactly accepted with equanimity is borne out by the immutable stance assumed by the principales of the district of Guano over their loss of autonomy. In a single year, 1575, the audiencia had to repeat a royal provision on three separate occasions urging the principales of the district to pay Don Sancho his annual salary of one hundred pesos and to fulfill the tribute and labor obligations owed him as a cacique principal. These included providing laborers from among their subjects to cultivate his fields, supply him with wood and fodder, repair his house, and weave twelve cotton or woolen shirts a year.[11]

Their failure to comply with any of these responsibilities was hardly an oversight, but rather a political problem. This became crystal clear in 1577, when they refused to obey Don Sancho Lema pending the outcome of a suit before the audiencia, in which they had challenged his legitimacy as cacique principal. They claimed that he had no authority over them because they were all of the same category as he; each of them considered himself to be the cacique principal of his own parcialidad and to have the right to collect tributes and pay them directly to Spanish authorities. Don Sancho Lema, they insisted, had never been a paramount lord before the arrival of the Spaniards and was, like them, only the principal of his own parcialidad.[12]

In 1578 the audiencia concluded this suit over legitimacy in favor of Don Sancho Lema and ordered the seven plaintiffs to recognize him as their cacique principal. Far from complying with the law of the land, these leaders retaliated by withdrawing whatever laborers they had begrudgingly assigned to Don Sancho's service, causing his fields and herds to fall into a state of ruin. The audiencia then issued a strong warning that the principales should acquiesce to these obligations, but they evidently did not comply for several years, as witnessed by yet more litigation.[13]

In 1583 Don Sancho Lema brought suit against his underlings, claiming that they and their subjects refused to fulfill their labor obligations to him and were conspiring with his bastard brother, Don Alejo Lema (also the principal of Suichi) to bring him down. Don Sancho succeeded in obtaining a provision from the audiencia to have the principales of the district punished. Once again they retaliated with a suit, charging that he had collected two thousand pesos in excess tributes and salaries and had engaged in all manner of abuses. In addition they claimed that his salary was exorbitant, calculating its value in cash and labor at eight hundred pesos annually for administering only five hundred subjects, while the cacique principal of Otavalo was charged with two thousand subjects and received only sixty pesos and six articles of clothing a year.[14] Interestingly they no longer questioned Don Sancho's legitimacy within the Andean context, but rather accused him of transgressions against the colonial system. As Spanish bureaucracy became more entrenched, the district's leaders apparently recognized the futility of basing their case solely on indigenous norms. As will be seen subsequently, they continued their battle for autonomy, but did so in increasingly oblique ways.

Apparently bewildered by the persistent tug-of-war in Guano, the audiencia finally issued a decree in 1586 to forestall litigation among the town's authorities. Lamenting the chaos and discontent engendered by the suits, it condemned "a new round of litigation and arguments over which Andean leaders had spent their fortunes and burned their passions." In exasperation it dispatched the oidor, Licenciado Francisco de Auncibay, to Guano to arbitrate, once and for all, each and every difference that had erupted over the years between Don Sancho Lema and the principales. Afterward the audiencia imposed perpetual silence on the community with regard to matters of previous litigation; the penalty for breaking the silence was the loss of all rights and exile to the City of Guayaquil for four years.[15]

Even these draconian measures, however, did not put an end to the intense backlash against political centralization. Don Juan Bueno, principal of the parcialidad of Guano, managed to find an indirect way to continue the struggle. In 1590 he sued in the audiencia for the right to sit on the *duho,* a wooden stool traditionally occupied only by the cacique. He also claimed that his possession of the duho and the fact that the corregidor had seated him on it after his father's death were sure proof of his status as a cacique.[16] The original conflict over the balance of power had now evolved into a seemingly petty but symbolically important fight over public seating.

When Don Sancho Lema objected that only the cacique principal might occupy the duho, the audiencia ruled that Don Juan could do so only in Don Sancho's absence. Unsatisfied with this compromise, Don Juan revealed his true intent by insisting on his right to occupy the duho in Don Sancho's presence, because he was his equal. Proudly he proclaimed that he had inherited the cacicazgo from his father, Pixan, and his grandfather, Titin. Indeed in another suit, the name "Pixana" appears in an excerpt from the Pizarran visita of 1539 as that of the autonomous cacique of the pueblo of Guano.[17]

Hence Don Juan's persistence in maintaining the distinction of his ancient lineage was probably fueled by the truth. At this juncture, however, he was willing to concede to all Spanish-imposed obligations of deference to Don Sancho Lema, if only he be permitted to keep the duho, traditional symbol of power. In apparent desperation he attempted once again to hold on to this vestige of Andean authority by rephrasing the argument in colonial terms—that he should have the right to sit on the duho, even in the presence of Don Sancho Lema, because "it would be an indignity for him to have to sit on the ground at public functions dressed, as he is, in Spanish garb."[18]

In short the original battle against centralization continued to be fought out indirectly, and by the end of the sixteenth century it had already assumed a distinctly colonial expression. Furthermore it hardly ended with the duho incident. In 1598 Don Sancho Lema died, giving the principales a perfect opportunity to begin yet another judicial odyssey, this time against his son and heir, Don Pedro Lema.[19] As in many similar cases, the new "secondary" elites transformed the death of a Spanish-imposed leader into an occasion to test the waters for a possible reinstatement of former political structures. Such tenacious efforts to maintain some semblance of power, no matter how muted, may reflect the deep-rootedness and importance of "autonomy" as a value among the local ethnic groups of the area.

That the Spaniards' centralization project had touched a sensitive chord in Riobamba is witnessed by the frequency with which this type of suit appears in the record and by the persistence and variation with which subordinated families attempted to recover power over time and even across generations. The following case of San Andrés is notable, not only for the disregard for local political norms with which the Spanish bureaucracy created a supreme leader, but for the duration of the intracommunity conflict engendered.

In a suit over the cacicazgo of the Taguan, Patulo, and Tunchucay parcialidades in the town of San Andrés, it comes to light that the sixteenth-century Spanish policy of concentrating indigenous power was still being hotly contested in 1691. Three times during the seventeenth century (1644, 1663, and 1676–91), the descendants of demoted leaders attempted to wrest control from the descendants of the externally imposed cacique principal.[20] In the suit of 1676, Don Joachín Chala, principal of the Patulo parcialidad, charged that his contender for the cacicazgo, Doña Lorenza Mazan (whose husband, Don Joseph Chapla y Lema, would rule), was the great-granddaughter of a commoner who had been raised to a position of power by the Spanish regime.[21] Town censuses reveal that his story is not only true, but also highly representative of blatant Spanish tampering with local political hierarchies.

Sometime prior to 1592, Andrés Lalligaña, a tributary member of the Tunchucay parcialidad, was appointed town accountant, because "he knew the whereabouts of all the town's inhabitants, even those in remote places and in other corregimientos, and could make a good accounting of them." As a result not only was he spared from tribute and the mita, but his talents also earned him the rank of *mandón* (lesser leader) of his parcialidad in the visita of 1592. Because he was not descended from caciques, however, the visitador stipulated that he and his subjects were to be under the formal jurisdiction of Don Hernando Chala, principal of the Patulo parcialidad.[22] Curiously Andrés Lalligaña appeared in the following census of 1620 as Don Andrés Apacagua, cacique principal of all three parcialidades. In addition the principal to whom he was subject in 1592 was now subject to him.[23]

For the leaders of San Andrés, this colonial reorganization represented an even more stinging political rebuke than that experienced by the leaders of Guano. In the latter town, the newly created cacique was, at the very least, one of several equivalent figures and not a mere commoner who had assisted the Spanish regime in its efforts toward demographic accuracy. In San Andrés the "accountant-turned-cacique principal" achieved sociopolitical advancement based on his ability to account for the absent population. Bountyhunting had apparently become a new requisite for power in a colonial society theoretically constructed on the tribute and labor of stationary Andean communities, but actually characterized by constant human movement and fiscal delinquency. Troubleshooters such as Don Andrés, who could keep the system working in spite of all the inherent contradictions, were most likely in high demand by the Spanish regime. Their legitimacy vis-à-vis indigenous society, however, was problematic, as witnessed by the serial suits described above. Those who had seen their power eroded seized each and every opportunity—official visitas, the cacique's death, the incompetence of his heirs—to challenge the authority of the imposed leader and restate the original grievance over and over again.

What makes these political conflicts more curious is that Riobamba was one of the areas where Inca administration had been most consolidated, yet it is the region where I have found the most telling data for this disunifying trend. Surely the principales of Guano and San Andrés, for example, must have been concentrated at one time under the command of a higher Incaic authority for at least a half century. So why the bitter feuds over Spanish-imposed centralization?

It has been posited in regard to other areas that once the Incaic superstructure was removed by the Spanish conquest, indigenous political organization returned temporarily to its pre-Incaic form. Ethnic lords then revelled in their newly recovered autonomy just long enough to be reluctant to surrender it; hence the staunch resistance to eventual Spanish efforts to centralize administration.

A closer look at the data for Riobamba, however, suggests an alternative, more plausible explanation, which might also be valid for other areas of the audiencia. It appears from the record that the administrative style of the Inca state allowed for more autonomy than that of the Spanish state. In several suits over centralization in Riobamba, "secondary" leaders insisted that they should have the right to deliver their subjects' tributes and labor directly to Spanish authorities, as they had always done under the Inca.[24] Apparently during the Incaic regime, each lord, no matter how small his constituency, was directly responsible to an official of the Inca state, and not to another local lord raised in status above him to act as intermediary. The latter scenario was eventually the case under Spanish rule and was precisely what the principales complained about most bitterly. The Inca state permitted the hierarchical structure of local political organization to remain intact, while imposing only an Inca representative to coordinate progressively more comprehensive state activities. The Spanish reorganization, however, was much more intrusive and upset the delicate balance of local politics, causing feelings of indignation on the parts of many indigenous authorities vis-à-vis their promoted cohorts and dividing Andean society further.

In short artificial political centralization gave rise to de facto political fragmentation. Spanish policies of concentrating power in a central figure chosen from among many equivalent local leaders was experienced as an erosion of power by those not selected. This led to bitter resentment and dissent, which was played out in the Spanish judicial system for decades and whose echoes reverberated in and out of the courts perhaps for centuries. Subsequently it will be demonstrated how descendants of these subordinated leaders took advantage of later demographic movements to realize their deferred dreams of autonomy.

Andean Demography, Human Agency, and the Political Weakening of the Early Colonial Cacicazgo

Much space has been devoted here to describing the political fragmentation of Andean society during the initial years of Spanish colonization. While not the direct result of population movements, the political trends described above are of more than tangential importance, because they weakened indigenous polities, setting the stage for further disintegration induced by demographic movements and human agency.

Early political atomization of Andean society resulted from externally imposed conditions occasioned by the conquest and new colonial bureaucracy; it was, however, both paralleled and followed by even more erosion that was internally motivated by Andean action—the decision to migrate in large numbers to escape Spanish tribute and forced labor. The rest of this chapter will focus on the dialectic that developed between Andean migration and bureaucratic responses, on the one hand, and the waning of the early colonial cacicazgo, on the other.

As the colony progressed, indigenous survival strategies based on both the subterfuge practiced by astute native leaders and the physical movements of ordinary Andeans came increasingly to light and became the subjects of numerous official discourses and experiments. From the Toledan reforms of the 1570s to the end of the colony, Spanish bureaucrats responded to Andean action by formulating and attempting to enforce a seemingly endless barrage of policies intended both to restrict migration and to incorporate unreported Andeans into the official tax and labor base. As detailed in chapter 3, demographic accountability became the centerpiece of an intense and enduring struggle between the audiencia and the Indian sphere, a struggle that would end in the decline of the early colonial cacicazgo.

As evident in previous discussion of the colonial reorganization of indigenous polities, the cacicazgo's downward spiral began at the inception of Spanish rule. Nevertheless the point at which it plummeted into irreversible descent can be traced to the Toledan reforms of the 1570s. The visita instructions that the Viceroy Francisco de Toledo forwarded to the Audiencia of Quito in 1570 stated that any native, whether cacique or commoner, who exposed ocultos would be rewarded with an appointment as the principal of those he reported; conversely the cacique responsible for hiding them would be punished by having them subtracted from his domain.[25] This measure, obviously an incentive for the resolution of the ocultos problem, was promptly translated into a juridical base for social climbing and political intrigue. Numerous suits over cacicazgos in the Audiencia of Quito attest to the frequent use of this practice and question time and again the legitimacy of the caciques that it produced and bolstered.

Once again the case of Guano is especially representative of the sociopolitical opportunism engendered by this measure. There Don Alejo

Lema reported more than four hundred Andeans who had allegedly been hidden by his brother, Don Sancho Lema.[26] In 1582 a suit was filed between the two brothers over the cacicazgo of Guano that typifies the manipulation of census data by caciques as a strategy for maintaining power and the manipulation of Spanish countermeasures by the caciques' political contenders as a strategy for assuming or expanding power.

As the story unfolds, it appears that Don Alejo Lema, bastard son of Guano's previous leader, had been deprived of his principalazgo by his brother, Don Sancho Lema, the natural son and present cacique principal of the town.[27] Supported by the encomendero, Juan de Galarza, Don Alejo Lema charged that in the censuses of 1572 and 1582, Don Sancho Lema failed to report 430 Andeans. He stipulated that during the visita of 1582, the oidor Ortegón had found 620 tributaries in Guano, but that Don Sancho had hidden 380 more for himself, intending to usurp their tributes, as he had done with 50 Indians whom he had managed to hide from the oidor Cárdenas in 1572.[28]

Prior to this accusation, it was claimed that Don Sancho, realizing that his brother was planning to expose the ocultos, reported 60 more Andeans as an addendum to the original census of 1582.[29] This move was intended to minimize the loss of his tax-exempt clientele, either to the Spanish regime through enumeration or to his brother through an official reward. That his efforts were in vain attests to the increasing administrative efficiency of the period and also depicts precisely how the accountability measures promulgated by the colonial bureaucracy intercepted and appropriated the caciques' strategies for the retention of power.

In response to Don Alejo's charges, the audiencia dispatched an investigator, Rodrigo de Argos, who, with the assistance of Don Alejo and thirty of his bountyhunters, succeeded in uncovering 300 more tributaries. Subsequently Don Alejo requested, as payment for his efforts, that these Andeans be subtracted from Don Sancho's domain and entrusted to him, presenting in support of his argument none other than a copy of the Toledan instructions of 1570. He then tried to push this mechanism one step further, by petitioning that Don Sancho Lema be deprived of the entire cacicazgo of Guano and that it be given over to him, in the interests of honest administration.

Don Alejo insisted that his brother should be removed from rule not only because he had hidden subjects from two Spanish census takers over the years, but also because he mistreated these ocultos. Among the abuses reported were: (1) that they paid no tribute to the encomendero, nor did they perform the mita; (2) that Don Sancho used them as personal servants for tending to his fields, livestock, and other enterprises; (3) that he collected excessive tributes from them, because they were not subject to the regularized tax rate established by the Spanish state; (4) that he prevented them from being indoctrinated in the Catholic faith, since it would be counterproductive if the priest were to know about them; and (5) that the state obligations of the hidden population then fell on the shoulders of the reported population and made their lives unbearable.[30]

In spite of all these alleged transgressions, however, the Spanish regime was reluctant to undertake such a radical solution. As it turned out, the audiencia at first agreed to give Don Alejo 150 of the Andeans he had reported and to return to him his principalazgo of 80 Andeans. This settlement was strongly opposed, however, by both Don Alejo and the encomendero, who pointed out that such a random distribution, uninformed by kinship and loyalty, would only exacerbate political divisions in the town; instead they proposed entrusting the entire cacicazgo to Don Alejo. The audiencia, apparently oblivious to the inner workings of indigenous society, but now better informed, accepted this advice in the interests of political stability. It did not, however, award the cacicazgo to Don Alejo, but rather instructed him to compose an ayllu from among his friends and relatives, to avoid further dissent.[31]

Clearly the suit was a test case for the effectiveness of Toledo's instructions; the audiencia reneged on the measure and opted for a more pragmatic solution that took into consideration the political stability necessary for the smooth functioning of the colonial system. While Toledo's instructions were not enforced to the letter, because they were considered impractical, they certainly did stimulate attempts at sociopolitical mobility as well as occasions for further political fragmentation.

The rather early date of the suit, 1582, a short ten years after the Toledan visita of Guano, indicates that indigenous contenders for power were quick to manipulate colonial legislation for their own political projects. The introduction of mechanisms intended to achieve demographic accuracy into communities that were already fragmented exacerbated divisions and resentments. These measures became vehicles for playing out existing political rivalries, adding to the chaos and turmoil already characteristic of many communities in the audiencia. Recall that Guano was also the site of an ongoing struggle between Don Sancho Lema (the cacique principal) and the town's secondary authorities over Spanish-imposed centralization.

The most serious, comprehensive efforts toward achieving demographic accountability took place in the Audiencia of Quito, between the years 1590 and 1630; one of the most effective policies to emerge from this period was the creation of crown parcialidades composed of forasteros. The official roundup of vagabonds and their aggregation into crown parcialidades had an especially adverse effect on the cacicazgo as an institution. As delineated in chapter 4, many of these roundups were equivalent to nothing more than the cooptation of the caciques' private, tribute-exempt work forces. The elimination of this economic survival mechanism, however, had equally deleterious social and political repercussions.

The formation of new crown parcialidades composed of forasteros provided Andean "upstarts" with an official vehicle for achieving social mobility and political power. The process through which "parcialidades de la Real Corona" were composed ended in the creation of numerous self-made caciques as well as the self-aggrandizement of some hereditary lords. This was especially true during the early aggregations of the late sixteenth and early seventeenth centuries, when the general roundup of vagamundos often took on the character of a free-for-all.

Those who came out on top in the aggregation process were frequently ordinary Andeans who recognized an opportunity for social advancement and seized it; they collected as many forasteros as possible, both through force and cajoling, offered them to the crown, and requested appointment as caciques of those they had rounded up. Similarly a select group of existing caciques took advantage of the same opportunity, in order to increase their wealth and power.

One name that appears repeatedly in the role of master aggregator of vagamundos is that of Jorge Llacta, supposedly of Nazca, Peru (although alternately from Cuzco). His grandson claimed that he was sent to Quito by the viceroy sometime in the late sixteenth century, to round up forasteros and attach them to the crown. In other documentation he appears as a carpenter from the city of Quito who was given a commission by the audiencia. While his background is unclear, he created crown parcialidades of vagamundos in Cuenca, Jaen de Bracamoros, Chimbo, Riobamba, Latacunga, and Ambato and became the cacique of some of them.[32]

Another pointed example is the famous Hati family of Latacunga, which increased its wealth and power through the systematic aggregation of hundreds of forasteros. In 1656 Don Guillermo García Hati, in a suit over the crown vagamundos of Latacunga, contended that these Andeans had been searched for, acquired, and naturalized ("buscados, adquiridos y naturalizados") by his father, Don Guillermo García Hati Zanipatín. In addition there are some questions raised in the suit as to whether the Hatis were descended from an ordinary Andean who had "made it" through the general roundup of the late sixteenth century.[33]

By using the forasteros as a political clientele, these ambitious individuals were able to acquire power through alternative means and to enhance their social position in both Andean and Spanish societies. Of more import, however, is that these feats undermined chiefly legitimacy in the Andean sense.

Perhaps more pertinent to the subject at hand is that the formation of crown parcialidades had the effect of further dividing Andean polities. The frequent Spanish practice of appointing separate leaders to these parcialidades—separate from the caciques of the towns' originarios—gave rise to further splintering in polities that were already badly fragmented. In short the creation of crown parcialidades of forasteros contributed heavily to the ongoing political destabilization of the Indian sphere.

Another policy similar in intent and effect was that of the manifestación. In the 1620s the visita of Matías de Peralta all but institutionalized the manifestación as a route to social mobility and even political status. At the opening of the visita, Spanish officials announced in each native town that any common Andean who exposed four unreported tributaries would be exempt from tribute and the mita for life.[34]

That this incentive succeeded in enticing many an ordinary Andean to turn informer is abundantly clear from both the census and judicial record. Some indigenous people took advantage of this measure to unburden themselves of state obligations and hence devote their time and energies to more lucrative pursuits, thereby achieving social mobility. Their descendants not only attempted to maintain this temporary privilege, but often sought to gain political power by claiming that they enjoyed exempt status because they were descended from caciques. An example would be the case of Juan Chunga, who claimed in 1686 that he should be exempt from tribute because he was the son of caciques. Don Pedro Sisalema, the cacique principal of Licto, however, claimed that Chunga's father had been reserved from tribute and the mita only because he had reported some hidden Andeans during an earlier census.[35]

The sociopolitical ascent of Andean commoners through the manipulation of the manifestación was paralleled by an elite version of the mechanism, in which native leaders could expand not only political control but economic power as well. The seventeenth-century record shows that both Andean authorities and Spaniards who reported potential tributaries were rewarded with the labor of those they had exposed. That this strategy must have produced significant results is borne out by the audiencia's reduction of the reward in 1691 to the labor of one-third of the Andeans reported.[36] A typical manifestación, for example, was that of Don Luis Zugo, principal of the Chuyupi ayllu in the town of Puni (alternately Punín) (Corregimiento of Riobamba), who "manifested" seventeen tributaries and their families. The latter were working on the haciendas of the vicinity and were absent from the town of Licto. He then requested that he be awarded the labor of one-fifth of those reported for the benefit of his own enterprises.[37]

The manifestación of both hidden and vagabond Andeans continued unabated throughout the colonial period. While it was a Spanish measure intended to incorporate as many uncounted and delinquent Andeans as possible into the tributary base, it also enabled Andean power contenders to challenge the rule of incumbent leaders on a systematic basis. One of many examples is that of the town of Carangue at the turn of the eighteenth century. In 1701 Doña María Roza de los Reyes, cacica principal of Carangue (Corregimiento of Otavalo) complained that one of her principales, Joseph Constantino de la Candelaria, was using his position as tribute collector to usurp the cacicazgo. In addition she mentioned in the suit that his father had "manifested" sixty tributary Andeans in the late seventeenth century, whose administration she was not contending. Seemingly the manifestación of a substantial number of tributaries by the prinicipal of one parcialidad changed the balance of power in the town and created conditions leading to his son's attempt to expand control to the whole cacicazgo.[38] On a more general note, the administrative measure known as the manifestación allowed for the almost instantaneous creation of new political bases from the forastero mass, causing frequent and radical shifts in the balance of power in some communities.

In short the excessive tribute and labor demands of the colonial regime prompted caciques and Andean commoners to formulate survival strategies based on demographic fraud and migration. The Spaniards countered with cooptative measures aimed at demographic accuracy, but which also created openings through which secondary Andean elites and even commoners could rise to power. This of course invoked further disunity in the Indian sphere and weakened chiefly authority. Political dilution, however, was not the only nor even the primary erosive trend to arise out of migration and related administrative phenomena. Rather the latter also became catalysts for important socioeconomic transformations that when combined with the political debasement of many established leaders, led to the eventual demise of the early colonial cacicazgo and to the advent of new-style leaders and new local politics.

Andean Migration and the Economic Deterioration
of the Cacicazgo

The political erosion of the early colonial cacicazgo was accompanied by the steady deterioration of its economic base. As described in the previous chapter, the events of the seventeenth century dealt a near-fatal blow to the Andean economy, as many communal resources were expropriated and channeled toward the Spanish sphere. This material flow was paralleled by an equally important human flow. As divestment accelerated the movement away from indigenous communities, labor passed increasingly to Spanish hands. As the exodus intensified, the ausentes-rezagos problem became accentuated, signaling the death knell of many early colonial cacicazgos.

As the divestment of the Indian sphere reached its colonial apogee at the end of the seventeenth century, the survival strategies of an earlier era, so carefully devised by the caciques, fell by the wayside. The land expropriations, labor appropriations, and out-migrations of the period not only left the Andean towns with scant material and human resources, but saddled the caciques with the personal burden of underwriting the tributes of a largely absent community. The larger the ausentes-rezagos problem loomed, the more destitute became early colonial leaders, whose lands, herds, and other private wealth were systematically confiscated in the interests of meeting tribute quotas and paying off arrears. Although the caciques had always been held personally responsible for their communities' tributes and had frequently forfeited their own possessions in order to fulfill their fiscal obligations, the divestment of their personal wealth did not become a generalized trend until the second half of the seventeenth century.[39]

Many Andean leaders who had managed to amass considerable fortunes in the sixteenth and early seventeenth centuries saw their assets dwindle as their subjects passed increasingly to the Spanish sphere but were not readily subtracted from the tribute rolls. With the personal payment of community tributes, the impoverishment and even incarceration of caciques became the order of the day. In the early 1670s, the caciques of all twenty-four Andean towns and urban parishes of the Corregimiento of Quito attributed their fiscal delinquency to the inclusion of dead and absent Andeans in the census rolls of their districts.[40] Furthermore the semantic format of tribute records and the high incarceration rate for this period confirm that the caciques' obligation to underwrite their communities' tributes was not just a legal formality but a genuine expectation.[41] The standard wording of the so-called "cartas cuentas" (tribute lists) regarding unpaid tributes is anything but ambiguous:

Under oath the cacique of such and such a town recognizes his tribute debts and attributes them to the many Indians who are absent from the town as well as to those who are dead, but who, in the absence of proper death certificates, have not been subtracted from the town's rolls. In addition, the cacique, in spite of a diligent search, has not been able to locate those who have fled, nor to collect their tributes. He will collect from them when they appear and will pay the difference in the interim or his person and possessions must be relinquished.[42]

That this was not an idle threat is attested by the systematic and prolonged imprisonment of large numbers of Andean leaders during the second half of the seventeenth century. In 1651 the caciques of Cuenca were subjected to group incarceration for their failure to pay the tributes of the district's many absentees. After filing a desperate petition in 1652, they were finally released, but only because it became apparent that if they were not free to search for their missing subjects, they would not be able to meet the current year's fiscal obligations either.[43]

Other examples of incarcerated leaders abound. All six caciques of the town of Yaruquís (Corregimiento of Riobamba) were imprisoned for a good part of the year 1666 because they were too poor to pay the tributes of the town's numerous absentees.[44] Likewise in the Corregimiento of Quito, the caciques of Ylambo, Zámbiza, Pomasque, Cotocollao, María Magdalena, and the urban parish of the cathedral were all jailed for nonpayment of absentees' tributes in 1673. One telling incident occurred in the town of Pomasque, where the cacique, Don Sebastián Morales, succeeded in getting a reprieve of twenty days, with the excuse that he would find the absentees within that time period and deliver their tributes. The twenty days passed, he was not able to comply, and he was summarily returned to prison.[45] Apparently catching up with runaway Andeans was not an easy task, nor did caciques have enough remaining wealth to meet these debts personally. Indeed incarceration for tribute arrears became so tightly associated with the position of cacique that in eighteenth-century litigation witnesses often correlated the legitimacy of a leader with the frequency with which he had been seen in the public jail.[46]

Toward the eighteenth century, the role of cacique took on such a sinister aura in some communities that an appointment to the position was often viewed as a misfortune. Many caciques even fled their cacicazgos, to avoid excessive demands and abuses; taking a cue from their subjects, they became caciques forasteros. As early as 1623, royal officials of Otavalo complained about "reluctant caciques" and those who fled their jurisdictions.

As the seventeenth century progressed, the "runaway cacique" became more prevalent.[47] Others stayed in their communities, lost power, and experienced such precipitous demotion that they were incorporated into the tributary base and assigned to the mita.[48]

Perhaps the progressive deterioration in the position of many established caciques and the breakdown of their legitimacy can best be illustrated by events in San Andrés (Corregimiento of Riobamba). There are three cases in the record that illustrate the steady impoverishment and demotion in status of that town's caciques. In 1672 the notarial records of Riobamba described Doña Luisa Bilcape, cacica of San Andrés, as so poor that she had no house in the town and had to rent one from her subjects.[49] In 1697 Don Joseph Vilcapi, son of caciques, was assigned to the mita.[50] And in 1771 the cacicazgo of San Andrés was allegedly purchased by a wealthy commoner.[51]

The political and economic decay of the early colonial cacicazgo reached its nadir in the second half of the seventeenth century and paved the way for the usurpation of authority by intruders.[52] From the 1660s through the early eighteenth century, the Spanish judicial system was bombarded with suits over the ubiquitous intruder caciques. The pathetic destitution and political degeneration of many established leaders created a power vacuum into which the intruders rushed headlong, completing the transition to a new-style rule that had been 150 years in the making.

Migration had finally resulted in such total political and economic divestiture that caciques could no longer fulfill the requisites of their dual contract. The outpouring of people from the communities, the tribute arrears they left in their wake, and the confiscation of chiefly wealth created conditions under which caciques were unable even minimally to meet their fiscal and labor obligations to the Spanish state.[53] These same conditions also impeded them from fulfilling, in Andean terms, the requisites of good leadership. The protection of community resources, institutionalized generosity, and other forms of reciprocity—the principal obligations of Andean rule—became unattainable goals even at the most reduced levels. The result was a loss of legitimacy, not only vis-à-vis the Spanish regime, but also in the eyes of their people. Consequently the turn of the eighteenth century saw the culmination of a process in which many established leaders were systematically challenged and frequently displaced by intruders who, in some cases, had already been laying in wait for propitious moments to assume control.

Intruder Caciques and the New Politics

Who were these intruders and how had they arrived to a position from which they could launch themselves into power? Although the social origins of the interlopers will be examined in more detail, a composite sketch of the typical intruder cacique would show him to be a forastero or dissident ayllu member who had left his community of birth to live and work in the Spanish sphere.[54] There he managed to accumulate wealth and establish important connections with powerful Spaniards, who usually proffered either financial or legal assistance in his bid for formal control over a particular cacicazgo.

In addition this local alliance typically had as its raison d'être a deal in which the newly installed cacique would facilitate Spanish access to land or labor or, at the very least, provide an opportunity to pilfer community tributes. The assumption of power could take the form of an appointment as cacique, if remote descent could be proven or at least falsified, or as governor, which was in some ways preferable, since the latter office frequently carried, by this point, more important responsibilities than that of cacique.

While there are probably myriad variations on this paradigm, it occurs in the documentation repeatedly and appears to represent a watershed in the arena of indigenous politics. The eventual failure of the early caciques' reproductive strategies gave way to the dawning of a new political era. The cacicazgo would now be dominated by collusive caciques, who were intricately woven into the local power structure and whose interests were more aligned with those of their Spanish cohorts than with those of the communities they ruled.[55]

Certainly caciques were integrated into local power groups in earlier periods as well and frequently engaged in alliances with powerful Spaniards for personal gain. Nevertheless they usually took care to walk a tightrope between the needs of their communities and the exigencies of their Spanish allies; that is, in spite of their deals with local luminaries, they still attempted to protect community lands, to fight for lower labor quotas, and to pay the tributes of the sick and unfortunate. The textural difference of the new politics of the late seventeenth century lies in its extreme departure from all Andean expectations of good leadership and its disavowal of the communities' interests. The disaffection of ordinary Andeans was consequently translated into accelerated out-migration.

Thus the new politics was equivalent to the plunder of the cacicazgo and in some areas ended in its collapse as an effective Andean institution.[56] Many caciques became Spanish-style officials administering groups of Andeans who were by now dispersed on haciendas and in cities—transformations that left their subjects essentially leaderless.

As witnessed by the cultural cohesiveness of many ethnic groups in contemporary Ecuador, however, it is evident that Andean society was decapitated by this process but not dismantled. It may very well be, as suggested by the work of Galo Ramón, that at this point, the reproduction of indigenous ways fell entirely to the ayllu members, who appear to have reconstituted their social organization inside the obraje-hacienda complex.[57] In addition one could embellish Ramón's model by positing that the hacendado replaced the cacique by assuming many of his functions: the distribution and administration of resources, the settlement of disputes, the collection of tribute, and at times the provision of protection and aid in moments of crisis.

Migration and Sociopolitical Mobility

What role did demography play in this transition and more specifically, how did migration factor into the apparent sociopolitical mobility of the intruder caciques? At the same time that population movements away from communities of origin undermined the political and economic base of early colonial leaders, migration also provided some migrants with a vehicle for social advancement. While the experiences of forasteros varied during the colonial period, depending on region, period, and economic conditions, migration did become a well-traveled route to social mobility for some.[58] An examination of the ways in which migration benefited the socioeconomic position of at least a segment of the forastero population will be instructive.

Although it is not always clear exactly how the forasteros who became intruder caciques rose to positions of wealth and power, it is possible to piece together from various sources a model for the socioeconomic ascent of forasteros in general. Extrapolating from this model and using the specific data on social mobility that appear in the suits over cacicazgos, it will be possible to determine with a fair degree of certainty the route of the intruders' ascent to leadership.

While the early record is replete with accounts of landless and desperately poor forasteros, as time goes on there is a qualitative change in the terms used to describe these "outsiders." As market opportunities and employment possibilities increased in the Spanish sphere, a somewhat stable group of forasteros emerged, who eventually enjoyed a better standard of living than their community counterparts. How precisely did this dichotomy develop? While the relatives they left behind in the Indian sphere became increasingly impoverished, some forasteros, through the migratory process, were able to improve the quality of their lives and move into higher socioeconomic categories. By migrating away from their communities of origin, forasteros escaped, at least temporarily, the tribute and labor obligations of the colonial regime, obligations that sapped the economic strength of those who remained, but that afforded those who departed the freedom to follow more lucrative pursuits.

The benefits that some forasteros derived from this freedom can be divided into three broad categories: (1) private ownership of the means of production as opposed to communal ownership, which, as will be demonstrated subsequently, may have warded off dispossession; (2) higher wages and lower tribute rates than mitayos; and (3) formal and informal education in Spanish ways and the opportunity to form important relationships with influential people.

How did forasteros gain private access to the means of production? Through what strategies were they able to acquire lands, herds, and even small textile mills? In some cases the higher wages of forasteros may have played a role in the accumulation of capital necessary for investments. Andeans who migrated to Spanish urban centers and became artisans, for example, often commanded extraordinary salaries. "Free" carpenters in the city of Quito were reported to have earned two pesos a day, while those of the mita earned two pesos a month.[59] Forasteros also worked on a regular basis in the textile industry and earned, as contract laborers, double the wages of mitayos. A mita carder, for example, received an annual salary of eighteen pesos, while a contracted carder received thirty-six.[60]

Occupations in trade and transport and even ownership of small textile workshops were also routes to capital accumulation, as were inheritances from Spanish employers and lovers, especially in the case of forastero women. In addition, as pointed out in chapter 3, the crown forasteros gave over a smaller percentage of their income in tribute payments than did originarios. This differential occasionally yielded a surplus sufficient to purchase small amounts of land and livestock. From the judicial record, it would also appear that the economic advantage sometimes provided forasteros with the wherewithal to protect their possessions against encroachment in the Spanish courts if need be.

Numerous forasteros, especially artisans and other urban Andeans, appeared in the notarials and lawsuits as purchasers and defenders of private lands. A case in point is that of Don García Lazo, a crown forastero from

the city of Quito, who in 1628 claimed to have purchased lands in Alausí, but
whose rights were contested by a cacique of the town, who insisted that the
former had intruded on community lands. A clear example of social mobility,
García Lazo had somehow assumed the title of "Don" and had accumulated
enough capital not only to buy the lands, but to finance the judicial proceedings necessary to protect them. Furthermore in a telling statement symbolic of
the resentment that originarios often held toward wealthy outsiders, the cacique of Alausí, Don Juan Bixay, warned the audiencia against giving preference to forasteros over the natives of the town.[61]

Ironically crown forasteros were exempt from the mita and paid less tribute precisely because they did not have access to communal lands, but these
exemptions may very well have given them an advantage in the acquisition
and maintenance of resources. Although systematic land studies are sorely
lacking for the Audiencia of Quito, an admittedly scattered and perfunctory examination of the record leaves one with the impression that forasteros
who were able to purchase titled lands as private individuals were in a better position than community Andeans as time went on.[62]

Contrary to the frequent claim for later periods that the privatization of
resources prejudiced the indigenous position because individualization
precluded the unity necessary for successful defense, the case of
seventeenth-century Quito appears to be the opposite. Originarios suffered
continual divestment as "surplus" lands were auctioned off to Spaniards
and community lands were officially reduced through composición.

Throughout the second half of the seventeenth century, Andean communities experienced sweeping losses each time there was a local claim of
underused resources or a royal demand for revenue.[63] Landed forasteros,
however, were not subject to these steamroller encroachments, since their
lands were privately owned and not exposed to blanket expropriations. They
may frequently have lost court cases to individual Spaniards, but they were
not the constant victims of sudden, generalized loss, as were originarios
during this period. In short their ability to acquire and protect resources
already put them in an enviable socioeconomic position compared to their
community cohorts.

By migrating some forasteros escaped, to a degree, the ascribed role of
exploitee assigned to the Indian republic and instead occupied a somewhat
more interstitial position in the colonial system. Perhaps a case can be made
that crown forasteros eventually represented a privileged class among the
colonized. They started out with the advantage of paying less tribute and
exemption from the mita. This then released them to work in more lucrative occupations, sometimes accumulating the capital necessary for the

purchase of private lands and other resources, resources that were then protected under Spanish law in that they were not subject to alienation by the state. Community Andeans, as a group, worked for low wages as mitayos, were stuck with the fiscal and labor burdens of the absentees, and lost land in composiciones, thereby becoming an underclass in colonial society.[64]

Higher salaries and reduced state obligations, however, were not the only components of strategies that resulted in significant social mobility for some members of this group. Under colonial conditions, survival alone required ingenuity; prosperity, such as that enjoyed by some forasteros, implied detailed planning and sometimes intrigue. An analysis of one family's strategies will be instructive.

In 1590 Francisco Ylagumba and Ynés Cuxilago, a forastero couple from Malchinguí and Lalchipichi (Corregimiento of Otavalo) accepted a contract to work as *vaqueros* (cowhands) for Francisco Méndez, an hacendado of Perucho (Corregimiento of Quito). According to the labor contract, a copy of which is presented as evidence in a suit of 1621, they were given subsistence lands, a hut, and an annual salary of fifteen pesos. Lacking specie, the owner often paid them in cattle; in addition they purchased cattle throughout the 1590s from surrounding neighbors. Also of importance in this case is that a relative, named Melchor Ylagumba, who was a shoemaker in the city of Quito, made significant investments in what apparently evolved into a family cattle business.[65] By 1621 the Ylagumbas were reported to have owned ninety head of cattle and four caballerías (45.12 hectares) of land in Perucho.[66]

The material success of this family appears to have been the result of a carefully planned joint venture. One branch migrated to a Spanish city to work for artisan wages and was responsible for providing investment capital, while another branch migrated to a Spanish hacienda on the outskirts of that city, where it received land in usufruct and cattle in payment. In this way the family was able to recuperate resources that had been slipping from their reach back home, and to establish, within a thirty-year period, a fairly prosperous enterprise, most likely supplying meat on the hoof to the Spanish market in Quito.

The good business sense of the Ylagumbas may also have been accompanied by a tinge of intrigue, since the hacendado, Francisco Méndez, charged in 1622 that the former were usurping his land and cattle. He claimed that only ten head of cattle were theirs and that while he was in prison for debts, Ynés Cuxilago and her son, Juan Ylagumba, had pilfered the rest from him, both by removing them from the hacienda little by little and selling them to various people and by branding, as their own, calves that were born to his cows during the period of his incarceration.

In addition Méndez charged that the four caballerías of land they claimed to own was land he gave them for subsistence, as part of their labor contract.[67] The forasteros insisted that they had acquired the cattle through payment and purchase and that the four caballerías were separate lands from those that Méndez had assigned them. Which party won the suit is unclear from the extant documentation. What is clear, however, is that whether they had amassed resources entirely through purchase or in part through pilfering from the hacendado, migration provided this family with all the means of production necessary to participate and prosper in the Spanish market economy. That there were many others like them is evident from the numerous cases in which forasteros were accused of trying to legalize hacienda lands that had been given to them in usufruct, as well as from abundant records that point to the investments of Andean artisans in lands and herds in the surrounding countryside.

The social mobility experienced by a segment of the forastero population was informed, however, not only by the economic opportunities that migration afforded them, but also by the political advantages inherent in their mere presence in the Spanish sphere. Having to make their way in an alien world, they developed an adroitness that enabled them to manipulate the colonial system more effectively than their community cohorts could. In more concrete terms, close and regular contact with the colonizers facilitated alliances in which forasteros both used Spaniards and were used by them in one or the other's political agendas. Countless are the accusations by "legitimate" leaders that their cacicazgos were being usurped by forasteros who, through the migration process, had cultivated important connections with powerful Spaniards.

That currying the favor of influential people in the Spanish sphere was a key component of the intruders' ascent to leadership is revealed in one suit after another during this period, but an especially illustrative example is that of Don Joseph Llaguargos. Don Joseph was an Indian of tributary status whose father, Hernando Tupa Toazo, had migrated from the town of Puni to the Spanish urban center of Riobamba, probably sometime in the 1640s. The latter worked as a cook in the Dominican monastery where his son, Joseph, learned to read and write and served the clergy as a page. When Don Joseph came of age, one of the friars reportedly arranged for him to marry an Andean woman who was remotely descended from the lateral line of the cacicazgo of Puni, his town of origin. Supported by the clergy and several local officials of Riobamba, Don Joseph Llaguargos took possession of the leadership of Puni, displacing Don Gonzalo Curi Argos in 1669.[68]

The ease of the takeover is a vivid reflection of the erosive effects of seventeenth-century trends on the cacicazgo. When asked to testify in a suit against Don Joseph in 1688, Don Gonzalo, the deposed cacique, stated that upon realizing that Don Joseph was backed by powerful Spaniards, he gave up the cause, because he was too poor to bring suit against the interloper and his allies.[69]

This case is far from unique among lawsuits over legitimacy; witnesses claimed repeatedly that intruders were able to acquire and maintain power because legitimate heirs were too impoverished to defend themselves in the Spanish judicial system. In contrast the interlopers were described time and again as having risen to positions of leadership because they had become "rico y ladino" (rich and Hispanicized).[70] Indeed entangling caciques in unending and expensive legal battles became a strategy for the assumption of power. Through a constant barrage of petitions and appeals, wealthy intruders and their Spanish allies frequently subverted the legal process by deliberately escalating costs, in an attempt to drive caciques out of power by divesting them of whatever wealth they still retained.[71]

The phrase "too poor to bring suit" became the leitmotif of seventeenth-century litigation and embodied the comprehensive impact of migration on the Indian sphere. While movement away from Andean communities made possible the frequent political and economic aggrandizement of ambitious individuals, it also gave way to the steady impoverishment and delegitimization of many established leaders. In the end the early colonial cacicazgo crumbled, in many instances, seemingly at the touch of a feather.

From the above discussion of the economic and political benefits of forasterismo, it is not difficult to identify the components of strategies for sociopolitical ascent. Migration facilitated private access to the means of production and gave rise to higher wages, exemption from the mita, and lower tribute rates, all of which created conditions conducive to the accumulation of wealth for some forasteros. In addition systematic relations with powerful Spaniards enabled them to form important political connections that served them well in their bid for power.

The Intruders: Social Origins and Political Motives

With the trajectory of ascent identified, attention should now be turned to an even more compelling issue: Who were the intruders and what were their social origins? Although they were described in the overwhelming majority of suits as forasteros, closer examination of the record reveals that

158 CHAPTER FIVE

they usually had at least some remote affiliation with the target cacicazgo.
More often than not, they were descendants of dissident ayllu members or
disgruntled secondary elites who had departed from the community sometime in the distant past. Since community members had little experience
with the migrants' progeny, they often referred uniformly to these intruders as forasteros. The condition of living and working outside their towns
of origin also qualified them for inclusion in this category. In some instances,
however, the intruders were, indeed, alien to the community, in which case
they usually attempted to gain power by marrying a female member of the
line of succession.[72]

Although the phenomenon of the "returned dissident" appears in the
litigation proceedings of many areas of the audiencia, it is once again the
judicial record of the Corregimiento of Riobamba that provides the richest
data on the subject. During the late seventeenth century, various cacicazgos
of this region were hotly contested in prolonged and bitter legal battles.
Since several cases in the towns of Guano and Puni lend themselves well to
deciphering the provenance and motives of the interlopers, they have been
selected for further analysis. By examining the sociopolitical contents of
these four lawsuits, it will be possible to draw a profile of the typical "intruder cacique."[73]

During the years 1669 to 1699, the Corregimiento of Riobamba was one
of several regions ravaged by an unrelenting wave of litigation over cacicazgos
that assumed an almost epidemic character. It is far from coincidental that
these were the years of greatest decline for early colonial leaders, years during which they had seen both their human and material domains dwindle,
years of the greatest tribute arrears and consequently of Spanish disaffection with their rule.

Everywhere the power of incumbent leaders, whether caciques or
principales, was challenged by a host of contenders from both inside and
outside the cacicazgo, some of whom succeeded in obtaining power and
some of whom did not. Although some challengers were forastero commoners whose migration to the Spanish sphere had resulted in significant
socioeconomic advancement, most power contenders of the period were
disaffected secondary elites who had managed, through migration, to maintain and even improve their status, while their ruling counterparts experienced socioeconomic erosion over the years.[74] They were typically bastard
or second sons, members of lateral lines of succession and descendants of
deposed leaders, people who were once close to the reins of leadership but
for whom power had been elusive.

An examination of these four cases should divulge important data on the exact social composition of the contending group, their motives and strategies for ascent and how the two were related to former colonial developments, and the textural change that took place in indigenous politics upon their assumption of rule.

One of the most politically straightforward suits is that of Don Joseph Roberto Amaguaña versus Don Joseph Quilpud over the Guano parcialidad in the town of Guano. The former charged in 1683 that Joseph Quilpud was a common Andean who had been absent from the community for years and who had now returned to take over the cacicazgo with the influence of powerful people.[75] It was claimed that he was really a mitayo called Joseph Puchig who migrated away, changed his name, and assumed the title of "Don." Furthermore several people declared that they had seen his brother, Mateo, working as a gardener, a shepherd, and a weaver in the obraje, all duties of common Andeans, and that Joseph had paid the Andean witnesses who testified on his behalf.[76]

Don Joseph Quilpud, however, insisted that he was descended from an ancient cacique named Don Francisco Quilpud and that Amaguaña was the intruder.[77] As the suit proceeded, the incumbent leader, Don Joseph Roberto Amaguaña, presented excerpts from the visitas of 1620, 1647, 1654, and 1663, all of which showed him in the chiefly line and none of which even mentioned the name Quilpud in association with the leadership of the Guano parcialidad. In addition the visitas listed the Puchig family as mitayos.[78] In the visita of 1663, Joseph Puchig was listed as a seventeen-year-old commoner, suggesting that shortly after this enumeration he had fled the community to avoid entering tributary status.[79] Presumably he returned twenty years later at the age of thirty-seven, a self-made man, to take over the cacicazgo.

At this juncture it would be easy to conclude that Amaguaña was the rightful heir and that Don Joseph Quilpud was a fiction created by Joseph Puchig, the commoner. Nevertheless Amaguaña and his lawyers never once denied that there existed an ancient cacique named Don Francisco Quilpud; apparently there was some community memory of such a leader, as demonstrated by the testimony of the contenders' Andean witnesses, and so the former preferred to assume a defense based on an accusation of imposture. This may imply that the line of Quilpud fell victim to dispossession prior to or during the visita of 1620, as a result of Spanish meddling in indigenous political organization. Was Don Joseph Quilpud, then, the embittered descendant of a deposed leader who returned to Guano at a propitious moment to vindicate his ancestors?

How this case was settled is unknown, nor can concrete conclusions be drawn from this type of litigation. Nevertheless, as will become clearer in subsequent cases, there was almost always an element of truth to the claims of the intruders, just enough to provoke some thought about aboriginal and colonial concepts of legitimacy. In a previous discussion of the Spanish reorganization of indigenous polities, it was demonstrated that secondary elites and even commoners were often raised in status during early Spanish visitas, in the interests of efficient administration. This created an optimal situation for those promoted, since they could always rely on the visitas as unambiguous evidence of provenance, while the descendants of those who were deposed had little legal ground to stand on in Spanish courts.

Since the obstinacy of demoted leaders and their descendants has already been addressed elsewhere in this chapter, it is not difficult to entertain the possibility that Don Joseph Quilpud, and others like him, may have had legitimate claims. And even if they were, indeed, commoners, it is significant that they could still manipulate legends regarding early leaders in an attempt to claim power; that is, they could continue to play on the community's persistent doubts about the legitimacy of Spanish-promoted caciques.

The second case is that of Don Miguel de Torres versus Don Manuel Sagñay over the cacicazgo of the Magssi parcialidad, town of Puni, in 1699. This suit points up the importance of both artisanry and enrollment in crown parcialidades as a route to acquiring sociopolitical status or, in this case, perhaps as a route to recuperating it.

Miguel de Torres, who was enumerated as a forastero in the crown parcialidad of Riobamba (Spanish center), sued for the cacicazgo of the Magssi parcialidad (town of Puni). He claimed that the incumbent leader, Don Manuel Sagñay, and his father before him were descendants of a tributary Andean, Don Gerónimo Sagñay. Torres charged that Don Gerónimo had been appointed as administrator of the parcialidad during the visita of Matías de Peralta (1620s), because the rightful heir was too young to rule, and that his descendants had illegally remained in control of the cacicazgo thereafter.[80]

Similar to the case of Quilpud, Torres insisted that before the infamous visita of 1620, his ancestors, descendants of the original cacique, Don Sancho Aquilema (alternately Daquilema), were the legitimate rulers of Magssi. He then claimed that when the last cacique from his line died, the intruders threw his father, Don Pedro de Torres, out of the ayllu, and he subsequently moved to the Spanish town of Riobamba, where he was forced to take up a trade (that of shoemaking) in order to sustain himself and his family. He was then logically enumerated in the parcialidad of the crown forasteros of

Riobamba. In addition a major objective of Miguel de Torres's suit was to gain access to the communal lands that he said were a part of his chiefly patrimony.[81]

The incumbent leader, Don Manuel Sagñay, presented excerpts from all the appropriate visitas dating from that of 1620, confirming his descent from the principales of Magssi; at the same time, it was apparently confirmed that Miguel de Torres was listed in the parcialidad of the forasteros.[82] Unfortunately neither the plaintiff nor the defendant presented the visitas of 1583 or 1592, two documents that most probably would have settled the matter more definitively. Instead the Matías de Peralta visita of 1620 was taken as the baseline, as always, and legitimacy was awarded to Don Manuel Sagñay.

Once again it is not possible to determine the veracity of either claimant's story, since many irregularities did, indeed, occur during the visita of Matías de Peralta. There are therefore two possible explanations. A forastero family of artisans (the Torres) made good and then attempted to gain access to land and prestige by challenging the leader of the Magssi parcialidad; or Miguel de Torres's ancestors were the rightful heirs to the parcialidad, but lost power during the official events of 1620, and that by 1688 their descendants had accumulated enough wealth and connections in the Spanish sphere to litigate for the cacicazgo.

The third case, one that has already been referred to above, is that of Don Augustín Argos Guaraca versus Don Joseph Llaguargos over the cacicazgo of the mitimaes of Puni in 1688.[83] This suit illustrates the importance of local Spanish-Andean alliances as a strategy for ascent on the part of intruders and the blatant disregard for Andean ways that became characteristic of their style of rule. Although the originally deposed cacique did not contest Don Joseph Llaguargos's takeover in 1669, the alleged heir to the cacicazgo, Don Augustín Argos Guaraca, brought suit in 1688. He charged that Don Joseph was a commoner who, bolstered by important contacts in the Spanish sphere, had usurped the leadership of the parcialidad. Nevertheless in a debate over genealogies that appears in the suit, it seems more likely that Don Joseph Llaguargos was descended from a bastard son of the original cacique, Yanaguaraca.[84] Don Augustín claimed descent from the legitimate son.

Upon the assumption of power, Don Joseph allegedly exiled Don Augustín from the town, by making him a shepherd in a remote area. He also assigned all the lateral heirs of the cacicazgo to the mita, forbidding them to return. He then took possession of the community's lands and town plots, sold them to various Spaniards through Andean proxies, and kept some for his own agricultural enterprises. When the mitayos of the parcialidad returned from their tours of duty, they found themselves dispossessed. Having no lands with which to sustain themselves, they abandoned the town. It was charged that this series of events became a vicious circle that ended in the near-total depopulation of the town. Land divestment prompted a general out-migration, leaving more lands vacant, which the cacique then usurped or sold.[85] The strategy was evidently intended to garner not only land but labor, since the overwhelming majority of those who fled ended up on the Spanish haciendas of the area.

Spanish involvement in this scam was underscored when Don Augustín, the heir apparent, requested that his witnesses not be interrogated by either of Riobamba's scribes, nor that the corregidor be involved in the suit. By way of explanation, he claimed that Juan de Garnica, the cabildo's scribe, was the friend, compadre, and confidante of Don Joseph Llaguargos and had helped him to gain the cacicazgo. He stipulated that neither should Captain Thomas de Herrera, the public scribe, serve on this case, since he was an intimate friend of both. Lastly he claimed that the corregidor could not be trusted either, because Juan de Garnica was his tribute collector.[86] The implication is that several important officials of the Spanish town of Riobamba participated in this project together. Ten years later the veracity of Don Augustín's story was borne out, when this entourage appeared again in the same capacity in the suit described below.[87] Here we have explicit evidence of a local power group, rooted in Spanish/Andean alliances and cemented by relations of compadrazgo, that operated in extreme prejudice of indigenous communities—the epitome of the new politics.

The last case, Don Fernando Duchinachay versus Don Luis Zugo over the governorship of the town of Puni (1699), involves nearly the same cast of characters, with the same project.[88] The town of Puni was divided into two large cacicazgos: that of the Inca mitimaes and that of the aboriginal Puruhá. The local power group, having succeeded in divesting the mitimaes of their land and labor, now attempted to repeat the same maneuver ten years later with the town's second cacicazgo. This case is also notable because, on the spectrum of intrusions, it falls on the extreme end, including as it does all the major elements of a successful takeover.

Don Fernando Duchinachay, who was the cacique principal of the ten Puruhá parcialidades of Puni, also traditionally held the office of governor of the town, until he became ill with *machaque*.[89] His poor health continued for four years, during which time his son, Don Martín, assumed the responsibilities of the position. Subsequently his son also fell ill and died, at which point Don Fernando once again took over the duties of governor. At this juncture local officials seized upon the death of Don Martín and Don Fernando's enfeebled state to dispossess the latter of his governorship. The corregidor allegedly made an unfavorable report about his performance at the urging of the notorious scribe, Juan de Garnica. This resulted in Don Fernando's loss of the governorship and its bestowal upon Don Luis Zugo (alternately Zubo).[90] A more profound investigation of the latter's identity is instructive.

Don Fernando Duchinachay, the plaintiff, described Zugo as a commoner who was raised in the Spanish center of Riobamba, a servant, since childhood, of the royal scribe, Juan de Garnica. He testified further that Don Luis had received the governor's position through the influence of his employer. Although his connection to the scribe was undoubtedly authentic, closer scrutiny and additional documentation reveal that Don Luis Zugo was not a commoner at all, but a disaffected secondary elite, with close ties to one of the parcialidades of Puni. The genealogical content of an earlier suit indicates that he was descended from a lateral line of a principalazgo of the Chuyupi parcialidad.[91] Indeed this case typifies, more than any other, the rise through migration of the "returned dissident." For a better understanding of this process, it will first be necessary to provide some background information on the colonial reorganization of the Puruhá cacicazgo of Puni.

In 1620 this cacicazgo consisted of ten parcialidades or ayllus, each with its own leader, all of whom were subject to the authority of a cacique principal; leaders of the individual parcialidades were designated as principales, according to the Spanish scheme, but called themselves caciques, a telling incongruity in itself.[92] Apropos of this and other data, it is not unreasonable to assume that the Puruhá polities of Puni experienced the same artificial centralization as other groups in the region during early Spanish visitas. That three different caciques vied for leadership during the 1583 visita supports this assumption. The original cacicazgo probably consisted of a constellation of separate, autonomous groups, who were "reduced" in Puni and politically concentrated under one cacique principal, selected out from among many equivalent leaders.[93]

The events of the visita of Matías de Peralta constitute more definitive proof of this Spanish-induced centralization process. In this census of 1620, Don García Duchinachay, Don Fernando's father, was registered as the cacique principal of the ten parcialidades of Culum (his own ayllu), Baleltul, Chusmote, Pangor, Chaupipachag, Malan, Magssi, Chuyupi, Tunchucay, and Bacum. Nevertheless it is stated that there were several contenders for the position and that Don Matías de Peralta had selected Duchinachay from among them, awarding him the duho.[94] Undoubtedly, as in previously cited cases, the Spanish centralization process must have generated feelings of demotion among those not selected, giving rise to intense political dissent.

Also of importance to the case of intrusion at hand is that the census of 1620 offers some confirmation of Don Luis Zugo's social origins. In the ayllu of Chuyupi, Matías de Peralta decided, as he frequently did, that the ruling principal, Don Juan Usco, was too old to administer the ayllu properly and his grandson, the direct heir, was too young. He therefore designated as administrator Don Juan's brother, Don Baltazar Gerónimo Zubo. It is likely, then, that Don Luis Zugo (Zubo) was the descendant of Don Baltazar, a member of the lateral line of succession.[95] However, in the visita of 1664, the rightful heir of the principalazgo was listed as Don Pedro Zugo, leaving us with the possibility that Don Luis might have been descended from the direct line.[96] Whether through lateral or direct succession, at some point Don Luis Zugo assumed the leadership of the Chuyupi ayllu, as well as the governorship of the town. It is more probable, however, that he was a lateral descendant with a hankering to bypass the direct heir; otherwise why would he or his ancestors have had to migrate to the Spanish sphere and assume power through the intercession of influential people?

Don Fernando Duchinachay's accusations of illegitimacy were followed by the usual charges of abuse on the part of the intruder. Just as Don Joseph Llaguargos had been accused of funneling community lands to his Spanish cohorts, it was reported that Don Luis Zugo, as governor, had subjected the community to excessive labor appropriations, incorporating elders and other reserved men into the mita, probably in fulfillment of promises made to his Spanish allies. Once again the cry was that this chaos and suffering had caused out-migration and the town's depopulation.[97]

Based on data presented in this suit and earlier related litigation, a somewhat conjectural sociopolitical sketch of this intruder can be drawn. Don Luis Zugo was most likely a secondary elite, whose ancestors migrated to the Spanish center of Riobamba. There he benefited from important Spanish connections and returned to his community first as principal of his parcialidad of origin and then as *gobernador* of the whole town of Puni.

Through this process of ascent, Don Luis was able to resolve two age-old conflicts: the secondary status of lateral descent in the Chuyupi ayllu, and the subordination of autonomous leaders during the earlier concentration of power under the Duchinachays. For Don Luis Zugo, migration made possible an assumption of power previously denied him on both levels. First by assuming rule of his ayllu, he attained a right denied to his ancestors by the Spanish regime, being as they were lateral descendants; second he recovered the position lost by his ayllu in the centralization process, by gaining control of the whole town through the position of gobernador, which now carried more political functions and prestige than that of cacique principal.

Nevertheless the benefits that disgruntled secondary elites derived from the migration process carried with them an exorbitant price; political hegemony could be attained and assured only through unabashed collusion with local Spanish power brokers. The payoff would have to be underwritten by the community; this was the essence of the new indigenous politics. Not surprisingly the rebellions of the late eighteenth century would be led not by caciques but by common Andeans. According to Moreno Yánez's definitive work on this topic, few caciques participated in these uprisings, and many colluded with Spanish officials to put them down.[98] In Otavalo, so vast had the breach become between leaders and community, that the people perceived native authorities as their enemies and even executed the province's Andean governor as a traitor during the 1777 rebellion of the town of San Pablo.[99]

Conclusion

The Spanish reorganization of indigenous polities in the sixteenth century precipitated the political weakening of Quito's cacicazgos. Colonial policies that centralized power under one Andean leader selected from among several equally ranked cohorts left a legacy of community conflict and undermined chiefly legitimacy.

The radical population movements of the late sixteenth and seventeenth centuries further fragmented an already divided Indian sphere. As migration and demographic fraud became Andean survival strategies, the Spanish regime countered with cooptative measures, such as the manifestación system and the creation of crown parcialidades of forasteros. While these measures were aimed at demographic accuracy, they produced alternative political bases upon which commoners, secondary elites, and existing caciques could establish or expand authority. This resulting multiplication of avenues to the assumption of power accelerated the political disunity of Andean society.

As Andean migration was increasingly redirected toward the Spanish sphere during the seventeenth century, the political erosion of the cacicazgo was paralleled by the economic divestment of early colonial leaders. Land expropriations and accelerated out-migration caused a serious deficit of human and material resources in the Indian sphere, leaving the caciques to resolve the ausentes-rezagos problem through the expenditure of their private wealth. The result was the political and economic destitution of many established leaders and the rise of intruder caciques.

In the late seventeenth and early eighteenth centuries, many descendants of "secondary" elites revived their deferred dreams of autonomy by attempting to exploit conditions that had their roots in the demographic and hence politico-economic weakening of the cacicazgo. This pattern was repeated throughout the period in the actions of bastards, second sons, lateral heirs, and descendants of the deposed and subordinated, many of whom had left their communities to avoid tributary status and its demoting implications. They migrated to the Spanish sphere where, free of state obligations, they often accumulated wealth and influential connections over the years. At the same time, their ruling cohorts—once objects of envy, but now personally saddled with increasing tribute and labor burdens—slipped into a pathetic state of economic and political decay.

At this critical juncture, when leaders of the direct line of succession, as well as those who were installed during the Spanish reorganization, were expended, so to speak, many lateral heirs and other disaffected elements returned to their communities to "take back" power. Through wealth, political influence, and downright, unobfuscated collusion, they attempted at last to realize dreams that had been secretly harbored and bitterly transmitted across generations.

Nevertheless those dreams had become somewhat altered over time and now included not only old political aspirations, but the acquisition of the means of production necessary to participate in a growing market economy. The duho, one-time symbol of traditional authority and prestige, was no longer enough, as witnessed by the land and labor that Llaguargos and Zugo accrued upon their ascent to power. The agreements they made with influential Spaniards to funnel community lands and labor in their direction carried with them significant material rewards. Llaguargos, for example, was accused by his community of first expropriating prime lands for himself and then partitioning the rest among his Spanish allies.[100] Zugo, while responsible for providing local elites with excessive labor from his community, was permitted to put together a private work force from among Andeans he had "manifested."[101] These were also compelling motives for repeated attempts to resume power on the parts of disaffected elites and commoners.

The tenacity with which some contenders held on and finally vindicated themselves can be better understood if examined in the light of contrasting

European and indigenous concepts of succession and legitimacy. It is important to consider that the deprivation of power that the "secondary" elites experienced at the hands of Spanish bureaucrats seemed to them arbitrary and incomprehensible. Surely it would have been easier for them to have gained power in pre-Hispanic times, before European concepts of legitimacy, primogeniture, and the nascent political ideal of the centralized nation-state made their American debut. People who appeared by European standards to be secondary, illegitimate, or laterally descended may very well have been selected as leaders within the context of Andean norms. This has been proven by many studies of Incaic and pre-Incaic succession, where the most able person from the line was chosen to rule, whether a direct or indirect heir.[102] Thus "secondary" elites were only trying to recoup what might have been much more easily theirs in pre-Hispanic times.

Conclusion

From migration and forasterismo, the indigenous peoples of Quito formulated a survival strategy that initially destabilized the Spanish administration and then evolved into a pervasive agent of change. Though developed as a personal and collective response to the abuses of conquest and colonization, it helped to determine the socioeconomic and political trajectory of both the indigenous and Spanish colonial worlds. Through this adaptation, native peoples both reproduced and transformed their own societies, impeded an assessment of their true numbers, and subverted the extractive system of the colony.

What was the demographic significance of this survival strategy? Central to an accurate population history of Spanish America is a careful evaluation of the credibility of the existing record. The study of Quito has underlined the tendency of native population movements to skew official demographic statistics. Migration, combined with irregular administrative practices and a high incidence of fraud, have made the use of tribute records problematic in assessing population trends.

This conclusion is borne out by an investigation of colonial Quito's anomalous population curve. By linking a variety of qualitative data to the quantitative record, I have concluded that Tyrer's and Alchon's projected demographic growth for the seventeenth century was the result of migrations from marginal areas to the center of the audiencia and the subsequent incorporation of return migrants, forasteros, and ocultos into official statistics.

The earliest interregional movements, those that took place from the 1550s to 1600, were, in part, organized movements whose infrastructure was founded upon pre-Hispanic and even pre-Incaic economic exchange mechanisms. As the Amerindians of the highlands died off during the depopulating events of the sixteenth century, they were replaced systematically by a migration from the adjacent lowlands and from marginal areas in the north and south. These regions harbored a large demographic reserve, created both by the displacements of the Inca and Spanish conquests and by the exigencies of native vertical economies.

Andean economies required the extraterritorial residence of large groups of people for the exploitation of needed resources. There is evidence that highland caciques orchestrated population movements from these peripheral colonies as a strategy for filling demographic shortages in their nuclear communities. In addition they engaged in the deliberate recruitment of outsiders—a strategy that had its roots in pre-Hispanic practices—and hid a considerable number of their subjects from Spanish census takers. Data also suggest that long-distance traders (mindalaes), who had once specialized in the acquisition of exotic goods, were transformed into migration agents. In these ways native leaders were able to meet the ever-increasing labor demands of the Spanish regime, ensure their own retention of power, and underwrite the community. Here political economy, demography, and geographic conditions formed an interconnected configuration that intersected with existing cultural forms. In short the caciques' reproductive strategies are fitting examples of Sahlins's "structure of the conjuncture," that is, how native peoples revalued pre-Hispanic cultural categories in order to fit new colonial imperatives.

As the Spanish invasion expanded to include marginal areas, the displaced people migrated back to their original communities in the central and north-central sierra. The return migrants, recruited outsiders, vagabonds, and hidden subjects of the second half of the sixteenth century were then systematically included in the census records of the seventeenth century and incorporated into the tributary base. This created an illusion of explosive demographic growth in the heartland of the audiencia. Clearly native migration, combined with tighter Spanish administration, were responsible for the tremendous leap in tributary population reported by Tyrer and Alchon for the years 1590 to 1670.

The above findings bear out Sánchez-Albornoz's suggestion that tribute records are not always accurate reflections of population trends. Regarding the Alto Peruvian data he asks, "demographic collapse or contraction of the tributary base?" In Quito the question is rather, "demographic growth or inflation of the tributary base?"—a reformulation that both demonstrates the wider range of the problem and underscores the need for demographic historians to combine complementary sources and methods.

Did migration bring about the reproduction or the destructuration of Andean communities? In Quito the answer rests with the particular migration patterns that arose out of conditions specific to different periods. The movements of the sixteenth century tended to take place within the Indian sphere, that is, from one native community to another. This pattern provided caciques with alternative labor and vacant lands for rental, enabling them to retain power and reproduce their communities. Thus intercommunity migration permitted substantial retention of pre-Hispanic cultural forms. In contrast the movements of the seventeenth century were characterized by a marked shift toward the Spanish sphere and were accompanied by considerable disruption of the politicoeconomic structures of the north Andean cacicazgo.

During the seventeenth century, the divestment of native resources and the growing domination of the Spanish economy compelled Andeans to migrate to Spanish cities, textile mills, and haciendas, both for subsistence and to escape tribute and forced labor. This was the kind of migration used typically throughout the Andes as a survival strategy; it was an ingenious manipulation of the Spanish legal system, which held that natives could only be taxed and drafted for labor in their towns of origin. Although this form of migration was a strategy that began with the inception of Spanish rule, it accelerated considerably during the seventeenth century.

What was the effect of this survival strategy on the Indian sphere in Quito? First migration accelerated the socioeconomic differentiation of Andean communities. The absent population created a severe problem of tribute arrears. According to Spanish law, caciques were held personally responsible for paying these back tributes. Consequently they were often forced to sell their possessions in order to fulfill their communities' tribute quotas and gradually became impoverished. This caused the demise of numerous hereditary leaders and the rise of intruder caciques, many of whom were secondary elites and ordinary Andeans who had migrated to the Spanish sphere, accumulated wealth, and established influential connections. The forasteros also represented a potential clientele upon which ambitious native commoners and members of lesser lineages could build a power base, further fragmenting the Indian sphere.

In addition some common Andeans achieved lesser degrees of upward mobility, as witnessed by the frequency with which migrants appeared in the records both purchasing and defending private lands. This group, however, was paralleled by a large category of indigenous peoples who sank to levels of extreme poverty; these were the migrants who ended as prisoners in textile mills, de facto slaves to caciques and Spaniards, and debt peons on Spanish haciendas.

Also throughout the seventeenth century, the steady out-migration from native communities caused the impoverishment of the Andeans who remained behind. Since the Spanish administration was often reluctant to adjust tribute and labor quotas downward, the originarios were forced to compensate for the quotas of those who had absented themselves. Thus while migration was a route up the social ladder for some Andeans, it undermined the socioeconomic position of Andeans as a group.

While migrations of individuals gave rise to a trend toward social differentiation and community disintegration, in some areas they were paralleled by collective migrations that functioned as a form of cultural resistance. These movements can be divided into two categories: those orchestrated by caciques and those arising from the group migrations of ordinary Andeans. The first type was prevalent in the central highlands and was often a calculated strategy for community survival that had its roots in pre-Hispanic economic structures. In much the same way that preconquest caciques dispatched Andeans to extracommunity locations to exploit needed resources, seventeenth-century leaders sent their subjects to Spanish textile mills, haciendas, and cities to exploit a new resource—wages. This income, while sometimes pocketed by unscrupulous caciques, was often used to pay tribute arrears and to subsidize the shrinking subsistence base, thereby ensuring community survival.

In the current historiographical debate over whether migration reproduced or destructured Andean society, proponents of reproduction often point to cacique-orchestrated movements as the sine qua non of cultural survival. Glave refers to seventeenth-century migration as a chiefly strategy "to manage exploitation," while Saignes underscores the reproductive role of the caciques' "new mitimaes." According to this view, Andean towns deliberately dispersed their populations, hoping to hide some of their residents from fiscal agents and to activate new resources in the form of capital.

While this study of Quito has certainly borne out the effectiveness of organized migration for some areas, it also cautions against assigning too much importance to the actions of the indigenous leadership in the process of cultural survival. First the caciques' intent with regard to these movements cannot be measured; some engaged in seemingly reproductive strategies for self-aggrandizement, others operated wholly in the interests of their communities, and still others devised ways to achieve both.

Second, as mentioned above, a substantial proportion of this movement took place at the individual level, thus tempering the reproductive process. Although Andeanists acknowledge that these two types of movements, individual and collective, occurred simultaneously, they have not found a way to determine whether one predominated, or if they were more or less equivalent in volume. Knowing this would color considerably our interpretations of the seventeenth-century history of Andean societies, since then we could conjecture about rates of destructuration and reproduction. Leapfrogging over this quantitative problem with regard to both the intent of caciques and the incidence of individual versus collective migrations has led to generalizations that most seventeenth-century movements were calculated community-survival strategies. In the absence of quantitative control and in the presence of contradictory qualitative data, these general claims remain unsupported.

Lastly the focus on the role of Andean elites in community reproduction has been somewhat misleading, and it is in this arena that the study of Quito makes a uniquely important contribution. There the institutional weakening of the cacicazgo left many of the region's ethnic peoples leaderless by the 1680s. In the final analysis, it was the migratory style of ordinary Andeans that militated most against group disintegration and eventual Hispanicization. According to computer analyses of the kin composition of migrating groups, Quito's peoples tended to move in family clusters to the same site—a migration pattern that ensured ethnic and cultural survival. Evidence suggests that Spanish textile mills and agricultural estates became new forms of aggregation, in which groups were recomposed and social organization reconstituted.

Thus the ethnogenesis of Ecuadorean groups under Spanish rule was strongly influenced not only by the deliberate reproductive strategies of native leaders, but also by the migratory style of ordinary Andeans. Migration and dispersed settlement patterns had been a fact of Andean life since time immemorial; ayllu members migrated in search of resources, whether as members of formal economic colonies or as informal barterers. The transformation of this pre-Hispanic cultural structure into a colonial survival strategy, however, led to a trifurcation of the ayllu's functions. The social, economic, and political life of the pre-Hispanic ayllu were interwoven threads of the same cloth, overlapping categories that could not be separated out, one from the other. The demographic movements arising from colonial conditions accelerated the process of resource divestment and the decline of the early colonial cacique. This led Ecuadorean peoples down an ethnogenetic path that stripped the ayllu of its political and economic functions. The latter were absorbed by the Spanish republic, but the ayllu's social function remained intact. In the end it was the cultural predilection of ordinary Andeans to reconstruct the social organization of the ayllu inside the Spanish obraje-hacienda complex that permitted ethnic and cultural survival. The Indian republic, now physically inserted into the Spanish republic, had disappeared as an economic and political entity, but lived on as a sociocultural organism. Indeed the study of Quito's migration patterns confirms that the social relations of the ayllu weighed more heavily than both territoriality and leadership in the endurance of the region's ethnic groups.

Although these findings hold specifically for the audiencia of Quito, the strength of the ayllu and vertical economy as pan-Andean institutions and the short-range migrations reported by other scholars lead me to suspect that the same migratory style occurred in the southern Andes, with similar results. This pattern may answer, in part, the oft-repeated question as to how Andean peoples have been able to maintain cultural cohesion in spite of five hundred years of demographic and social destabilization.

Ironically both individual and collective migrations permitted Andeans to survive as a people and as a culture, but they also contained the seeds for the general weakening of Andean society vis-à-vis the colonizers. Migration brought prosperity to some Andeans and gave rise to a native sector that benefited from its connections with the Spanish sphere. This laid the foundation for closer and more widespread collaboration between the colonizers and the colonized, creating the typical colonial situation in which part of the nation turns into the anti-nation and permits structures of domination to become self-perpetuating.

Using the study of migration as a vehicle, this book has attempted to give a more nuanced historical meaning to the actions of Ecuador's ethnic peoples. By migrating to escape the formal demands of their colonizers, they ended up stimulating important changes not only in their own societies, but in the society of their oppressors as well. Although there can be no doubt about which of these contending forces was in control of the colony at any given moment, it is also clear that Andean agency played a significant role in the historical outcome. In the words of one seventeenth-century bureaucrat, the Andeans were, after all, "prendas con pies" (assets with feet).

Appendix:
Census Analysis for Chapter Two

The censuses surveyed—those of the Corregimiento of Otavalo and of the towns of Guaca and Calpi—were arranged by household and recorded the kin position and age for each individual, as well as the manner in which each was reported—that is whether the individual was seen in person by the census taker, was reported by a cacique or relative, or was included simply because he or she was registered in the last census. In the censuses of the Audiencia of Quito, the specific ages of wives were not recorded; rather it was always stated that they were the same age as their husbands ("de la misma edad"). Although this is impossible in every case, it appears that most women must have been approximately the same age as their husbands, because on the rare occasions that a man was much older than his wife, the census taker would indeed list her specific age.

In addition information was recorded for the head of household concerning his marital status, tributary status, whether he was present or absent, and if absent, his place of residence. The absentee's residences were frequently recorded in the census as local places names (Perucho, Guayllabamba, and Alausí, for example), but their presentation as such would have made the tables unwieldy and the flows incomprehensible. For this reason, all geographic designations in the census materials have been compressed into the larger category of corregimiento or province.

For the purposes of this study, the most important information was the head of household's residential status. Although this data was not provided specifically for other members of the kin group, it is evident throughout the censuses that in the overwhelming majority of cases, they lived with the head; when they did not, the census taker designated their specific places of residence. Hence the analysis presumes that all family members were living in the same location with the head of household, unless otherwise stated.

The format of the census also divulges other important kin relationships, since each household head was described in relation to the household head listed in the previous position—"Joan Cacoango, hermano del sobredicho," for example. Conversely the format obscures the consanguineal relationships of married women, since they are listed in the same entry with their husbands and children, ignoring the other members of the community to whom they were most certainly related. Nevertheless a limited family reconstruction has been possible through the use of nuclear- and extended-family codes.

Although the census of Otavalo (1645) has survived only in a fragmentary state, it has been possible to standardize the data to the extent necessary for viable analysis. This was achieved by comparing the population totals of ayllus arrived at by counting all individuals recorded in the document with the census taker's official counts, or *sumarios*, which appear at the end of each section of the census. If the computerized count is equivalent to or greater than the official count of the census taker, than it has been assumed that the data for that ayllu has been preserved in its entirety and the ayllu has been included in the analysis of the region's towns.

In addition to the tables on absenteeism and migration patterns that appear in the text (tables 1–25), demographic profiles have also been compiled for the Corregimiento of Otavalo and for the towns of Guaca (Corregimiento of Ibarra) and Calpi (Corregimiento of Riobamba). Statistics on census reporting, gender distribution, age structure, and marital status for these population centers are recorded below in tables 26–38.

Demographic Profiles

I. Demographic Profile of Repartimiento of Otavalo, 1645 (Corregimiento of Otavalo)

The data recorded here for the repartimiento of Otavalo are limited to the five towns of Otavalo, Cotacache, Tontaquí, Ynta, and Urcuquí and to the ayllu of Yacelga; that is to the parts of the census that were well preserved. The analysis, therefore, does not include the entire repartimiento, Tumbaviro and Cayambe, for example, being important omissions, but treats a population substantial enough for an analysis of general trends.

Table 26: Census Reporting in Repartimiento of Otavalo, 1645

Manner Reported in Census	Number of Individuals	% Total Pop.	% Valid Cases
Appeared in person	2,057	39	70
Registered in previous census	412	8	14
Reported by cacique	187	4	6
Reported by relative or friend	304	6	10

These figures are derived from 2,960 valid cases; that is, data were reported for this variable for 2,960 individuals out of a total population of 5,214. The cases for whom these data are missing were mostly children.

Table 27: Gender Distribution in Repartimiento of Otavalo, 1645

	Number of Individuals	Valid Percentages
Male	2,925	63
Female	1,707	37

This striking gender imbalance is most probably due to serious underreporting of females in the census and will be investigated further below, in an age-specific analysis of gender distribution.

Table 28: Gender Distribution by Age in Repartimiento of Otavalo, 1645

Age	Male	Female
Infants	62	47
1–9 years	890	373
10–17 years	296	115
18–29 years	613	413
30–39 years	560	381
40–49 years	235	192
50–89 years	243	176

Figures were derived from 4,596 valid cases for which both gender and age were reported in the census.

Table 28 indicates that the sex imbalance in the Repartimiento of Otavalo cut across all generations but was especially evident among young children, ages one to nine years. A likely explanation would be that the census takers made less serious efforts to count females accurately, since the latter were not, nor ever would be, nominally responsible for tribute and forced labor. Ann Zulawski has found similar gender-distribution patterns for colonial censuses in Bolivia (personal communication).

Table 29: Age Structure of Repartimiento of Otavalo, 1645

Age	Number of Individuals	Percentages
Infants	109	3
1–9 years	1,263	27
10–17 years	412	9
18–29 years	1,027	22
30–39 years	941	21
40–49 years	427	9
50–89 years	419	9

Figures derived from 4,598 valid cases.

The repartimiento's age structure may be somewhat skewed by the apparent underreporting of females. Nevertheless some of the same relationships between generations can be noted in the age-specific gender-distribution analysis above, where males were less likely to have been omitted from the census, due to their tribute and labor functions. Note, for example, that the age category "10–17 years" is very small in both tables 28 and 29 suggesting that this generation had been decimated by epidemic disease.

Table 30: Marital Status in Repartimiento of Otavalo, 1645

Marital Status	Number of Individuals	Percentages
Married	2,079	79
Single	362	14
Widowed	191	7

Sources: All above data were derived from Freile G., Numeraciones, and AN/Q, Indígenas 4, 23-III-1645.

II. Demographic Profile of Town of Guaca, 1650
(Corregimiento of Ibarra)

Table 31: Census Reporting in Town of Guaca, 1650

Manner Reported in Census	Number of Individuals	% Total Pop.	% Valid Cases
Appeared in person	353	36	69
Registered in previous census	99	10	19
Reported by cacique	44	4	9
Reported by relative or friend	15	1	3

Figures derived from 511 valid cases out of a total population of 801. Most cases for whom this variable was not reported were children.

Table 32: Gender Distribution in Town of Guaca, 1650

	Number of Individuals	Valid Percentages
Male	367	48
Female	404	52

Figures derived from 771 valid cases out of a total population of 801.

Table 33: Age Structure of Town of Guaca, 1650

Age	Number of Individuals	Valid Percentages
Infants	15	2
1–9 years	170	22
10–17 years	89	12
18–29 years	174	23
30–39 years	77	10
40–49 years	138	18
50–96 years	102	13

Figures derived from 764 valid cases out of a total population of 801.

The small size of the age category "10–17 years" is evident again, although now accompanied by a paltry population for the 30–39 age group as well. Since the latter group is likely to have been the parent generation of the 10–17 age group, it may be that the 30–39 population was affected by disease in childhood or adolescence and then produced a small 10–17 age generation.

Table 34: Marital Status inTown of Guaca, 1650

Marital Status	Number of Individuals	Valid Percentages
Married	337	70
Single	78	16
Widowed	70	14

Source: All above data were derived from AN/Q, Indígenas 5, 20-VII-1650.

III. Demographic Profile, Town of Calpi, 1663
(Corregimiento of Riobamba)

Table 35: Census Reporting in Town of Calpi, 1663

Manner Reported in Census	Number of Individuals	% Total Pop.	% Valid Cases
Appeared in person	339	21	26
Registered in previous census	773	48	59
Reported by another	195	12	15

Figures derived from 1,307 valid cases out of a total population of 1,500. Most cases for whom this variable was not reported were children.

Table 36: Gender Distribution in Town of Calpi, 1663

	Number of Individuals	Valid Percentages
Male	751	51
Female	731	49

Figures derived from 1,482 valid cases out of a total population of 1,500.

Table 37: Age Structure of Town of Calpi, 1663

Ages	Number of Individuals	Valid Percentages
Infants	36	3
1–9 years	302	21
10–17 years	188	13
18–29 years	315	22
30–39 years	132	9
40–49 years	222	16
50–89 years	223	16

Figures derived from 1,418 valid cases out of a population of 1,500.

Thirteen to eighteen years after the censuses of Otavalo and Guaca, Calpi also exhibits the same depopulated pattern for the 10–17 and 30–39 age groups.

Table 38: Marital Status in Town of Calpi, 1663

Marital Status	Number of Individuals	Valid Percentages
Married	625	77
Single	119	15
Widowed	68	8

Source: All above data were derived from AN/Q, Cacicazgos 9, 1749-V-21.

Ayllu Nomenclature

Both midseventeenth-century censuses and late seventeenth-century absentee lists were organized first by town and then by ayllu. Since many of the ayllu names that appear in these census materials have not come to light before this study, they have been recorded below in table 39.

Table 39: Ayllu Names by Town, 1645–1698

Towns (census dates in parentheses)	Ayllus (by order of appearance in text)	Towns (census dates in parentheses)	Ayllus (by order of appearance in text)
Otavalo (1645)	Camuinto Sicañaro Pirance Sarance	Licto (1690–94)	Nabug Chumu Malad Gaurun Dutñap Salahole Chuyupi Puninguil
Cotacache (1645)	Pangobuela Cotacache Cotacache 2 Gualcaquí Cuchisquí Aguaborín Cuchagro y Salinero Tocagón	San Andrés (1690–94)	Chalca Cullagua Hazaco Sogsi Chibunga Chibunga (Camayos) Langos Guanando Chazo Tunchucay
Tontaquí (1645)	Tontaquí Mindalaes Tupián Apulrro		Taguan Patulo
Ynta (1645)	Pincaquí Tulla		
Malchinguí (1645)	Malchinguí	Ylapo (1698)	Lanlansi Zasguansi Ylapo Milaniat Camayos
Urcuquí (1645)	Urcuquiango Yacelga		

Sources: Freile, G. Numeraciones; AN/Q, Indígenas 18, 1690-7-II; AN/Q, Religiosos 7, 1698-II-7.

Note: The ayllus of the towns of Guaca, Calpi, and Chambo are recorded in tables 10, 14, and 22 in the text. The census materials used for the towns of Patate and Mulahaló were not organized by ayllus.

Notes

Introduction

1. Ethnogenesis is the process by which distinct ethnic cultures are continually recreated over time, especially cultures that have experienced colonization.

2. Eric Wolf, *Europe and the People without History* (Berkeley: University of California Press, 1982), p. x.

3. Charles Gibson, *The Aztecs under Spanish Rule: A History of the Indians of the Valley of Mexico, 1519–1810* (Stanford: Stanford University Press, 1964).

4. The most noted of these works are Andre Gunder Frank's *Capitalism and Underdevelopment in Latin America* (New York: Monthly Review Press, 1967); Fernando Henrique Cardoso and Enzo Faletto's *Dependency and Development in Latin America* (Berkeley: University of California Press, 1979); and Immanuel Wallerstein's *The Modern World System: Capitalist Agriculture and the Origins of the European World Economy in the Sixteenth Century* (New York: Academic Press, 1974).

5. Eduardo Galeno, *Open Veins of Latin America: Five Centuries of the Pillage of a Continent* (New York: Monthly Review Press, 1973); Stanley and Barbara Stein, *The Colonial Heritage of Latin America: Essays on Economic Dependence in Perspective* (New York: Oxford University Press, 1970).

6. For a fine critique of Wallerstein's world-system, see Steve Stern's, "Feudalism, Capitalism, and the World-System in the Perspective of Latin America and the Caribbean," *American Historical Review* (October 1988):829–72.

7. Miguel León-Portilla, *The Broken Spears: The Aztec Account of the Conquest of Mexico* (Boston: Beacon Press, 1962); Nathan Wachtel, *The Vision of the Vanquished: The Spanish Conquest of Peru through Indian Eyes, 1530–1570* (New York: Barnes and Noble, 1977).

8. Nancy Farriss, *Maya Society under Colonial Rule: The Collective Enterprise of Survival* (Princeton: Princeton University Press, 1984); Luis Miguel Glave, *Trajinantes: Caminos indígenas en la sociedad colonial, siglos XVI y XVII* (Lima: Instituto de Apoyo Agrario, 1989); Grant Jones, *Maya Resistance to Spanish Rule: Time and History on a Colonial Frontier* (Albuquerque: University of New Mexico Press, 1989); Brooke Larson, *Colonialism and Agrarian Transformation in Bolivia: Cochabamba, 1550–1990* (Princeton: Princeton University Press, 1988); Galo Ramón, *La resistencia andina: Cayambe, 1500–1800* (Quito: Centro Andino de Acción Popular, 1987); Thierry Saignes, *Caciques, Tribute, and Migration in the Southern Andes: Indian Society and the Seventeenth Century Colonial Order* (London: University of London, 1985); Karen Spalding, *Huarochirí: An Andean Society under Inca and Spanish Rule* (Stanford: Stanford University

Press, 1984); Steve Stern, *Peru's Indian Peoples and the Challenge of the Spanish Conquest: Huamanga to 1640* (Madison: University of Wisconsin Press, 1982).

9. James Lockhart, *The Nahuas After the Conquest: A Social and Cultural History of the Indians of Central Mexico, Sixteenth Through Eighteenth Centuries* (Stanford: Stanford University Press, 1992); S. L. Cline, *Colonial Culhuacan, 1580–1600: A Social History of an Aztec Town* (Albuquerque: University of New Mexico Press, 1986); Robert Haskett, *Indigenous Rulers: An Ethnohistory of Town Government in Colonial Cuernavaca* (Albuquerque: University of New Mexico Press, 1991); Rebecca Horn, "Postconquest Coyoacan: Aspects of Indigenous Sociopolitical Organization in Central Mexico, 1550–1650" (Ph.D. diss.: UCLA, 1989); Susan Schroeder, *Chimalpahin and the Kingdoms of Chalco* (Tucson: University of Arizona Press, 1991); Stephanie Wood, "Corporate Adjustments in Colonial Mexican Indian Towns, Toluca Region" (Ph.D. diss.: UCLA, 1984).

10. Kevin Gosner, *Soldiers of the Virgin: The Moral Economy of a Colonial Maya Rebellion* (Tucson: University of Arizona Press, 1992); Susan Kellogg, *Law and the Transformation of Aztec Culture, 1500–1700* (Norman: Oklahoma University Press, forthcoming); Cheryl English Martin, *Rural Society in Colonial Morelos* (Albuquerque: University of New Mexico Press, 1985); Robert Patch, *Maya and Spaniard in the Yucatan* (Stanford: Stanford University Press, forthcoming); Judith Zeitlin, "Ranchers and Indians on the Southern Isthmus of Tehuantepec: Economic Change and Indigenous Survival in Colonial Mexico," *Hispanic American Historical Review* (February 1989):23–60; Judith Zeitlin and Lillian Thomas, "Spanish Systems in Sixteenth-Century Tehuantepec," *Ethnohistory* (Summer 1992):285–315.

11. Sherburne Cook and Woodrow Borah, *The Aboriginal Population of Central Mexico on the Eve of the Spanish Conquest* (Berkeley: University of California Press, 1963).

12. Noble David Cook's *Demographic Collapse: Indian Peru, 1520–1620* (Cambridge: Cambridge University Press, 1981) and Murdo MacLeod's *Spanish Central America: A Socioeconomic History, 1520–1720* (Berkeley: University of California Press, 1973) are excellent examples.

13. John Murra, ed., *Visita de la Provincia de León de Huánuco, 1562,* 2 vols. (Lima: Villanueva, 1968, 1972); Waldemar Espinosa Soriano, ed., *Visita hecha a la provincia de Chucuito por Garci Diez de San Miguel en el año 1567* (Lima: Talleres Gráficos Quiros, 1964).

14. Nicolás Sánchez-Albornoz, *Indios y tributos en el Alto Perú* (Lima: Instituto de Estudios Peruanos, 1978).

15. Nicolás Sánchez-Albornoz, "Mita, migraciones y pueblos: Variaciones en el espacio y en el tiempo, Alto Perú, 1573–1692," *Historia Boliviana* 3 (1983) 1:38.

16. Peter Bakewell, *Miners of the Red Mountain: Indian Labor in Potosí, 1545–1650* (Albuquerque: University of New Mexico Press, 1984); Jeffrey Cole, *The Potosí Mita, 1573–1700: Compulsory Indian Labor in the Andes* (Stanford: Stanford University Press, 1985); Peter Evans, "Migration Processes in Upper Peru in the Seventeenth Century," in *Migration in Colonial Spanish America,*

ed. David M. Robinson (Cambridge: Cambridge University Press, 1990), pp. 62–85; Glave, *Trajinantes*; Ann Zulawski, "Migration and Labor in Seventeenth-Century Alto Peru" (Ph.D. diss., Columbia University, 1985).

17. Thierry Saignes, "Las etnías de Charcas frente al sistema colonial: Ausentismo y fugas en el debate sobre la mano de obra indígena, 1595–1665," *Jahrbuch fur Geschichte von Staat, Wirtschaft und Gesellschaft Lateinamerikas* 21 (1984):27–75; Nicolás Sánchez-Albornoz, "Migración rural en los Andes: Sipesipe (Cochabamba), 1645," *Revista de Historia Económica* 1 (1983):13–36; Ann Wightman, *Indigenous Migration and Social Change: The Forasteros of Cuzco, 1570–1720* (Durham: Duke University Press, 1990); Mesoamerican migrations have also been a focus of ethnohistorical research in the works of Nancy Farriss and Grant Jones.

18. Robson Brines Tyrer, *La historia demográfica y económica de la Audiencia de Quito: Población indígena e industria textil, 1600–1800* (Quito: Banco Central del Ecuador, 1988), p. 45; Suzanne Alchon, *Native Society and Disease in Colonial Ecuador* (Cambridge: Cambridge University Press, 1991), p. 80.

19. Nicolás Sánchez-Albornoz, *The Population of Latin America: A History* (Berkeley: University of California Press, 1974), pp. 103–4.

20. In *Native Society and Disease in Colonial Ecuador,* Alchon concludes that Quito suffered many of the same sixteenth- and seventeenth-century pandemics as Peru and Bolivia and was hit decidedly harder by some of them. She also draws a consistent picture of earthquakes, volcanic eruptions, floods and famine for the seventeenth century (pp. 35–43 and 57–66). Linda Newson of Kings College, London has also conducted independent research on epidemics and Andean labor in the Audiencia of Quito (personal communication, Summer 1989).

21. Sánchez-Albornoz, *Indios y tributos,* pp. 20–34.

22. The Spanish empire in America was theoretically divided into two separate republics based on race. Within this construct, Spaniards were required by law to live in Spanish-style cities in polity with other Spaniards; Amerindians were to remain in native towns or *reducciones* in the countryside where the colonial administration resettled them in concentrated fashion to facilitate tribute collection, labor extraction, and Christian indoctrination.

23. Sánchez-Albornoz, *Indios y tributos,* p. 14; "Migración rural en los Andes," pp. 13–36; "Mita, migraciones y pueblos."

24. Ann Wightman, *Indigenous Migration and Social Change,* pp. 151–53.

25. Saignes, *Caciques, Tribute and Migration*; "Las etnías de Charcas."

26. Glave, *Trajinantes.*

27. Marshall Sahlins, *Islands of History* (Chicago: University of Chicago Press, 1985).

28. Also useful to this analysis is William Roseberry's integrated view of history, culture, and political economy—a view that seeks to wed historical materialism to cultural anthropology. William Roseberry, *Anthropologies and Histories: Essays in Culture, History and Political Economy* (New Brunswick: Rutgers University Press, 1989).

Chapter 1

1.John V. Murra, "Historic Tribes of Ecuador," in *Handbook of South American Indians*, ed. Julian H. Steward (Washington, D.C.: U.S. Government Printing Office, 1946), 2:786.

2. The Palta and the Panzaleo are thought to have Amazonian origins. Ibid., p. 791; Jorge Carrera Andrade, *El fabuloso reino de Quito* (Quito, 1963), p. 147.

3. Frank Loewen Salomon, *Native Lords of Quito in the Age of the Incas: The Political Economy of North Andean Chiefdoms* (Cambridge: Cambridge University Press, 1986), pp. 158–67; Nathan Wachtel, *The Vision of the Vanquished*, p. 111; Marcos Jiménez de la Espada, ed., *Relaciones geográficas de Indias* (Madrid: Ministerio de Fomento, 1881–87), 2:254–55; RAH/M, Colección Muñoz, Tomo 24 (A/66). "Relación de . . . Morales Figueroa," 1591.

4. Suzanne Alchon estimates that a population of 1,080,000 declined by 33–50 percent during the pandemic of 1524–28 and again by 25–30 percent during the pandemic of 1531–33; *Native Society*, pp. 15–18.

5. Sánchez-Albornoz, *Indios y tributos*, p. 9.

6. AGI, Justicia 683, "Residencias tomadas del licenciado Juan de Salazar Villasante . . . , 1563–65," also cited in Salomon, *Native Lords*, pp. 119–20.

7. Alberto Landázuri Soto, *El régimen laboral indígena en la Real Audiencia de Quito* (Madrid, 1957), pp. 44–45.

8. Jiménez de la Espada, *Relaciones geográficas*, 2:310–11.

9. Hugo Burgos Guevara, "La población del Ecuador en la encrucijada de los siglos XVI y XVII," International Congress of Americanists *Atti* 2 (1972):485.

10. They were outsiders not only in the sense that they were outside their communities but also outside Spanish control.

11. José Rumazo González, *La región amazónica del Ecuador en el siglo XVI* (Sevilla: Estudios Hispanoamericanos de Sevilla, 1946), pp. 30–31; Emilio Bonifaz, "Extractos de los libros del cabildo de Quito: 1534–1657," *Museo Histórico*, 17 (April/June 1971):133–38; *Libro primero de cabildos de Quito*, descifrado por Jorge A. Garces (Quito: Archivo Municipal, 1935), p. 97; Oswaldo Romero Arteta, "El indio quiteño en el siglo XVI," *Boletín de la Academia Nacional de Historia*, 47 (July/December 1964):55.

12. José María Vargas, *Historia del Ecuador: Siglo XVI* (Quito: Pontifícia Universidad Católica, 1977), p. 55. Vargas reports that four thousand Andean men departed from Quito and that many were accompanied by their wives and children.

13. Ibid., p. 86.

14. John Phelan, *The Kingdom of Quito in the Seventeenth Century* (Madison: University of Wisconsin, 1967), p. 47.

15. Rumazo G., *La región amazónica*, pp. 45, 133 (source uncited).

16. Bonifaz, "Extractos," p. 144; Jiménez de la Espada, *Relaciones geográficas*, 2:173–74, 308–9; Vargas, *Historia del Ecuador*, p. 246.

17. Alchon, *Native Society*, p. 37; Linda Newson, "Old World Epidemics in

Early Colonial Ecuador," in *"Secret Judgments of God": Old World Disease in Colonial Spanish America*, ed. Noble David Cook and W. George Lovell (Norman: University of Oklahoma Press, 1991), p. 111; Tyrer, *Historia demográfica*, p. 24; Gualberto Arcos, "Evolución de la medicina en el Ecuador," Universidad Central del Ecuador *Anales*, 61 (October/December 1938):1061; Aquiles Pérez, *Las mitas en la real audiencia de Quito* (Quito: Ministerio de Tesoro, 1947), pp. 344–46.

18. Alchon, "Disease, Population, and Public Health in Eighteenth Century Quito," in *"Secret Judgments of God,"* ed. Cook and Lovell, p. 159.

19. Rumiñawi, for example, has been described in most literature on the conquest of Quito as escaping to Quijos with four thousand followers after the final battle in the sierra. Gil Ramírez Dávalos claims to have found as many as forty thousand tributary Amerindians in the province of Quijos upon his conquest of that region in 1559; Jiménez de la Espada, *Relaciones geográficas*, 1:74.

20. See Alchon, *Native Society*; Tyrer, *Historia demográfica*; Javier Ortiz de la Tabla Ducasse, "La población ecuatoriana en la época colonial: Cuestiones y cálculos," *Anuario de Estudios Americanos* 37 (1980):235–77; and Hugo Burgos Guevara, "La población del Ecuador."

21. Alchon, *Native Society*, p. 57; Tyrer, *Historia demográfica*, p. 36.

22. Sánchez-Albornoz, *Population of Latin America*, p. 104; Tyrer, *Historia demográfica*, pp. 76–77.

23. Alchon, *Native Society*, pp. 76–79; Tyrer, *Historia demográfica*, pp. 77–78.

24. Suzanne Alchon (*Native Society*, p. 46) attributes this confusion to an increase in areas that had been severely depopulated before the Spanish arrival and specifically names Otavalo, Quito, and Cuenca. However, I have found reports of growth for highland regions other than these and for the audiencia as a whole.

25. Jiménez de la Espada, *Relaciones geográficas*, 2:202, 224, 169, 267, 183, 286; Phelan, *Kingdom of Quito*, p. 45.

26. AGI, Justicia 683, "Residencias tomadas." Noble David Cook has uncovered substantial evidence indicating that many of the totals recorded for Peru in the Morales Figueroa census of 1591 were copies of those that appeared in the Toledan Visita of the 1570s. This appears not to obtain for the Audiencia of Quito, however, where an intervening census was conducted in the early 1580s, which was then used as a base for the 1591 census. Furthermore, even if the Morales Figueroa figures for Quito were a copy of those of the Toledan Visita, the essential argument would not change. There would still be a precipitous demographic increase in Chillos, but within an even shorter period of time (1559–70s). Noble David Cook, *Demographic Collapse*, p. 78; AN/Q, Cacicazgos 4, "Numeración de San Miguel, 1582–92," copy inserted in "Doña Lucía Pusana contra don Guillermo Hati sobre el cacicazgo de San Miguel, 1687," ff. 287–91.

27. Tyrer, *Historia demográfica*, p. 270. Tyrer concluded that 4.7 was an accurate factor for the sierran communities of the 1580s.

28. Alchon, *Native Society*, pp. 47–49; Tyrer, *Historia demográfica*, p. 75;

Gualberto Arcos, "Evolución de la medicina en el Ecuador," p. 1061; Aquiles Perez, *Las mitas,* pp. 344–46; and Newson, "Old World Epidemics," pp. 97–99.

29. Burgos and Ortiz de la Tabla suggest that Quito's anomalous population curve may be related to internal migrations; this study is, in part, a response to their suggestion. Burgos G., "La población del Ecuador," pp. 483–87; Ortiz de la Tabla D., "La población ecuatoriana," p. 246.

30. Alchon attributes the dramatic rise of population in the heartland to a combination of natural increase and immigration from outside the audiencia (*Native Society,* p. 79). Although the author of the "Relación de Zaruma" reported the presence of Amerindians from "Popayán, Nuevo Reino [de Granada] and other areas of Peru," in the Ecuadorean highlands, there is much more evidence that most of the heartland's immigrants emanated from other parts of the audiencia rather than from outside it (Jiménez de la Espada, *Relaciones geográficas,* 3:241–43). In addition Popayán was at that time part of the Audiencia of Quito and, as will be demonstrated, was the sending area for a substantial migration to the heartland.

31. Tyrer (*Historia demográfica,* pp. 28–29), Newson ("Old World Epidemics," p. 108), and Ortiz de la Tabla D. ("La población ecuatoriana," p. 276) mention demographic variation between highlands and lowlands ("tierra fría y tierra caliente"), but none posits a migratory connection between them.

32. Jiménez de la Espada, *Relaciones geográficas,* 2:169–82. Yaguarzongo was also known as Bracamoros.

33. Ibid., p. 183.

34. Vargas, *Historia del Ecuador,* p. 244; Cieza de León, *The Travels of Pedro Cieza de León, 1532–50* (New York: Franklin, n.d.) p. 203.

35. The term *montaña* specifically refers to the interstitial, subtropical areas between lowlands and highlands, but will frequently be subsumed under the term *lowlands* when describing migration flows.

36. Phelan, *Kingdom of Quito,* p. 46; Salomon, *Native Lords,* p. 122.

37. *Libro Primero de cabildos de Quito,* 1:443.

38. Cieza de León, *Del señorío de los incas* (Segunda parte de la crónica del Perú) (Buenos Aires: Ediciones Argentinos "Solar," 1943), p. 132; also cited in Salomon, *Native Lords,* p. 149.

39. Salomon, *Native Lords,* p. 184.

40. Jiménez de la Espada, *Relaciones geográficas,* 3:87–90; also cited in Salomon, *Native Lords,* p. 185.

41. Murra, "Historic Tribes of Ecuador," pp. 807, 817.

42. AGI, 76-6-2, 2, "Relación de Fray Pedro Bedón Agüero," 1598; cited in Rumazo G., *La región amazónica,* p. 246.

43. This is a subject developed at length in the works of Frank Salomon and Udo Oberem; see Salomon, *Native Lords*; Udo Oberem, "El acceso a recursos naturales de diferentes ecologías en la sierra ecuatoriana (siglo XVI)," in *Contribución a la etnohistoria ecuatoriana,* ed. Segundo Moreno Yánez and Udo Oberem (Otavalo: Instituto Otavaleño de Antropología, 1981), pp. 45–71.

44. In his study of pre-Incaic Quito's political organization, Hugo Burgos Guevara found that strong provincial relationships existed between certain sierran chiefdoms that were further enhanced by relations with peoples of the eastern lowlands. He describes this network of relationships as the Quito-Oriente axis. "El guaman, el puma y el amaru: formación estructural del gobierno indígena del Ecuador," (Ph.D. diss., University of Illinois at Urbana-Champaign, 1975), p. 331; see also Salomon, *Native Lords*, chap. 4.

45. Murra, "Historic Tribes of Ecuador," p. 807; see also Salomon, *Native Lords*, p. 155, and Oberem, "Acceso a recursos naturales," p. 271.

46. Salomon, *Native Lords*, p. 136.

47. Pedro Ignacio Porras Garcés, *Contribución al estudio de las valles Quijos y Misaguallí en la región oriental del Ecuador* (Quito: Fenix, 1961).

48. Vargas, *Historia del Ecuador*, p. 138.

49. For the treatment of migrations from Quijos to the sierra see Karen Powers Vera, "La migración vertical en la audiencia de Quito: El caso de los Quijos en el siglo XVI," *Revista Ecuatoriana de Historia Económica* 2 (1987):103–30.

50. Salomon, *Native Lords*, pp. 106, 202.

51. The term *destructuration* is used throughout this book to describe the process by which the social, economic and political structures of indigenous societies were undermined by conquest and colonization. This process could occur slowly or rapidly depending on local conditions and could result in levels of deterioration ranging from structural weakening to structural collapse. For more detailed analyses of destructuration in Quijos, see Udo Oberem, *Los quijos: Historia de la transculturación de un grupo indígena en el oriente ecuatoriano, 1538–1856* (Otavalo: Instituto Otavaleño de Antropología, 1980); Powers, "La migración vertical"; and Alicia Garces Dávila, "La economía colonial y su impacto en las sociedades indígenas: El caso de los quijos, siglos XVI–XVII," in *Opresión colonial y resistencia indígena en la Alta Amazonía*, ed. Fernando Santos Granero (Quito: Flacso/Abya-Yala, 1992), pp. 49–75.

52. AGI, Justicia 671, ff. 241–57, "Visita de los Puruháes, 1557."

53. Alchon, *Native Society*, pp. 155–57.

54. Jiménez de la Espada, *Relaciones geográficas*, 2:280; Wachtel, *Vision of the Vanquished*, pp. 100–101.

55. Salomon, *Native Lords*, p. 85.

56. Tyrer, *Historia demográfica*, pp. 29, 46–47; Powers, "La migración vertical," pp. 114–16.

57. *Libro segundo de cabildos de Quito* (Quito: Archivo Municipal, 1934) 2:383.

58. Vargas, *Historia del Ecuador*, p. 187.

59. Jiménez de la Espada, *Relaciones geográficas*, 3:335–36.

60. RAH/M, "Relación de . . . Morales Figueroa," 1591. There has been some discrepancy about this figure, which according to Tyrer could be adjusted upward to 1,500. Whichever figure is accepted, the precipitous decline of the Yumbos population remains evident.

61. Tyrer, *Historia demográfica*, p. 29.

62. See Tyrer (*Historia demográfica*, p. 29) for statistical tables on coastal areas and western montañas.

63. Vargas, *Historia del Ecuador*, p. 82.

64. Ibid., p. 187.

65. AGI, Quito 23, "Carta de los caciques e indios de la provincia de Yaguarzongo y distrito de Jaen a la audiencia," March 10, 1591, cited in Alchon, *Native Societies*, p. 42, and Newson, "Old World Epidemics," p. 99.

66. Jiménez de la Espada, *Relaciones geográficas*, 1:74; see also Vargas, *Historia del Ecuador*, p. 139.

67. Burgos G., "La población del Ecuador," p. 483.

68. Cited in Tyrer, *Historia demográfica*, p. 32.

69. Ibid.

70. Jiménez de la Espada, *Relaciones geográficas*, 3:326. Frequently population disasters are followed by an almost instinctual increase in fertility rates. Nevertheless the demographic recovery described by Auncibay seems too immediate to be explained by reproduction alone.

71. AGI, Justicia 683.

72. Jiménez de la Espada, *Relaciones geográficas*, 2:259.

73. BN/M, Ms. 3044, f. 478, "Memorial tocante a las cosas de la gobernación de los Quijos" [ca. 1570].

74. Jiménez de la Espada, *Relaciones geográficas*, 2:311.

75. Ibid., pp. 267–68.

76. Wachtel, *Vision of the Vanquished*, p. 89.

77. "Segundo tomo de recopilación de cédulas despachadas en diferentes tiempos por su magestad y señores de su Real Consejo de Indias, para la Audiencia y Cancillería Real de la Ciudad de San Francisco del Quito del Pirú [hecho] por El doctor Antonio de Morga, Presidente de la misma Audiencia y Cancillería Real," Cédula de 1626 (Popayán), reproduced in *Anuario Histórico Jurídico Ecuatoriano*, 4:146; AN/Q, Indígenas 20, "El fiscal protector de los naturales por Don Gerónimo Tamayo, cacique principal y gobernador de Inta (Ibarra) sobre entero de mitayos a los cañaverales, 1693."

78. Jiménez de la Espada, *Relaciones geográficas*, 2:271.

79. AN/Q, Indígenas (Hojas Sueltas): 174, 25-V-1712; AN/Q, Obrajes 8, Licencias de obrajes, Pichincha, 1682–1701, [Gabriel de Yerobi, vecino de Quito, sobre la mita de forasteros, 1694].

80. It is also interesting that contemporary Andean migrations have, until the recent advent of north-south roads in the oriente, occurred traditionally between vertically contiguous areas, that is, between the highlands and their adjacent eastern and western lowlands. Most colonists, for example, in the new agrarian schemes sponsored by the Ecuadorean government in the eastern province of Morona Santiago are Cañaris from the nearby highland area of Cuenca. Personal communication with Thomas Rudell, sociologist at Rutgers University, who has done research recently in this area.

81. BN/M, Ms. 3044, f. 478. The recruiting activities of native leaders will be explored further in subsequent chapters.

82. F. M. Renard-Casevitz, T. Saignes, and A. C. Taylor, *Al este de los Andes: Relaciones entre las sociedades amazónicas y andinas entre los siglos XV y XVII*, 2 vols. (Quito: Abya-Yala, 1988), p. 14.

83. AGI, Quito 16, f. 35v, "Toma de residencia de Pedro de Agreda, gobernador de Popayán, por el Licenciado Valverde, 3 de noviembre de 1564."

84. RAH/M, tomo 24, A/66, ff. 188–209, "Relación de Popayán [hecha por] Fray Gerónimo Descobar, predicador de la Orden de San Agustín como procurador general de la provincia de Popayán," [n.d., sixteenth century]; RAH/M, tomo 24, A/66, ff. 214–21, "Memoria de los pueblos de la gobernación de Popayán y cosas y constelaciones que hay en ellos . . . , 1583"; RAH/M, tomo 24, A/66, f. 222, "Relación para los muy poderosos señores del Real consejo de Indias de S. M. así de la descripción de la tierra que llaman gobernación o provincia de Popayán, como de los indios que hay en ella . . . ," [n.d., sixteenth century]. In his recent study of the Pasto region, Cristóbal Landázuri shows a depopulation rate of nearly 50 percent for the towns of Tulcán, Guaca, Tusa/El Angel, and Mira between 1582 and 1598. "Territorios y pueblos: La Sociedad pasto en los siglos XVI y XVII," *Memoria* (Quito: MARKA) 1(November 1990),66.

85. AGI, Quito 16, f. 35v, "Toma de residencia de Pedro de Agreda, 1564."

86. AGI, Quito 9, f. 14v, "Carta de Fray Pedro Bedón de Aguero, Provincial de los Dominicos de la Provincia de Quito, 10 de marzo de 1598." Personal service was also reported to be a routine practice in Quijos and Yaguarzongo at this time.

87. AGI, Quito 8, doc. 1, cap. 20, "Carta del Presidente Santillán al Rey, 1564."

88. AGI, Quito 18, "Instrucción de lo que ha de hacer Francisco Ponce, Procurador desta gobernación de Popayán por esta ciudad y en su nombre en los negocios que lleva a su cargo tocantes a los vecinos y república della . . . [1557]."

89. AGI, Quito 18, ff. 15v–16r, "Memorial instrucción de las cosas mercedes y negocios que ha de pedir y hacer pedir el muy illustre señor licenciado Fernando de Santillán del Consejo de su magestad en nombre de la ciudad de San Juan de Pasto de la gobernación de Popayán . . . , 1568."

90. AGI, Quito 8, doc. 65, ["Carta del Doctor Barros, Presidente de Quito, al Rey, 12 de mayo de 1589"].

91. AGI, Quito 18, ff. 6v–7v, "Las ciudades de Pasto, Popayán y Quito sobre ciertas mercedes que piden [Carta del Cabildo de Pasto a su magestad, 7 de agosto de 1571]."

92. In 1646, however, the *visitador* (inspector), Andrés de Sevilla, had enumerated them, and they were made to pay their annual tributes in full. AGI, Quito 55, doc. 28, ff. 453–60, "Don Pedro de Bolívar y la Redonda pide confirmación de una encomienda de indios que le dió el gobernador de la provincia de Popayán, 1649."

93. AGI, Quito 156, doc. 8, "Don Miguel Gregorio Zambrano, vecino de San Juan de Pasto, Provincia de Popayán pide confirmación de una encomienda, 1712."

94. According to Spanish chronicles—Cieza de León, for example—the Inca conquest had a decidedly negative impact on the southern highlands, leaving it with a paltry population in comparison to the central and north-central sierra.

95. AGI, Quito 7, ["Petición de Juan Sevillano, 21 de enero de 1586"].

96. AGI, Quito 8, doc. 48, "Carta del Oidor Licenciado Francisco de Auncibay, 18 de febrero de 1587."

97. Newson, "Old World Diseases," p. 99.

98. AGI, Quito 76, doc. 32, ff. 579r–79v, "Carta del Obispo de Quito a su Magestad, 1581."

99. Tyrer, *Historia demográfica,* p. 102.

100. This is a topic that will be developed in chapter 4.

101. Sánchez-Albornoz, *Population of Latin America,* p. 82.

102. Vargas, *Historia del Ecuador,* p. 280. Christiana Borchart de Moreno's study of sixteenth-century land grants concurs with this picture of agrarian monopolization. "Orígen y conformación de la hacienda colonial," in *Nueva historia del Ecuador,* ed. Enrique Ayala Mora (Quito: Corporación Editora/ Grijalbo, 1989), 4:147–53.

103. Bonifaz, "Extractos," pp. 128, 129, 149, 158, 164.

104. Ibid., p. 137.

105. AGI, Quito 76, doc. 51, "Carta de Fray Luis López de Solís, Obispo de Quito, 1598."

106. Bonifaz, "Extractos," p. 147.

107. *Libro segundo de cabildos de Quito,* p. 342–44.

108. Ibid., pp. 349, 354.

109. Ibid, p. 155.

110. AN/Q, Cedularios: 1, título 12, cédula 51.

111. AGI, Quito 9, doc.108, ff. 672r–72v, "Carta de la Audiencia al rey, 22 de marzo de 1611."

112. AGI, Quito 27, "Carta de Don Sancho Díaz de Zurbano, 13 de febrero de 1609."

113. AGI, Quito 10, doc. 55, "Carta del Presidente Antonio Morga a su magestad, 15 de abril de 1620"; AGI, Quito 30, "Relación del General Pedro Ponce Castillejo sobre el estado de la Provincia de Otavalo, 1623."

114. This phenomenon will be further examined in chapter 4.

Chapter 2

1. See the works of Nicolás Sánchez-Albornoz, Ann Wightman, Brian Evans, Thierry Saignes, Jeffrey Cole, and Luis Miguel Glave.

2. Yanaconaje was an institution that had its roots in the Incaic past. During the colony it continued, with the wartime attachment of an Andean to a Spaniard and his continued personal service to that Spaniard thereafter. Later, however, it often came to mean any Indian who migrated to a Spanish enterprise to become the retainer of its owner.

3. AC/Q, "Sinodales del Obsipado de Quito celebradas en la Ciudad de Loja por el illustrísimo y reverendísimo señor don Fray Luis López de Solís, Obispo de la Santa Iglesia de Quito, 1596," cap. 53 [1594], ff. 37v–38v.

4. Richard Konetzke, *Colección de documentos para la historia de la formación social de Hispanoamérica, 1493–1810* (Madrid: Consejo Superior de Investigaciones Científicas, 1953), p. 447.

5. Pérez, *Las mitas*, pp. 67–68.

6. AMQ, "Colección de cédulas reales dirigidas a la Audiencia de Quito, 1601–1660," p. 199; AN/Q, Cacicazgos: 9 (1738-VIII-26).

7. The time span between the censuses of Otavalo and Calpi (18 years) is not as problematic as it seems at first. Overall conditions in the audiencia did not change drastically during those years; major changes came about first in the 1690s. Hence although the 1663 census is slightly outside midcentury, it is still a viable unit of analysis.

8. For analytic details on these censuses, see Appendix.

9. A breakdown of absentee rates by ayllus reveals even more pronounced variation. The ayllu of Sarance in the town of Otavalo, for example, had an absentee rate of 17 percent, while that of Yacelga (an ayllu dispersed in several locations) suffered the absence of 79 percent of its members. See tables 29 and 33 in Karen M. Powers, "Indian Migration and Sociopolitical Change in the Audiencia of Quito" (Ph.D. diss., New York University, 1990), pp. 449 and 452.

10. Short-range migration was also prevalent in the southern Andes. See Wightman, *Indigenous Migration*, p. 62; Evans, "Census Enumeration in Late Seventeenth-Century Alto Peru: The Numeración General of 1683–1684," in *Studies in Spanish American Population History*, ed. David J. Robinson (Boulder: Westview Press, 1981), p. 38; Sánchez-Albornoz, "Migración rural," p. 26 and "Migración urbana y el trabajo: Los indios de Arequipa, 1571–1645," in *De historia a historiadores: Homenaje a José Luis Romero* (Mexico: Siglo XXI, 1982), p. 275; Ann Zulawski, "Migration and Labor in Seventeen Century Alto Peru" (Ph.D. diss., Columbia University), pp. 193–94.

11. Neither did the migration patterns of individual ayllus deviate significantly from this compact configuration. See Tables 34–38 in Powers, "Indian Migration," pp. 452–55.

12. These political changes will be elaborated upon in chapter 5.

13. A more detailed analysis by ayllu is also available in Tables 39–43 in Powers, "Indian Migration," pp. 456–60.

14. For migratory styles of individual towns in the Repartimiento of Otavalo, see tables 44–48 in Powers, "Indian Migration," pp. 461–64.

15. The kin composition of this ayllu's absent groups and their specific places of residence are recorded in tables 49 and 50 in Powers, "Indian Migration," pp. 464–69.

16. This trend will be illustrated in chapter 5.

17. Tyrer (*Historia demográfica*, p. 281) claims that Ibarra lost 50 percent of its tributary population between 1582 and 1679–80. Even more poignant is Landázuri's study of the Pasto region which shows Guaca's tributary popula-

tion declining from 800 in 1582 to 140 in 1666. He attributes depopulation to personal service, excessive tribute demands, and forced labor in the hot valleys ("La sociedad pasto," p. 67). Rosario Coronel Feijoo's *El valle sangriento: De los indígenas de la coca y el algodón a la hacienda jesuita, 1580–1700* also points to a history of depopulation and land divestment (Quito: Abya-Yala, 1991).

18. Suzanne Alchon's analysis (*Native Society,* p. 87) of Guaca's marriage patterns showed a 35 percent incidence of extra-ayllu and extracommunity marriage—another possible sign of destructuration.

19. See Appendix for a more detailed demographic profile of the town of Guaca.

20. Tyrer, *Historia demográfica,* p. 281.

21. For a more detailed demographic profile of the town of Calpi, see Appendix.

22. Chimbo was the site of numerous peripheral colonies, especially for cotton, in pre-Hispanic times.

23. AN/Q, Indígenas 9, "Memorial de los ausentes del pueblo de Yaruquís, 1666."

24. Also in the 1680s Palata's census was reported to have caused massive migration all over the Viceroyalty of Peru, as forasteros responded to attempts to register them as tributaries and mitayos in their places of residence (Wightman, *Indigenous Migration,* p. 35; Evans, "Census Enumeration," p. 34).

25. The other two issues are the result of population movements and will be examined at greater length in subsequent chapters.

26. That nearly 60 percent of Ylapo's tributary population was absent is not surprising, since the Ylapo list was made immediately after the earthquake of 1698. For an analysis of individual ayllus, see tables 51–55 in Powers, "Indian Migration," pp. 469–73.

27. Note that there was indeed out-migration in Riobamba during the seventeenth century, as witnessed by continual complaints that many Andeans fled immediately after official enumerations, in order to escape the consequences of overzealous population counts. Given the rest of the demographic record on Riobamba, however, this did not represent a deficit migration until the end of the seventeenth century.

28. Rates of absenteeism among the economically active populations of the towns of the Corregimiento of Otavalo and the town of Guaca in Ibarra were 61 percent and 47 percent, respectively, for the period 1645–50, while that of the five towns surveyed in Riobamba during the 1690s was 52 percent. Thus the latter had surpassed Guaca and were not far behind Otavalo.

29. For a breakdown by ayllus of migratory flows, see tables 56–60 in Powers, "Indian Migration," pp. 473–76

30. ASF/Q, 8-22, "Seis padroncillos de indios de diversos pueblos, 1710."

31. These political changes will be examined in detail in chapter 5.

32. Six of the seven ayllus had members in Quito. It is unclear whether this was a retention of pre-Hispanic structures or an adaptation to post-Hispanic conditions; most likely these Indians were in the employ of their *encomendero.*

33. AN/Q, Religiosos 7, 1698-II-7.

34. Christiana Borchart de Moreno, "Las tierras de comunidad de Licto, Punín, y Macaxí: Factores para disminución e intentos de restauración," *Revista Andina* (December 1988):503:24. Many late-seventeenth- and early-eighteenth-century suits point to disruptive agrarian episodes ending in land divestment, labor appropriation, or out-of-area migration for the Andean population of Riobamba. These are discussed in chapter 5.

35. The other 81 absentees were not locatable.

36. ASF/Q, 8-3, ff. 94–103, "Para que todos los enhacendados paguen salarios por los indios forasteros, Latacunga, 1702"; ASF/Q 8-5: ff. 10–17, "Edicto episcopal para que los caciques de Latacunga acudan a Quito a informar sobre el cobro de salarios a los indios forasteros, 1724."

37. AN/Q, Indígenas 11, "Cartas cuentas de Latacunga, 1672"; ASF/Q, 8-22, "Padroncillo . . . del pueblo de Mulahaló . . . de los tercios de navidad de 1706, San Juan y navidad de 1707 y San Juan de 1708."

38. AN/Q, Indígenas 37, 1720-VIII-15, "Quaderno de los yndios pertenecientes al corregimiento de la Villa de Ybarra que residen en este de Otavalo . . . , 1720."

39. Galo Ramón, *La resistencia andina: Cayambe 1500–1800* (Quito: Centro Andino de Acción Popular, 1987), p. 177.

40. AN/Q, Indígenas 37, 1720-VIII-15.

41. Tyrer, *Historia demográfica,* p. 86.

42. Ibid., p. 89.

43. Their pre-Hispanic experience was rooted in cotton-cloth production, but one assumes that some part of those skills was transferable.

44. Glave (*Trajinantes,* p. 191) also makes this point about the labor force at Potosí. He reports that there was a population decline in the southern Andes between 1570 and 1620, the years of the silver economy's apogee. Silver production was not tied to population size, but to the relocation of the work force and other factors.

45. Quito's problems were also exacerbated by the growing contraband trade in English and French textiles in Lima; Tyrer, *Historia demográfica,* p. 168.

Chapter 3

1. Salomon, *Native Lords,* pp. 127–29.

2. Nathan Wachtel, *Vision of the Vanquished,* p. 89.

3. AN/Q, Cacicazgos 4 ["Numeraciones de San Miguel, 1582–92"], copy presented as evidence in "Doña Lucía Hati Pusana con Don Guillermo Hati sobre el cacicazgo de San Miguel, 1687," ff. 287–91.

4. AN/Q, Cacicazgos 4, "Petición de Don Francisco Hati, 1614," copy inserted in "Doña Lucía Pusana con . . . , 1687," ff. 167v–68r.

5. Interestingly enough these eight concertados were now devoted to sheep raising and not coca tending, a possible reflection of migration from lowland

colonies to nuclear communities in the highlands, as well as an indication of changes in the Andean economy and its integration into the Spanish market economy.

6. AN/Q, Cacicazgos 4 ["Numeraciones de San Miguel, 1582–92"], presented as evidence in Doña Lucía Pusana con . . ., 1687," f. 290.

7. AGI, Justicia 683, "Residencias tomadas del licenciado Juan de Salazar Villasante . . . , 1563–65"; also cited in Salomon, *Native Lords,* p. 15.

8. AN/Q, Cacicazgos: vol. 8, "Pleito de Don Sancho Lema, cacique principal de Guano, con el Capitán Juan de Galarza y Don Alejo Lema, 1582," presented as evidence in "Autos de Rafael Pillcolema contra Felipe Lema sobre el cacicazgo de las parcialidades de Ñacchucay, Llando, pueblo de Guano, 1674," ff. 114r–37v.

9. AN/Q, Indígenas, (Hojas Sueltas): 171, "Tasa de Guambahaló y de los carpinteros de Quero, 1575."

10. AGI, Quito 9, ff. 185r–85v ["Autos de una visita de la Audiencia de Quito, Licenciado Miguel de Ybarra, Presidente de la Real Audiencia de Quito, 27 de noviembre de 1600"].

11. I say approximately because one must take into account the young men who entered tributary status between the years 1591 and 1600, although their numbers would have been offset at least partially by those deducted from the rolls due to old age or death.

12. AGI, Quito 9, doc. 57, ff. 286–87, "Provisión real para que el corregidor del partido de Chimbo visite al repartimiento del pueblo de Chimbo, 1598." He responded in 1600.

13. Recall that these "indios vagamundos" were reported to have totaled six thousand by the year 1600; see chapter 1.

14. AGI, Quito 10, doc. 55, "Carta del presidente Antonio de Morga a su magestad, 15 de abril de 1620."

15. This was a pan-Andean strategy that became more common in the second half of the seventeenth century, as caciques and local Spanish bureaucrats colluded to extort tributes from the absentees.

16. In the early seventeenth century, general reducciones of the audiencia and of the viceroyalty were ordered by the king or the viceroy in 1618, 1634, and 1638. There is evidence that Quito complied haphazardly with the first order but apparently ignored the others. AGI, Lima 38, Libro III, f. 297, "Carta del Virrey Esquilache a S. M., 1618"; AGI, Lima 47, no.1, ff. 64–64v; AGI, Lima 50, no. 1, f. 140.

17. AGI, Lima 47, no.1, ff. 64r–64v, "Carta del Virrey Chinchón a su magestad, 1636."

18. AGI, Quito 8, "Carta del Presidente Santillán al Rey, 1564, cap. 25."

19. AGI, Quito 8, doc. 10, f. 102v, "Instrucción que se le dió al Licenciado Francisco de Cárdenas para el modo de hacer la visita de los repartimientos de términos [de Quito], 1570." That this was a somewhat successful strategy is borne out in chapter 5.

20. Jiménez de la Espada, *Relaciones geográficas,* 2:181; Vargas, *Historia del Ecuador,* p. 280. It was also proposed in the 1590s that tributes should even be

collected from the audiencia's population of color—the mulattos, zambos, and free blacks. Whether this ever came to pass is uncertain.

21. Aggregations of Andean vagabonds took place in the southern Andes in accordance with the Toledan instructions of the 1570s. There they were called "yanaconas del rey" and were both taxed and incorporated into the mita (Wightman, *Indigenous Migration,* p. 18). In Quito they were called "vagamundos de la corona real" and were taxed, but for reasons that are apparently unique to Quito, they remained exempt from the mita.

22. Sources on the aggregation of vagamundos into crown parcialidades: AGI, Quito 8, cap. 25, "Carta del Presidente Santillán al Rey, 15 de enero de 1564"; AGI, Quito 8, doc. 29, "Carta de la Audiencia de Quito a su Magestad, 22 de enero de 1578"; AN/Q, Real Hacienda: 3, "Libro de la Real Hacienda deste año de 1593 de la cuenta del contador Francisco de Cáceres," f. 57; AGI, Contaduría: 1536, doc. 26, "Cuentas tomadas por el contador, Pedro de Zorrilla a los oficiales reales, 1594," ff. 30–31.

23. All available treasury records for the seventeenth century list a tribute rate of between two and three pesos a year for crown Indians, while Tyrer reports that the tribute rates of encomienda Indians varied greatly according to region and economic possibilities, but usually hovered between five and nine pesos a year from the 1620s to the end of the colony. AN/Q, Presidencia de Quito, Tributos, and Indígenas series; Tyrer, *Historia demográfica,* pp. 110–11.

24. The terms *forastero* and *vagamundo* are used interchangeably in the documentation on Quito.

25. AGI, Quito 9, doc. 132, f. 818, "Carta del Licenciado Diego Zorrilla a su Magestad, 20 de abril de 1613."

26. AGI, Quito 8, doc. 1, cap. 7, "Carta del Presidente Santillán al Rey, 1564."

27. AGI, Lima 43, no. 2, "Cédula real sobre la edad de tributar y el problema de asentar indios de encomienda en las parcialidades de la real corona como forasteros en perjuicio de los encomenderos en Quito, 23 de marzo de 1626."

28. AGI, Contaduría 1536, "Cuentas tomadas por el contador Pedro de Zorrilla a los oficiales reales, 1594"; AGI, Contaduría 1537, "Cuentas tomadas por los señores presidente y oidores desta Real Audiencia de Quito a los oficiales reales desta ciudad de la Real Hacienda en principio del año de 1598 de lo del año pasado del 1597."

29. There are numerous documents in both Quito and Seville that refer to this wage difference. Two are AN/Q, Obrajes: caja 8, no. 2, which reports that the carders of the mita made only eighteen pesos a year, while contracted carders earned thirty-six pesos; and AN/Q, Indígenas: caja 171 (29-VII-1595) describes "free" carpenters in the city of Quito as earning two pesos a day, while those of the mita earned two pesos a month. This may be an exaggeration, but it nonetheless makes a point.

30. Tyrer, *Historia demográfica,* p. 276.

31. AN/Q, Indígenas 28, 1705-21-V.

32. Forasteros in other parts of the audiencia were engaged in a constant judicial battle to maintain their exemption from the mita; apparently there was

a local decree in the 1640s demanding that forasteros perform the mita in their places of residence. The validity of this decree became the center of unending litigation, as elites used it to invigorate the mita, while forasteros clung tenaciously to their royal exemption, sometimes citing the Latacungan forasteros' success in having it overturned in their province. The Indígenas section of the Archivo Nacional de Historia in Quito (boxes 26, 28, 173) contains many examples of these cases.

33. This oscillation of policy also took place at the viceregal level, when the marqués de Montesclaros (1607–15) attempted the radical reform of extracting tribute and labor from forasteros in their places of residence, a reform that was undermined by his successor, the prince of Esquilache (1615–21). The Duque de Palata (1681–89) tried to implement the same policy, but the reform was once again reversed by his successor, the Conde de Monclova (1689–1705) (Wightman, *Indigenous Migration*, pp. 25–36).

34. Similar conflicts among competing interest groups over Andean migration and forastero labor are also reported for colonial Peru and Bolivia; Cole, *Potosí Mita*, p. 54; Glave, *Trajinantes*, pp. 272–73; Saignes, *Caciques*, p. 3.

35. AGI, Quito 10, doc. 31, f. 160v, "Carta del Presidente Doctor Antonio de Morga a su Magestad, 20 de abril de 1618"; AGI, Lima 44, no. 9, ff. 86–94, "Parecer de la Audiencia de Quito sobre la reducción general de indios, 1 de abril de 1631."

36. BN/M, no. 3.069/30, ff. 76–82, "Relación que hizo de su gobierno el duque de la Palata . . . Virrey del Peru . . . al Conde de Moncloa, su sucesor, 18 de diciembre de 1689."

37. AN/Q, Indígenas: caja 9 (12-I-1666), "Petición de los forasteros de la Real Corona de Cuenca sobre la mita, 1666."

38. AN/Q, Indígenas: caja 19 (28-VII-1692), "Juicio de Don Fulgencio Santi, cacique principal del pueblo de Chapacoto (Chimbo) de los indios arrieros forasteros y camayos contra Doctor Juan González de Ortega, presbítero y los vecinos hacendados del dicho asiento de Chimbo, 1692." The ten-year rule was originally instituted by Toledo in the 1570s, but was altered by Viceroy Salvatierra (1648–55), to allow forasteros to remain in communities where they had resided for ten years or more, as tribute payers but exempt from the mita (Wightman, *Indigenous Migration*, p. 29). In Quito ten-year residents were to be incorporated into the mita.

39. AGI, Lima 44, no.9, ff. 86–94.

40. AGI, Quito 74, "El fiscal, Antonio de Ron, sobre fraudes de tributos en la provincia de Quito, 15 de julio de 1694."

41. AN/Q, Indígenas, caja 9 (22-III-1666), "Pleito de Pablo Gordillo y consortes, indios naturales del pueblo de San Pedro Sicchay, jurisdicción de la ciudad de Cuenca con el Capitán Don Urban de Aredondo . . . , 1666."

42. A buscador searched for absent Andeans, ostensibly to return them to their communities of origin. In the second half of the sixteenth century, buscadores were usually favored Indian caciques and prominent Spaniards, officially appointed by the audiencia. During the seventeenth century,

buscadores were the agents of caciques and corregidores, as well as self-appointed thugs, all of whom engaged more frequently in blackmailing Andean migrants for financial gain than in their repatriation. AGI, Quito 26, "Probanza de Don Pedro Zámbiza, indio principal y señor del pueblo de Zámbiza en la Provincia de Quito, 1600," ff. 24v–29; BN/M, ms. 3044, "Memorial tocante a cosas de la gobernación de los Quijos, ca. 1569–70," f. 478; AGI, Quito 33, "Carta de los caciques de Quito sobre agravios, 1 de septiembre de 1677"; AGI, Quito 72, "Autos de la visita hecha a dicha audiencia por Don Mateo de Mata Ponce de León, 1679–1697," ff. 186v.

43. AGI, Lima 44, no.9, ff. 86–94.

44. Both Thierry Saignes and Ann Zulawski have suggested this type of planned collective migration for their Bolivian data.

45. Personal communication with Drs. Segundo Moreno Yánez and Christiana Borchart de Moreno.

46. The instructions given at the commencement of all the Matías de Peralta censuses offered this incentive. An example is included in the census of the town of San Andrés (Riobamba) presented in AN/Q, Cacicazgos: 5, "Joachín Chala con Joseph Chapla y Lema . . . , 1676."

47. AN/Q, Cacicazgos 9, "Visita y numeración del pueblo de Calpi . . . 1663."

48. This model has been corroborated by Sylvia Benítez' recent demographic study of the cacicazgo of Sangolquí. "Apuntes demográficos del cacicazgo de Sangolquí, siglos XVI al XVII," *Memoria* (Quito: MARKA) 2(November 1991): 68.

49. Untoward practices of the Matías de Peralta census are either discussed or can be extrapolated from the following suits over cacicazgos in Riobamba: AN/Q, Cacicazgos: 5, "Joachín Chala con Joseph Chapla y Lema"; Cacicazgos: 18, "Autos de Fernando Duchinachay"; Cacicazgos: 14, "Autos de Augustín Argos"; Cacicazgos: 11, "Autos de Juan Lema."

50. These subjects will receive more attention in chapter 5.

51. AGI, Quito 29, "Carta de Don Diego de Sandoval a su magestad, 1617."

52. Ibid. Don Christóval de Bonilla, the encomendero of whom Sandoval complained, was allegedly related to the majority of the Spanish population of the city of Quito and was the husband of Doña Clara de Larrea, Matías de Peralta's niece. Juan de Vera, the official scribe, was married to Doña Clara de Bonilla, Don Christóval's sister.

53. Ibid. Other accusations included staying in Latacunga for one whole year, during which time he received a stipend from the native communities, and getting married in Latacunga that year and demanding that the vecinos and indigenous population pay for the festivities.

54. Don Gabriel Sañay Lema, gobernador of Licán (Riobamba) claimed that most of the ausentes of his town had absented themselves after the census of Matías de Peralta. AN/Q, Indígenas: 6, I-VII-1656.

55. AN/Q, Indígenas 9, "Memoria de los indios ausentes del pueblo de Yaruquís, 1666."

56. Christiana Borchart de Moreno, "Camayos," p. 10.

57. An excellent study of the decline of crown power and the creolization of

colonial rule by the late seventeenth century is Kenneth Andrien's, *Crisis and Decline: The Viceroyalty of Peru in the Seventeenth Century* (Albuquerque: University of New Mexico Press, 1985).

58. Glave, Larson, and Saignes also report extensive tribute and census fraud for turn-of-the-century Peru and Bolivia, while Glave describes a similar manipulation of ausentes and rezagos. Glave, *Trajinantes,* p. 266; Brooke Larson, *Colonialism and Agrarian Transformation in Bolivia: Cochabamba, 1550–1900* (Princeton: Princeton University Press, 1988), pp. 110–11; Thierry Saignes, "Las etnías de Charcas," pp. 53–59.

59. AGI, Quito 72 ["Autos sobre la forma de cobranza de tributos, 1691"] in "Autos de la Visita hecha a la Audiencia por Don Mateo de Mata Ponce de León, 1679–1697," ff. 180–214.

60. AGI, Quito 33, "Carta de los Caciques de Quito sobre agravios, 1 de septiembre de 1677." Glave (*Trajinantes*) claims that most Indian forasteros of the southern Andes ended up paying tributes too, although not necessarily to the state.

61. AGI, Quito 33 ["Carta de Juan Guerrero Salazar, 20 de mayo de 1678"].

62. Ibid. He reports alternately 388 Indians in Guayaquil.

63. Ibid.

64. AGI, Quito 5 ["Carta de Don Juan Guerrero de Salazar, vecino de la Ciudad de Quito, 24 de julio de 1694"].

65. In reality they had retained 56 percent of the tributes collected.

66. AGI, Quito 6 ["Real Provisión sobre los ausentes en la gobernación de Popayán, 1690"].

67. Ibid.

68. AGI, Quito 72 ["Autos sobre la forma de cobranza de tributos, 1691"], f. 205v, in "Autos de la Visita hecha a [la Audiencia de Quito] por Don Mateo Ponce de León: año de 1679 a 1697," ff. 180–214.

69. Ibid., f. 187r.

70. Ibid., f. 186v. Similar suspicions of large gaps between potential and real tributaries were also reported for the southern Andes, but were not borne out by the Palata census of the 1680s, which was purportedly an overcount. Evans reports, for example, that Cuzco's alleged population of 30,000 potential tributaries was in reality only 3,320. While southern Andean hyperbole gives reason for caution, concrete evidence for extensive ausente-rezago fraud in Quito cannot be ignored. That it occurred is undeniable, though its magnitude may have been exaggerated.

71. Ibid., ff. 192v–93r.

72. Matías de Lagúnez made a mathematical error; the number of Spanish and native officials actually totals 586.

73. AGI, Quito 74 ["El fiscal, Antonio de Ron, sobre fraudes de tributos, 15 de julio de 1694"].

74. AGI, Quito 17 ["Carta del fiscal Antonio de Ron a su magestad sobre fraudes de tributos, 1695"].

75. Examples are AGI, Quito 128, "Carta del Presidente Juan de Lozaya a su

magestad, 13 de noviembre de 1711"; AGI, Quito 128, "Carta del presidente Larrayn a su magestad, 3 de septiembre de 1718"; AGI, Quito 129, "Carta de Dr. Don Diego de Zaráte, fiscal de Quito, sobre tributos que deben los corregidores desde 1640, 11 de febrero de 1724"; AGI, Quito 128 ["Carta de la Audiencia de Quito a su magestad, 9 de junio de 1723"]; AGI, Quito 138 ["Carta de Jacinto González, diputado de los vecinos de la ciudad de Quito, 26 de enero de 1719"], ff. 18r–24v.

76. Ibid. These charges of undercounts were made in spite of the high mortality rates produced by the epidemics of the 1690s. Alchon (*Native Society,* p. 98) claims a 40–50 percent depopulation rate, while Tyrer (*Historia demográfica,* p.48) claims one-third.

77. AGI, Quito 72, ["Autos sobre la forma de cobranza, 1691"], ff. 180–214. In his study of the southern Andes, Glave (*Trajinantes,* pp. 265–66) also reports that royal tributes were undermined and siphoned off to local power groups during this period.

Chapter 4

1. Sources for sixteenth-century dispossessions are: AGI, Quito 76, "Carta del obispo de Quito Maestro Don Fray Pedro de la Peña, escrita en su nombre por Alonso de Herrera y Fray Domingo de Hugalde, 1569," cap. 27; BN/M, no. 3035, "Instrucción de Su Magestad para el Licenciado Hernando de Santillán, Presidente de Quito, 1563"; AN/Q, Cedularios: 1, título 12, cédula 9, 1558; ibid., cédula 8, 1566.

2. For biographical information on these families see Waldemar Espinoza Soriano, *Etnohistoria ecuatoriana: Estudios y documentos* (Quito: Abya-Yala, 1989), pp. 193–243, and *Los Cayambes y carangues, siglos XV–XVI: El testimonio de la etnohistoria* (Otavalo: Instituto Otavaleño de Antropología, 1988), 2:136–46; Fernando Jurado Noboa, *Sancho Hacho: Orígenes de la formación mestiza ecuatoriana* (Quito: Abya-Yala, 1990); Udo Oberem, *Sancho Hacho: Un cacique mayor del siglo XVI* (Quito: Abya-Yala, 1993); Karen Powers, "Resilient Lords and Indian Vagabonds: Wealth, Migration, and the Reproductive Transformation of Quito's Chiefdoms, 1500–1700," *Ethnohistory* 38 (Summer 1991):225–49; and Frank Salomon, "Don Pedro de Zámbiza, un varayuj del siglo XVI," *Cuadernos de Historia y Arqueología* 42 (1975).

Some outstanding examples of services rendered and awards received by these caciques and their descendants are found in AGI, Quito 27, "Probanza de Don Sancho Hacho, cacique principal de Latacunga, 1591"; AGI, Quito 26, "Probanza de méritos de Don Pedro Zámbiza, indio principal y señor del pueblo de Zámbiza en la provincia de Quito, 1600"; AGI, Quito 22, "Probanza de Don Hierónimo Puento, cacique principal del pueblo de Cayambe, 1583"; AGI, Quito 32, "Probanza de Don Francisco Hati, 1592," included as evidence of services in "Probanza de Don Francisco García Hati, 1633"; and AGI, Quito 32, "Probanza de Don Guillermo García Hati Zanipatín, 1633".

3. Good management and institutionalized generosity have been found to be the main attributes of successful indigenous leaders in Peru and Bolivia. That these criteria also applied to the ethnic groups of Ecuador is illustrated by the number of colonial petitions and suits brought by ayllu members against their caciques for squandering community resources and by the works of Frank Salomon and José Rumazo González, which demonstrate that gift giving was an important component of leadership in the northern Andes; Salomon, *Native Lords*, pp. 208–11; Rumazo González, *Región amazónica*, p. 87.

4. Sánchez-Albornoz, *Indios y tributos*; Steve J. Stern, *Peru's Indian Peoples*; Wachtel, *Vision of the Vanquished*; Cook, *Demographic Collapse*; Carlos Sempat Assadourian, *El sistema de la economía colonial* (Lima: Instituto de Estudios Peruanos, 1982); Wightman, *Indigenous Migration*. These studies have focused, at least in part, on the erosive effects of migration on Andean society. In contrast Thierry Saignes has put forth a model of migration as an adaptive strategy that may have resulted in cultural continuity; see, for example, his "Las etnías de Charcas." Ann Zulawski's model, "Migration and Labor," argues for more continuity than change.

5. Franklin Pease, *Curacas, reciprocidad y riqueza* (Lima: Pontificia Universidad Católica del Perú, 1992), pp. 147–69; Karen Powers, "Resilient Lords and Indian Vagabonds," pp. 230–34; Karen Spalding, *De indio a campesino: Cambios en la estructura social del Perú colonial* (Lima: Instituto de Estudios Peruanos, 1974), p. 81; Susan Ramírez, "The 'Dueño de Indios': Thoughts on the Consequences of the Shifting Bases of Power of the 'Curaca de los Viejos Antiguos' under the Spanish in Sixteenth-Century Peru," *Hispanic American Historical Review*, 67(1987)4:609; Frank Salomon, "Don Pedro de Zámbiza," p. 307.

6. Some Andeanists posit that the cacique's and the community's enterprises were one and the same, since the cacique's wealth was traditionally funneled back to his subjects through the Andean norms of reciprocity and redistribution. Admittedly the caciques of the Audiencia of Quito frequently subsidized their communities by financing tribute arrears and litigation to protect community lands. Nevertheless, some sixteenth- and seventeenth-century leaders accumulated immense private wealth, to which the community had no access. Hence I list chiefly and community enterprises as separate entities.

7. AGI, Quito 80, "Avisos en cosas de gobierno [escritos por el licenciado Pedro Rodríguez Aguayo, arcediano del Quito, juez eclesiástico]," cap. 23, n.d. (appears to date from late sixteenth or early seventeenth century).

8. Jorge Llacta de la Nasca, commissioned by the audiencia to round up forasteros in the late sixteenth and early seventeenth centuries, was reported to have aggregated vagabonds in Quito, Latacunga, Ambato, Riobamba, Chimbo, Jaén de Bracamoros, and Cuenca. That many were in the service of caciques is born out by his petition of 1613, in which he emphasized the need to protect these Andeans from the abuses of the native leaders where they resided. He claimed that the caciques forced them into personal service, employing them in agricultural tasks and in guarding livestock. AN/Q, Cacicazgos: 14, "Don

Francisco Llacta de Anasca sobre el cacicazgo de la Real Corona de Ambato, 1706," ff. 2r–2v and 32r–33r.

9. Chantal Caillavet, "La Artesanía textil en la época colonial: El rol de la producción doméstica en el Norte de la Audiencia de Quito". *Cultura* (Quito) 8(January–April 1986):521–30.

10. It is evident, for example, from the last will and testament of Don Francisco Hati, cacique of San Miguel (Latacunga), that his cotton transactions with other Andean groups were still an important component of the region's native economy in 1582. In addition Galo Ramón has found that Otavalo's indigenous communities continued to reap substantial benefits from cotton-textile production until the 1640s. See Ramón, *Resistencia andina*, p. 131.

11. In the residencia of the corregidor, Juan de Salazar Villasante, one witness claimed that if the cotton-textile enterprises of the corregidores, caciques, and private Spaniards were legitimized, the crown could sell each license for sixty or seventy thousand pesos, because the putting-out system yielded a 200-percent profit without risks. AGI, Justicia 683, no. 1, "Residencia tomada al Licenciado Juan de Salazar Villasante, 1564," ff. 760–62. This same document also attests to the monopolization of Indian labor, especially that of women, in cotton-textile production, as do the following native petitions and ecclesiastical reports: AN/Q, Indígenas: 1, "Autos sobre el hilado del algodón del rey . . . Chillogallo, 1617"; AGI, Quito 76, doc. 51, "Carta de Fray Luis López de Solís, Obispo de Quito, 1598"; AGI, Quito 82, "Memorial de las cosas que hay necesidad de orden y remedio en la provincia de San Francisco de Quito," no. 6, n.d. (ca. 1577–86); on the "perpetual weaving" of the Quijos Indians in the sixteenth century, see Rumazo González, *Región amazónica*, p.241.

12. AGI, Quito 76, doc. 51, "Carta de Fray Luis López de Solís, Obispo de Quito, 1598," f. 727v.

13. Accounts that portray forasteros as the caciques' "slaves" are included in the following documents: AN/Q, Cacicazgos: 14, "Real Provisión de 1613," presented as evidence in "Don Francisco Llacta de Anasca sobre el cacicazgo de la Real Corona de Ambato, 1706," ff. 32–33; BN/M, ms. 3044, "Memorial tocante a cosas de la gobernación de los quijos, ca. 1569–70"; AN/Q, Cacicazgos: 3 (1-VIII-1656), "Don Guillermo García Hati, cacique principal del pueblo de San Miguel, y Don Luís de Figueroa sobre el gobierno de los indios vagamundos de la Real Corona de Latacunga, 1656."

14. Salomon, *Native Lords*, pp. 119–20.

15. *Libro de cabildos*, pp. 351, 353, 356–57.

16. AGI, Justicia 683, no. 1, "Residencia tomada al Licenciado Juan de Salazar Villasante, 1564," ff. 760r–63r, 773v.

17. AGI, Justicia 683, no. 1, ff. 798–874; *Libro de cabildos, 1593–1597*, pp. 351–57.

18. AGI, Justicia 683, ff. 760–62. Note that these Andean servants must have been extraofficial retainers, above and beyond the yana reported in the visita of 1559; otherwise the encomendero's threat would have been an idle one.

19. AN/Q, Indígenas: 1 (1616-IV-24) ["Reparticiones de algodón que se dió a hilar a los pueblos de las cinco leguas . . . , 1617"], also cited in Caillavet, "Artesanía textil," pp. 6–10.

20. AN/Q, Cacicazgos: 3, "Auto de la paga del algodón del pueblo de Amaguaña . . . , 1617"; AN/Q, Indígenas: 1, "Autos sobre el hilado del algodón del rey . . . Chillogallo, 1617."

21. AN/Q, Indígenas: 1, "Autos sobre el hilado del algodón del rey . . . Chillogallo, 1617."

22. Ibid.; Frank Salomon and Sue Grosboll, "Names and Peoples in Incaic Quito: Retrieving Undocumented Historic Processes through Anthroponymy and Statistics," *American Anthropologist* (June 1986):387–99.

23. Married Indian women retained their own surnames but were registered in the ayllus of their husbands for the duration of their marriages. This could explain the presence of women with local surnames in the ayllu of the forasteros.

24. AN/Q, Cacicazgos: 3, "Auto de la paga de algodón del pueblo de Amaguaña, 1617."

25. A correlation between the surnames of caciques and commoners reported in the census of 1559 and the payment record of 1617 indicates that Amaguaña is the former Anan Chillo, although the geographic boundaries and ethnic composition of the town may have been altered slightly by the reducciones of the 1570s. Ibid.; Salomon and Grosboll, "Names and People," pp. 392–94.

26. AN/Q, Indígenas: 2, "Francisco Auqui Guacra y otros indios Tomaicos de Amaguaña contra Juan Vizcayno el mozo sobre despojo de tierras, 1626," f. 35v.

27. AN/Q, Indígenas: 25 (1701-II-16), "Don Marcos Camuento, cacique principal de Otavalo con Gabriel Pasto, Thomas Latacunga, Miguel Pasto y otros forasteros Pastos Tontaquíes, 1701." Spalding (*De indio a campesino*, p. 194) describes this exchange as customary in Huarochirí. There outsiders who married into the kin group were given access to land in return for community labor.

28. Ibid; data from the census of 1645 also coincides with this claim. Many originarios are registered in the census as mitayos de obraje, but only one appears as a mitayo de obras. Freile Granizo, *Numeraciones.*

29. Between 1574 and 1628, the number of population centers in the Audiencia of Quito increased by 50 percent and the size of the Spanish population increased eightfold; Sánchez-Albornoz, *Population of Latin America*, p. 82.

30. AN/Q, Indígenas: 25, "Don Marcos Camuento . . . , 1701"; AGI, Quito 76, "Carta del Obispo de Quito . . . , 1598," f. 730.

31. AN/Q, Indígenas: 25, "Don Marcos Camuento . . . , 1701."

32. Ramírez, Saignes, and Wightman have also reported these agreements for Peru and Bolivia. See Ramírez, "'Dueño de Indios'"; Saignes, *Caciques*, p. 18; Wightman, *Indigenous Migration*, pp. 132–35.

33. AN/Q, Indígenas: 25; Freile Granizo, *Numeraciones*, 1:107-42. "Potosí" is not of Pasto derivation, but a place-name that Spaniards assigned to mines in the region in reminiscence of the Potosí mines of Alto Perú. Also although the

census of 1646 is preserved in a highly fragmented state, the ayllu of Camuento is one for which there is complete data.

34. AN/Q, Cacicazgos: 3, "Comisión dada a Don Guillermo García Hati Zanipatín, 1633," presented as evidence in "Don Guillermo García Hati, cacique principal de San Miguel contra Don Luis de Figueroa sobre el gobierno de los indios vagamundos de la Real Corona de Latacunga, 1656," f. 7v.

35. AN/Q, Cacicazgos: 3, "Título de gobernador de los indios vagamundos, enero de 1633"; "Posesión del cacicazgo de los indios vagamundos de San Miguel, 1635," both presented as evidence in "Don Guillermo García Hati . . . , 1656," ff. 8v–10r. It is more than probable that these two hundred were only part of the forastero mass. Subsequent data point to a holding back on the part of caciques in reporting the true number of vagamundos in their service.

36. AN/Q, Cacicazgos: 3, "Auto sobre los indios vagamundos de Latacunga, noviembre de 1633," presented as evidence in "Don Guillermo Hati . . . , 1656," ff. 7v–8r.

37. Ibid.

38. AN/Q, Cacicazgos: 3, "Título del gobernador . . . , 1634," in "Don Guillermo Hati . . . , 1656," ff. 8v–9r.

39. Considering the dates that appear in the documentation, the period of the roundup could not have lasted more than one or two months.

40. Juan Carrera Colín, "Apuntes para una investigación etnohistórica de los cacicazgos del corregimiento de Latacunga, siglos XVI y XVII," *Cultura* 11(1981):152–53.

41. Christiana Borchart de Moreno ("Origen y conformación de la hacienda colonial," p. 160) shows that numerous land grants were made to Spaniards in Latacunga from 1583 to 1587. Most of the documentation on "land for labor" arrangements with forasteros, however, occurs prior to those dates.

42. José María Vargas, "Los cacicazgos," *Boletín de la Academia Nacional de Historia* 53(1970):260–61, original source uncited.

43. Ibid.

44. BN/M, ms. 3044, f. 478, "Memorial tocante a cosas de la gobernación de los quijos," ca. 1569–70. Since Quijos was famous for cotton-textile production, it is also possible that they were deliberately recruited for their spinning and weaving talents. Don Sancho Hacho was mentioned in the residencia of 1566 (AGI, Justicia 683) as having a cotton contract with the encomendero of Chillos and was also described during the conquest of Quijos in 1559 as having close ties with the inhabitants of that region.

45. AN/Q, Indígenas (Hojas Sueltas): 173, "Indios de Quijos en Sigchos, Latacunga, 1703." Other cases in which forasteros were recruited and land was exchanged for labor in Latacunga are AN/Q, Indígenas: 2, 27-VI-1627, "Andrés Pichucho de los mitímas de Saquisillí y consortes contra Juan Sánchez de Sigura sobre tierras en Tanicuchi, 1617," presented as evidence in "Francisco Sánchez de Sigura contra Juan Sánchez de Sigura sobre tierras en Tanicuchi, 1628," which in turn was presented as evidence in "Martín Chunato y Estéban Aluissa yndios

contra Juan de Vergara contradiciendo la posesión de las tierras que compró de Francisco Sánchez Sigura, 1628"; AN/Q, Indígenas (Hojas Sueltas): 172, Carpeta 1686–88, "Phelipe Guanín Annapilla y consortes contra Alonso Quilapa, García Guanoluisa y otros yndios sobre tierras de Saquisillí, 1686." In this last suit, it is reported that the ancestors of these forasteros were granted land by Don Sancho Hacho, cacique principal of Latacunga, in return for fifty years of personal service. See also Tyrer, *Historia demográfica*, p. 40.

46. This seems to have been part of a viceroyalty-wide policy. In other parts of Peru, those who uncovered hidden Indians were made caciques of separate ayllus called "ayllus de manifestados." Personal communication with Efraín Trelles.

47. That labor reserves were hard-won is witnessed by the terms that caciques used in litigation to describe their recruitment efforts. An oft-repeated phrase with regard to the forasteros was that they were "buscados, adquiridos y naturalizados con maña e industria" ("searched for, acquired, and naturalized with skill and hard work"). Examples are found in AN/Q, Cacicazgos: 3, 1-VIII-1656, "Don Guillermo García Hati . . . , 1656" and AN/Q, Cacicazgos: 14, "Don Francisco Llacta de Anasca . . . , 1706."

48. AN/Q, Cacicazgos: 3, I-VIII-1656, ff. 20, 26–27v; AN/Q, Indígenas: 11 (1672-9-I), "Cartas Cuentas de Latacunga, 1672–1674," f. 1r.

49. Glave, *Trajinantes*; Saignes, "Las etnías de Charcas"; Sánchez-Albornoz, *Indios y tributos*; Wightman, *Indigenous Migration*.

50. Ramírez, "'Dueño de indios,'" pp. 587–88.

51. That forasteros often married into the communities where they resided appears repeatedly in the documentation. An example would be the Pastuzo forasteros of Tontaquí, who claimed to have permanent rights to the land that the cacique had assigned them because they and their ancestors had married local women. AN/Q, Indígenas: 25, "Don Marcos Camuento . . . , 1701."

52. Ramón, *Resistencia andina*, p. 169 and "La cara oculta de la hacienda: La visión andina en Cayambe, siglo XVII," in *Reproducción y transformación de las sociedades andinas, siglos XVI–XX*, eds. Segundo Moreno Yánez and Frank Salomon (Quito: Abya-Yala, 1991) 2:425–31.

53. Although Burgos Guevara found evidence in his early study ("El guaman, el puma y al amaru," p. 313) that forasteros had lower status than originarios in eighteenth-century Otavalo, his recent research reveals a more varied picture. Personal communication with Burgos G. in November 1993. At complete variance with the southern Andean data, however, is Loreto Rebolledo's study of Lumbisí and Tumbaco (Corregimiento of Quito) in which she states that originarios, rather than discriminating against forasteros, formed bonds of solidarity with them (*Comunidad y resistencia: El caso de Lumbisí en la colonia* (Quito:Flacso/Abya-Yala, 1992), pp. 114–15). For data on Alto Perú, see Sánchez-Albornoz, "Migración rural," pp. 28–30, 34; and Larson, *Colonialism*, p. 139.

54. Salomon, *Native Lords*, p. 43.

55. Ibid., pp. 208–10.

56. The cases of Tontaquí (Otavalo) and Tanicuchi (Latacunga) are two of many. AN/Q, Indígenas: 2, 27-VI-1627, "Andrés Pichucho . . . y consortes contra Juan Sánchez de Sigura; AN/Q, Indígenas: 25, "Don Marcos Camuento . . . , 1701."

57. Glave, *Trajinantes,* p. 348; Saignes ("Las etnías de Charcas," p. 70) calls this the creation of new mitimaes.

58. AGI, Quito 33, "Carta de Juan Guerrero Salazar, 20 de mayo de 1678."

59. Salomon, *Native Lords,* pp. 196–201.

60. Although considerably weakened as a reproductive adaptation, the formation of private work forces never ceased to function entirely. Throughout the colonial period, caciques continued to attach forasteros to their communities both through official roundups and unofficial contracts.

61. For land-rental strategies in Peru and Bolivia, see Saignes, "Las etnías de Charcas," p. 59; Spalding, *De indio a campesino,* pp. 195–96; Stern, *Peru's Indian Peoples,* p. 162; Wightman, *Indigenous Migration,* p. 133.

62. In a recent work on Indian and Spanish conceptions of land and tenure in colonial Peru, Susan Ramírez defines the Andean concept of land rights as based on use and occupation. "Land was a place [to plant a field] and a medium, not an item or possession belonging to someone." *The World Upside Down: Cross-Cultural Contact and Conflict in Sixteenth-Century Peru* (Stanford: Stanford University Press, forthcoming), chap. 3.

63. Spalding, *Huarochirí,* pp. 195–96.

64. That land rentals were a pan-audiencia strategy is demonstrated by the geographic range of the documentation. The following documents contain seventeenth-century examples for the Corregimientos of Ibarra, Otavalo, Quito, Latacunga, Ambato, and Cuenca. AN/Q, Cacicazgos: 3, Carchi (1586-IX-4), "El pueblo de Puntal con el pueblo de Tusa sobre tierras, 1791"; AN/Q, Cacicazgos: vol. 3, "Autos de Don Sevastián Cabezas, cacique principal y gobernador del pueblo de Urcuquí, Corregimiento de Otavalo, [1647–1669]"; AN/Q, Indígenas: 22, "El fiscal protector general de los indios por Domingo Zimbaña y consortes, indios del valle de Aloa (Chillogallo) de la Real Corona sobre tierras, 1696"; AN/Q, Indígenas: 10, "Bartolo Chanalacta, Christóval Toaquicha y consortes, naturales del pueblo de Saquisillí (Latacunga) contra el comisario Rodrigo Gonzáles de Alcoser sobre tierras, 1669"; AN/Q, Indígenas: documento suelto, "Don Clemente Yunapanta, cacique principal de la parcialidad de los indios hambatillos del pueblo de Quero (Ambato) sobre tierras, 1739"; AN/Q, "Don Francisco Anquisaca, cacique de Paute, sobre venta de tierras, 1683."

65. AN/Q, Cacicazgos: 3, Carchi (1586-IX-4), "Composición de tierras del pueblo de Tusa, 1647," inserted in "El pueblo de Puntal con el pueblo de Tusa sobre tierras, 1791," ff. 25v–32v.

66. AGI, Quito 10, doc. 115, "Carta del presidente Morga al rey, 15 de abril de 1623," ff. 677–78. The cacique, Don Francisco Paspuel, reported that the three towns had 900 tributaries in the visita of Mateo de Aguirre (probably during the 1580s), 878 in the Visita of Zorrilla (early 1590s), and only 600 in

1623. The bulk of these tributaries probably lived in Tusa, since it was traditionally reputed to be the largest of the three towns.

67. AN/Q, Cacicazgos: 3, Carchi (1586-IX-4), ff. 25v–32v. This decline is corroborated by the census of 1647 (AN/Q, Cacicazgos: 3) cited by C. Landázuri in "La sociedad pasto," p. 74.

68. Ibid.

69. Salomon, *Native Lords*, pp. 208–10.

70. This conflict may be rooted in the multiethnic composition of many reducciones.

71. AN/Q, Cacicazgos: vol.3, "Composición de tierras del pueblo de Urcuquí, 1647" inserted in "Autos de don Sevastián Cabezas, cacique principal y gobernador del pueblo de Urcuquí, Corregimiento de Otavalo, (1647–1669)," ff. 25v–26v.

72. Freile G., *Numeraciones*, 2:81–112. According to the census carried out in 1646, members of the Yacelga ayllu were resident in the towns of Urcuquí, Tontaquí, Azangues, Yaruquí, and other places, both inside and outside the Corregimiento of Otavalo. Some of the more local dispersion, however, may reflect pre-Hispanic settlement patterns or even postconquest reducciones.

73. AN/Q, Cacicazgos: vol. 3, "Autos de Don Sevastián Cabezas . . . , [1647–1669]."

74. AN/Q, Cacicazgos: vol. 3, "Pleito entre Don Sevastián Cabezas, cacique principal de Urcuquí y consortes y Juan Gonzáles de Escobedo y Diego Paes Altamirano sobre tierras, 1666," included in "Autos de Don Sevastián Cabezas . . . , [1647–1669]," f. 106.

75. Tom Dillehay refers to these arrangements as "resource sharing." See his "Pre-Hispanic Resource Sharing in the Central Andes," *Science* (1979) 204:24–31. See also Ramírez's "Social Frontiers and the Territorial Base of Curacazgos," in *Andean Ecology and Civilization: An Interdisciplinary Perspective on Andean Ecological Complementarity*, ed. Shozo Masuda (Tokyo, 1985), pp. 423–42.

76. AN/Q, Cacicazgos: vol. 3, "Pleito entre Don Sevastián Cabezas . . . ," ff. 107r–8r and ff. 117r–27v.

77. AN/Q, Cacicazgos: vol. 3, "Composición de tierras, 1647," ff. 25v–26r.

78. Susan Ramírez, "Social Frontiers," pp. 432–35 and *The World Upside Down*, chap. 3.

79. AN/Q, Cacicazgos: vol. 3, "Pleito entre Don Sevastián Cabezas . . . ," f. 26.

80. AN/Q, Cacicazgos: vol. 3, "Petición de Don Sevastián Cabezas Urcuquiango, 1668," ff. 156r–58r.

81. AN/Q, Cacicazgos: vol. 3, "Tanto de la Numeración de Pedro Porras y Toledo de los indios naturales del pueblo de Urcuquí, 1665," ff. 128r–28v; Freile G., *Numeraciones*, vol. 2.

82. AN/Q, Cacicazgos: vol. 3, "Memoria de los gastos que se hacen con la plata de los arrendamientos de las tierras de los naturales del pueblo de Urcuquí y censos que paga Joseph de Ribera desde el año de 1654," presented as evidence in "Autos de Don Sevastián Cabezas . . . , 1647–1669." Out of 803 pesos

collected for rentals and censos, 662 pesos were spent on church-related donations and activities, 110 pesos on litigation over lands, and 31 pesos on the
tributes of sick Indians. Examples of items purchased for the church were dam-
ask clothing from China for the statue of San Miguel and a *sagrario.*

83. Spalding, *De indio a campesino,* pp. 61–87.

84. AN/Q, Cacicazgos: vol. 3, "Memoria de los gastos," ff. 159–60.

85. Saignes (*Caciques,* p. 13) shows that in the Sapahaqui Valley in Bolivia,
Spanish officials took advantage of the nontributary status of the area's seven
hundred forasteros to dispossess the Quirua repartimiento of forty-nine
estancias at midseventeenth century.

86. AN/Q, Cacicazgos: vol. 3, "Autos de Don Sevastián . . . ," ff. 130–34.

87. Borchart de Moreno, "Tierras de comunidad." For more detailed analy-
ses of the seventeenth-century land transfer in the Audiencia of Quito, see
Borchart de Moreno, "Composiciones de tierras en el valle de los Chillos";
"Composiciones de tierras en la Audiencia de Quito"; "Origen y conformación;
La transferencia de la propiedad agraria indígena en el corregimiento de Quito
hasta finales del siglo XVII," *Caravelle* 34(1980):5–19; Segundo Moreno Yánez,
"Traspaso"; Ramón, *Resistencia andina* and "La cara oculta." Wightman also
notes for Cuzco that the composiciones of midseventeenth century severely
limited the ability of Andean communities to absorb forasteros on their lands.

88. AN/Q, Presidencia de Quito: 5, "Carta de la Audiencia al Virrey, 1647,"
ff. 183r–84r. Audiencia officials reported to the viceroy that the Andean communities complained bitterly about land divestment during the composición
of 1647. The 1660s were also a time of widespread state-sponsored divestment
as well as illicit land-grabbing by private Spaniards. Numerous suits of this
period attest to the summary designation of the lands of ausentes as surplus
and their auction in the interests of the royal coffers. Two examples are found
in AN/Q, Cacicazgos: vol. 3, "Autos de Don Sevastián Cabezas . . . , 1647–1669";
AN/Q, Indígenas: 10, "Bartolo Chanalacta, Christóval Toaquicha . . . , 1669."
The composiciones of Antonio de Ron in the 1690s were also reported to have
been very prejudicial to the agrarian interests of the audiencia's Andean communities. Lastly the earthquake of 1698 finalized the land transfer from Andean
to Spanish hands in the central highland provinces of Riobamba, Latacunga,
and Ambato, as Spaniards scrambled to grab whatever land was still cultivable
after the disaster.

89. Caciques often prided themselves on their ability to convince ausentes
to return to their communities and frequently cited this ability in litigation as
an indicator of good leadership.

90. Here the term *early colonial leaders* refers to caciques of the period ca.
1534–1650.

Chapter 5

1. For example, see Charles Gibson, *The Aztecs under Spanish Rule*; Franklin
Pease, *Del Tawantinsuyu a la historia del Peru* (Lima: Instituto de Estudios
Peruanos, 1972).

2. Chantal Caillavet and Galo Ramón both propose this polarization for the northern sierra. Caillavet, "La adaptación de la dominación incaica a las sociedades autóctonas de la frontera septentrional del imperio (Territorio Otavalo-Ecuador)," *Revista Andina* 3(December 1985)2:412–13; Ramón, *Resistencia andina,* p. 91.

3. Salomon, *Native Lords,* pp. 122–24. Burgos Guevara ("El guaman, el puma y el amaru," pp. 335–37) emphasizes that Quito's aboriginal, political organization was characterized by the "separation, independence, primacy and individuality of its many cacicazgos." He states further that Quito's microvertical economy did not require a centralized state; its multiplicity of affiliated cacicazgos was an appropriate, politico-cultural adaptation whose efficiency the Inca understood and respected in their imperial reorganization of the region. Oberem's work on Latacunga (*Sancho Hacho,* pp. 15–21) also points to a series of independent cacicazgos, as does Landázuri's study of the Pasto region ("La sociedad pasto," p. 59). Both Burgos Guevara and Oberem argue for provincial alliances among these cacicazgos; Oberem makes a case for the existence of a small group of provincial leaders called "caciques mayores," whose pre–Incaic role was wartime leadership of intertribal confederations and whose power was enhanced by the Spanish regime during the sixteenth century in the interests of more efficient colonial rule. Caillavet ("La adaptación de la dominación incaica," p. 409) has found evidence for a somewhat more centralized organization in the north under a supreme leader named Otavalango. It is unclear whether this concentration of power predated the arrival of the Inca. In a more recent work ("Las jefaturas prehispánicas del norte del Ecuador," p. 24), she uncovered thirty-five ethnic lords in Otavalo but noted that four appeared to have more importance than the others. For a fine overview of the pre-Incaic political organization of Quito's ethnic groups, see Moreno Yánez, "Formaciones políticas."

4. After the breakup of the Incaic administrative system, many south Andean polities also experienced decentralization, as local leaders claimed their autonomous rights. Nevertheless these groups, the Huancas for example, already had large populations with central authority figures and thus did not require their creation by the Spanish regime.

5. AGI, Camara 922A, doc. 2, f. 10v, cited in Chantal Caillavet, "La estructura básica de las sociedades autóctonas de la Sierra Norte de Ecuador en el siglo XVI, (las "parcialidades" indígenas: unidades étnicas mínimas.)," in *Reproducción y transformación,* 1:175.

6. Caillavet, "Estructura básica," pp. 9–11.

7. AN/Q, Cacicazgos: vol. 12 ["Don Sancho Lema, cacique principal del pueblo de Guano con Don Juan Bueno de Galarza y los otros principales de Guano, 1575–1600"] presented as evidence in "Don Joseph Roberto Amaguaña, cacique principal de la parcialidad de Guano con Don Joseph Quilpud sobre el cacicazgo de Guano, 1683."

8. There were seven principales who contested Don Sancho Lema's rule. They

were listed in the suit as: Don Juan Bueno de Galarza, principal del pueblo de
Guano; Don Juan Lata, principal del pueblo de Olti; Don Marcos Buela, prin-
cipal del pueblo de Olti; Don Martín Yunga, principal del pueblo de Calpi; Don
Joan Auqui and Don Alejo Lema, principales del pueblo de Suichi; Don
Hernando Ayna and Don Miguel Ayunynna, principales del pueblo de Ylapo.
Ibid.

9. Excerpts from the visita of 1539 are presented in AN/Q, Cacicazgos: vol.
8, "Pleito de Don Sancho Lema, cacique principal de Guano con el capitán Juan
de Galarza y Don Alejo Lema," presented as evidence in "Autos de Rafael
Pillcolema contra Felipe Lema sobre el cacicazgo de las parcialidades de
Ñacchucay, Llando, pueblo de Guano, 1674," ff. 134r–35v. The 1570 data is
contained in AN/Q, Cacicazgos: vol. 12, "Don Sancho Lema con Don Juan Bueno
de Galarza . . . "; AN/Q, Cacicazgos: vol. 7, "Autos de Don Augustín Lema contra
Don Joseph Chapla y Lema sobre el cacicazgo de la parcialidad de Suichi, pueblo
de Guano, 1664."

10. Evidence of the reducción and the unsettling repercussions it left in its
wake is cited in AN/R, PJ: 25, "Don Marcos Cambal, cacique principal del pueblo
de Ylapo contra Don Sancho Lema, Don Juan Bueno, Don Marcos Navarro, y
Don Juan Lata sobre casas en Guano, 1586."

11. AN/Q, Cacicazgos: vol. 12, "Don Sancho Lema con Don Juan Bueno . . . "
12. Ibid.
13. Ibid.
14. Ibid., ff. 113v–16r.
15. Ibid., ff. 120r–22r.
16. Ibid.

17. AN/Q, Cacicazgos: vol. 8, "Pleito de Don Sancho Lema . . . con el Capitán
Juan de Galarza," in Autos de Rafael Pillcolema," ff. 134r–35v.

18. When one considers the cacique's colonial role as mediator between two
worlds, this quote poses a strikingly symbolic image. AN/Q, Cacicazgos: vol.
12, "Don Sancho Lema con Don Juan Bueno . . . ."
19. Ibid., f. 129.

20. AN/Q, Cacicazgos: vol. 5, "Joachín Chala con Joseph Chapla y Lema
sobre el cacicazgo de San Andrés, 1676." This suit contains evidence presented
in two previous suits, one brought by Don Hernando Chala in 1644, and another by Don Pedro Caxo in 1663.
21. Ibid., f. 124.
22. Ibid., f. 44.

23. Ibid., f. 16. An analysis of vital data presented in the censuses of 1592
and 1620 confirms that Andrés Lalligaña and Andrés Apacagua were indeed
the same man. The ages and names of household members exhibit too many
similarities for any other interpretation.

24. The seven principales of the town of Guano, for example, insisted that
they be permitted to deal directly with the Spanish state. AN/Q, Cacicazgos:
vol. 12, "Don Sancho Lema con Don Juan Bueno . . . ."

Nevertheless Salomon (*Native Lords*, p. 193), in his comparison of the 1557 visita of the Puruhá with the 1559 visita of Chillos, claims that while small groups in the latter area tributed directly to the Inca, evidence of this type of autonomy was absent for the Riobamba area.

25. AGI, Quito 8, doc. 10, f. 102v, "Instrucción que se le dió al Licenciado Francisco de Cárdenas para el modo de hacer la visita de los repartimientos de términos [de Quito], 1570."

26. AN/Q, Cacicazgos: vol. 8, "Pleito de Don Sancho Lema . . . con el Capitán Juan de Galarza . . . , 1582," presented as evidence in "Autos de Rafael Pillcolema," ff. 114–37.

27. Although Don Alejo Lema claimed that both he and Don Sancho were natural sons of the previous cacique and were therefore equals, it is fairly certain that he was a bastard. Don Sancho presented his father's will as evidence that the latter recognized him as his son and heir, while no mention was made of Don Alejo. Ibid.

28. Ibid.

29. Ibid.

30. Ibid.

31. Ibid.

32. AN/Q, Cacicazgos: 14, "Don Francisco de Anasca sobre el cacicazgo de la Real Corona de Ambato, 1706."

33. AN/Q, Cacicazgos: 3 (I-VIII-1656), "Don Guillermo García Hati, cacique principal del pueblo de San Miguel y Don Luis de Figueroa sobre el gobierno de los indios vagamundos de la Real Corona de Latacunga"; AN/Q, Cacicazgos: 4 (San Miguel, 1687), "Probanza de Doña Lucía Hati Pussana contra Don Guillermo García Hati," f. 81v.

34. This incentive is described in many documents which refer to the Matías de Peralta visita. One such description appears in AN/Q, Cacicazgos: vol. 7, "Autos de Don Augustín Lema contra Don Joseph Chapla y Lema sobre el cacicazgo de la parcialidad de Suichi, pueblo de Guano, 1664," ff. 29v-30r.

35. AN/R, PJ: 5, "Don Pedro Sisalema, cacique principal de Lito, con Juan Chunga, 1686."

36. AGI, Quito 72, "Autos de la Visita hecha a dicha audiencia por don Mateo de Mata Ponce de León: 1679–1697," ff. 180–214.

37. AN/Q, Cacicazgos: vol. 18, "Autos de Fernando Duchinachay sobre el gobierno del pueblo de Punín, 1699," ff. 8–12.

38. AN/Q, Indígenas (Hojas Sueltas): 173, 19-V-1701.

39. The record for the second half of the seventeenth century contains numerous accounts of caciques dissipating their personal fortunes to meet tribute quotas. Examples are included in AN/Q, Cacicazgos: 3 (1654-II-12), "Don Felipe Saplay, Cacique de la parcialidad de Ciguán (Provincia de Chimbo) pide que se relieve de cobrar tributos, pues todos los indios son ausentes, 1654."

40. AN/Q, Presidencia de Quito: 10, "Cartas Cuentas de Quito y las cinco leguas, 1673–1675," ff. 7–157.

41. Although the imprisonment of caciques for nonpayment of tribute quo-

tas was commonplace in earlier periods, incidents were isolated, sporadic, and short-lived, owing to the availability of chiefly wealth. In 1633, for example, the cacique of Yaruquís (Riobamba) was imprisoned for three hundred pesos in tribute arrears but put one of his agricultural estates up as collateral and was released. AN/R, PJ: 4, "Don Juan Duchisela, cacique principal y gobernador de Yaruquís encarcelado por rezagos, 1633."

42. AN/Q, Indígenas: 10, "Cartas Cuentas del Pueblo de Guangópolo de la Real Corona, 1674."

43. AN/Q, Indígenas: 6, "En la ciudad de Cuenca . . . Joseph de Landivar . . . a la defensa de Don Mateo Quispilema, Don Juan Chavancalva y demás caciques presos de este partido por tributos . . . 1652."

44. AN/Q, Indígenas: 9 (24-X-1666), ff. 2v–5v, "Memoria de los indios ausentes del pueblo de Yaruquís, 1666."

45. AN/Q, Indígenas: 10, "Cartas Cuentas de la Real Corona de Santa Clara de Pomasqui, 1669–1672"; "Cartas Cuentas de la Real Corona de Ylambo en la provincia de los Yumbos, 1669–1673"; "Cartas Cuentas de los indios del pueblo de María Magdalena de Machanganilla de la Real Corona, 1668–1673"; "Cartas Cuentas del pueblo de Zámbiza de la Real Corona, 1670–1673"; Indígenas: 11, "Cartas Cuentas de los Indios bagamundos de la Corona Real que residen en la collación de la Santa Iglesia Catedral desta ciudad [Quito], 1669–1673"; Indígenas: 12, "Cartas Cuentas de los indios del pueblo de Cotocollao de la Real Corona, 1669–1673."

46. A prime example is the cacique of Azogues, who in 1786 tried to prove his legitimacy by gathering several witnesses who testified that they had seen him in jail on numerous occasions for tribute arrears. AN/Q Cacicazgos: 1, "Azogues, 1786."

47. AGI, Quito 30, "Relación del general Pedro Ponce Castillejo sobre el estado de Otavalo, 1623"; later examples appear in AN/Q, Indígenas: 18, (10-XI-1690), "Don Antonio Cazeres, indio cacique de Latacunga, connaturalizado en Otavalo contra Don Juan Salas sobre tierras, 1690"; AN/Q, Indígenas: 11, (1673-I-12), "Don Juan Chacón de la Vega, Don Gerónimo Amagua, Don Miguel Sinchugna y Don Miguel Yansapagssi, caciques principales del pueblo de Uyumbicho, sobre abusos del gobernador, Don García Zumba, 1673"; AN/Q, Indígenas (Hojas Sueltas): 173 ["Don Pablo Lema Carbajal sobre las parcialidades de Ñagchucay y Llanto, pueblo de Guano"], 1701; AN/Q, Cacicazgos: vol. 10, "Alejo Lema pide se le reconozca el cacicazgo de Guano, 1683"; AN/Q, Indígenas (Hojas Sueltas): 173 ["Don Christóval García Paspuel Tusa sobre el cacicazgo de Tusa, Puntal, y Angel"], 1701.

48. Many examples are included in AN/Q, Indígenas (Hojas Sueltas): 173.

49. AN/R, PJ: 5 ["Doña Luisa Bilcape, natural de San Andrés, cacica del pueblo, sobre donación de tierras"], 1672.   ,

50. AN/Q, Cacicazgos: 9 (San Andrés, 1697) ["Don Joseph Vilcapi, hijo de caciqués de San Andrés sobre la mita"], 1697. Vilcapi is a variation on Bilcape.

51. AN/Q, Cacicazgos: 9 (San Andrés, 1697) ["Melchor Quigyachi, indio particular que por compra que hizo de los papeles se halla al presente en el ejercicio del cacicazgo . . . "], 1771.

52. Glave (*Trajinantes,* p. 212) and Sinclair Thompson (personal communication) also report intruder caciques for the southern Andes in the late seventeenth and eighteenth centuries.

53. Tyrer's statistics (*Historia demográfica,* pp. 277, 282, 290, 292, 294) on rates of tribute payment indicate that the second half of the seventeenth century exhibited the lowest collection rates of the colonial period. The years 1670–99 represented the nadir for most of the corregimientos in the heartland. Some examples of corregimientos with especially low rates of payment are Otavalo (1693–95), 35 percent; Latacunga (1672–74), 39 percent; Ambato (1678–80), 39 percent; Riobamba (1691–94), 46 percent. Quito's payment rate reached its nadir in the years 1673–75, although a specific percentage has not been calculated, due to the diffusion of the data.

54. The intruder group also included, on many occasions, the descendants of those who had left.

55. Similarly, Stern, in his study of Huamanga (*Peru's Indian Peoples,* pp. 163–73), addresses the formation of local power structures that incorporate an elite Andean minority whose role is to facilitate extraction from native communities for mutual gain.

56. Galo Ramón (*Resistencia andina,* p. 234) describes the cacicazgos of the repartimiento of Otavalo as empty shells by the end of the seventeenth century. This certainly seems to have been the case in Latacunga and Riobamba as well, areas that have come under close scrutiny during this study.

57. Ramón (*Resistencia andina,* pp. 219–35 and "La cara oculta") has constructed a model of social reproduction inside the haciendas for the region of Cayambe in the second half of the seventeenth century.

58. I am addressing mainly those who benefited from migration to the Spanish sphere, as opposed to those who migrated to other Andean communities. The latter forastero population frequently represented a type of underclass, especially in other parts of the Viceroyalty of Peru, as witnessed by Sánchez-Albornoz' case study of Sipe-Sipe ("Migración rural," pp. 13–36). Conversely in his work on Huamanga, Steve Stern (*Peru's Indian Peoples,* chapter 7) also devotes a great deal of attention to migration to the Spanish sphere as a path to social mobility.

59. AN/Q, Indígenas: 171 (29-VII-1595).

60. AN/Q, Obrajes: 8, no. 2.

61. AN/Q, Indígenas: 2 (1628-IV-29), "Don García Lazo, natural del pueblo de Alausí de la Corona Real contra Don Juan Bixay, cacique y gobernador del dicho pueblo sobre tierras de la comunidad, 1628." Other representative examples of crown forasteros from the city of Quito who were involved in land suits include the cases of Don Ventura Chuqui Condor, whose father was a blacksmith in the Parish of San Roque; Diego Rimache, a sacristan in the Church of San Roque; Juan Paca, a butcher. AN/Q, Indígenas: 7, "Agustín de Villena contra Don Ventura Chuqui Condor sobre tierras, 1657"; AN/Q, Indígenas: 8, 1662-VI-6, "Diego Rimache, indio de la ciudad de Quito de la Real Corona con los padres de San Francisco sobre tierras, 1662"; AN/Q, Indígenas: 1, "Venta de

tierras a Juan Paca, carnicero, y Ana Quilago, indios de la ciudad de Quito, 1609."

62. Stern (*Peru's Indian Peoples*, pp. 161–63) also finds that this was true in Huamanga.

63. See chapter 4.

64. This is not to imply that originarios did not amass wealth, buy lands, and climb the social ladder, but only that this trajectory was more common for those who left their communities, even if only temporarily.

65. AN/Q, Indígenas: 1 (1621-VIII-9), "Francisco Méndez contra Ynés Cuxilago y Francisco Ylagumba sobre tierras y ganado, 1621," ff. 2–4.

66. Ibid., f. 109.

67. Ibid.

68. AN/Q, Cacicazgos: 14, "Autos de Augustín Argos Guaraca contra Joseph Llaguargos sobre el cacicazgo de los pueblos de Andaguaillas, Punín y Macaxí, 1688."

69. AN/Q, Cacicazgos: 14, "Probanza de Don Gonzalo Curi Argos," f. 14.

70. One especially illustrative case is that of the cacicazgo of San Miguel (Latacunga), where witnesses testified that the intruder, Don Francisco Hati, and his descendants were able to maintain power because the legitimate heirs were too poor to litigate. AN/Q, Cacicazgos: 3 (San Miguel, 1678), "Doña Lucía Pusana contra Don Guillermo Hati sobre el cacicazgo de San Miguel (Latacunga), 1678."

71. As early as 1582, Don Sancho Lema, cacique principal of Guano, pleaded with his bastard brother, who was supported by the encomendero, not to force him to spend his fortune in litigation. AN/Q, Cacicazgos: vol. 8, "Autos de Rafael Pillcolema, 1674." One hundred years later, Don Joachín Chala, the leader of San Andrés, was so impoverished after fifteen years of litigation with the intruder, Don Joseph Chapla y Lema, that his petition of 1691 was used to notify the opposing parties of the decision in lieu of a royal provision, because Don Joachín had not sufficient funds to pay for a single additional bureaucratic transaction. AN/Q, Cacicazgos: vol. 5, "Joachín Chala con Joseph Chapla y Lema sobre el cacicazgo de San Andrés, 1676."

72. The incidence of wealthy forasteros marrying their way into a cacicazgo is considerable. Two cases that generated bitter intracommunity conflict are AN/Q, Cacicazgos: 3, "Doña Barbara Paybata Cando, cacica principal de la provincia de Angamarcas (Latacunga) sobre el dicho cacicazgo con Don Alonso Cunsi, 1656"; AN/Q, Indígenas: 26, (1703-VI-23) ["Cacica y su marido forastero venden tierras de comunidad en Otavalo"], 1703.

73. The four cases from Guano and Punín are AN/Q, Cacicazgos: vol. 12, "Don Joseph Roberto Amaguaña, cacique principal de la parcialidad de Guano, pueblo de Guano, con Don Joseph Quilpud sobre el cacicazgo de Guano, 1683"; AN/Q, Cacicazgos: vol. 19, "Miguel de Torres contra Manuel Sagñay sobre el cacicazgo de Puni, 1699"; AN/Q, Cacicazgos: vol. 14, "Autos de Augustín Argos Guaraca contra Joseph Llaguargos sobre el cacicazgo de los pueblos de Andaguaillas, Punín, y Macaxí, 1688"; AN/Q, Cacicazgos: vol. 18, "Autos de

Fernando Duchinachay sobre el gobierno del pueblo de Punín, 1699." Representative examples of similar intrusions and suits for other towns in Riobamba and other areas of the audiencia are as follows: AN/Q, Cacicazgos: vol. 7, "Autos de Don Augustín Lema contra Don Joseph Chapla y Lema sobre el cacicazgo de la parcialidad de Suichi, pueblo de Guano (Riobamba), 1664"; AN/Q, Cacicazgos: vol. 11, "Autos de Juan Lema contra Fernando Duchinachay sobre el cacicazgo del pueblo de Punín (Riobamba), 1683"; AN/Q, "Acuerdos de Phelipe Sango Panta a favor de su sucesor Alonso Sango Panta, sobre el cacicazgo de San Phelipe (Latacunga), 1664"; AN/Q, Cacicazgos: 4, "Doña Lucía Hati Pusana con Don Guillermo Hati sobre el cacicazgo de San Miguel (Latacunga), 1687"; AN/Q, Cacicazgos: 3 (1668-XI-5), "Don Phelipe Sancho Hacho, cacique de San Phelipe con Don Bartolomé Sancho Hacho sobre cacicazgo de los indios camayos y de las parcialidades de Tuguan y Patatuan (Latacunga), 1668"; AN/Q, Cacicazgos: 3 (Guaranda, 1694), "Don Estéban Captusi, cacique principal de Guaranda con Don Lázaro Quinabanda sobre el cacicazgo de Camayo Salinas (Chimbo), 1694"; AN/Q, Cacicazgos: 2 (Chimbo, 1706), "Don Juan Pilamunga y consortes con Miguel Guaman sobre el cacicazgo de la parcialidad de Cañi, pueblo de Santiago (Chimbo), 1706"; AN/Q, Indígenas: 25 (14-II-1701) ["Don Blas Sogsso Tobón, cacique principal de los indios hambatillos con Don Christóval Sid"], 1701 (Ambato); AN/Q, Cacicazgos: 14, "Memorial de Don Andrés Alomunga Mudin, cacique principal del pueblo de Tisaleo (Ambato) con Don Sebastián Hallo Zumba sobre cacicazgo, 1699"; AN/Q, Cacicazgos: 14, "Don Christóval Tubón con Don Nicolás Yunapanta sobre cacicazgo de Pasa (Ambato), 1672"; AN/Q, Indígenas (Hojas Sueltas): 173 (19-V-1701) ["Doña María Roza de los Reyes, cacica principal del pueblo de la Asunción de Carangue con Joseph Constantino de la Candelaria"], 1701 (Otavalo).

74. Thierry Saignes (*Caciques,* pp. 26–27) also discusses caciques of lesser lineages who arose during the seventeenth century in Bolivia.

75. Many of the conflicts described here are really over principalazgos, but the litigants, true to their traditional resistance to centralization, refer to themselves as caciques and to their jurisdictions as cacicazgos. For this reason the terms *cacique* and *cacicazgo* are applied uniformly to all contenders and units under litigation.

76. AN/Q, Cacicazgos: vol. 12, "Don Joseph Roberto Amaguaña, 1683," ff. 25, 32–33, 84–88v.

77. Ibid., ff. 35r–35v.

78. Ibid., ff. 39v–40r, 70–74.

79. Ibid., f. 74.

80. AN/Q, Cacicazgos: vol. 19, "Miguel de Torres . . . , 1699." It is true that Matías de Peralta installed Don Gerónimo Sagñay as administrador of the Magssi parcialidad, as evidenced in an excerpt from the 1620 visita that appears in AN/Q, Cacicazgos: vol. 11, "Autos de Juan Lema . . . , 1683." It was also a common complaint that the descendants of temporary administrators often remained in power long after the conditional circumstances of their rule had dissolved.

81. AN/Q, Cacicazgos: vol. 19, "Miguel de Torres . . . , 1699."

82. Ibid.

83. There were two cacicazgos in Puni, one for the Inca mitimaes and one for the local Puruhá; both were contested during this period.

84. AN/Q, Cacicazgos: vol. 14, "Autos de Augustín Argos Guaraca, 1688." Yanaguaraca was said to have participated in the Incaic conquest of Riobamba and was consequently awarded lands and a cacicazgo of mitimaes in Puni.

85. Ibid.

86. Ibid.

87. AN/Q, Cacicazgos: vol. 18, "Autos de Fernando Duchinachay, 1699."

88. Ibid.

89. An unidentified but apparently chronic disease.

90. AN/Q, Cacicazgos: vol. 18, "Autos de Fernando Duchinachay," ff. 2r–2v.

91. AN/Q, Cacicazgos: vol. 11, "Autos de Juan Lema, 1683," f. 38v.

92. Ibid. The leaders of all ten parcialidades were recorded in the "Cabeza de la Numeración del pueblo de Puni de la Real Corona, hecha por el oidor Don Mathías de Peralta en 1620," ff. 41r–42v.

93. Ibid., ff. 4–5. The major caciques of the town are listed in the "Cabeza de la numeración del pueblo de Puni de la Real Corona, hecha por Juan de Sepúlveda en 1583."

94. Ibid, f. 41v.

95. Ibid, f. 42v.

96. Ibid, f. 38v.

97. AN/Q, Cacicazgos: vol. 18, "Autos de Don Fernando Duchinachay, 1699," ff. 26–27.

98. Segundo Moreno Yánez, *Sublevaciones indígenas en la Audiencia de Quito desde comienzos del siglo XVIII hasta finales de la colonia* (Quito: PUCE, 1985), pp. 394–95.

99. Ibid., p. 184.

100. AN/Q, Cacicazgos: vol. 14, "Autos de Augustín Argos Guaraca, 1688," f. 6.

101. AN/Q, Cacicazgos: vol. 18, "Autos de Fernando Duchinachay sobre el gobierno del pueblo de Punín, 1699," ff. 8–12.

102. Charles Gibson, *The Inca Concept of Sovereignty and the Spanish Administration in Peru* (Austin: University of Texas Press, 1948). Karen Spalding, *Huarochirí*, p. 33.

Glossary

Alcalde de encomienda. Indian official in charge of an encomienda; usually
    entrusted with tribute collection and labor organization.
Archipélago. Extensive network of economic colonies characteristic of
    Andean vertical economies.
Asiento. Spanish urban center.
Audiencia. Spanish colonial court in charge of a particular territory; also
    refers to the territory.
Ausentes. Andeans who absented themselves from their communities of
    origin and who were frequently maintained on their communities'
    tribute rolls in spite of fiscal and labor delinquency.
Ausentes perdidos. Andean absentees whose places of residence were un-
    known and who had severed ties with their communities of origin.
Ausentes seguros. Andean absentees whose places of residence were known
    and who probably fulfilled their tribute obligations to their commu-
    nities of origin in spite of their absence.
Auto. Local decree.
Ayllu. Andean social unit based on kinship, which owned land collectively
    and engaged in reciprocal obligations.
Cabildo. Spanish town council.
Cacique principal. Supreme leader or paramount lord of a cacicazgo.
Cacicazgo. An aboriginal polity that, in the north Andes, assumed the politi-
    cal form of a chiefdom.
Camayo. Native member of an economic colony who lived outside his
    nuclear community for the extraction of needed resources; part of a
    pre-Hispanic economic exchange mechanism.
Cartas cuentas. Tax records of Andean communities.
Cédula. A royal decree.
China. Indigenous female, domestic servant.
Composición. Legalization of formerly illegal lands or other resources
    through payment of a fee to the crown.
Corregidor. Spanish official entrusted with tribute collection, labor recruit-
    ment, and local justice in a corregimiento.
Corregimiento. Jurisdiction akin to a province.
Duho. Wooden stool belonging to the cacique principal of a north Andean
    polity and symbolizing his authority over his subjects.

Ejido. Common pasturelands.

Encomienda. Award of Amerindians to a Spaniard for the purposes of extracting tribute and labor from them.

Encomendero. Spanish grantee of an encomienda.

Fiscal. Attorney to the audiencia.

Forastero. Andean who had abandoned his/her community of origin. His/her descendants were also called forasteros.

Gobernador. Andean governor of a community who was entrusted with some of the responsibilities of Spanish administration and who rivaled the power of the traditional cacique when both offices were not vested in the same person.

Hacendado. Owner of a large landed estate, usually a Spaniard in colonial times.

Hacienda. Large landed estate dedicated to both agriculture and ranching.

Kuraka. Quechua term for an Andean leader or cacique.

Llajta. Place of origin.

Mandón. Local leader below the principal in the indigenous hierarchy.

Manifestación. An official exposure of truant Andeans.

Mindalá. Long-distance merchant who worked in the service of an Andean lord in both pre-Hispanic and early colonial times; prevalent in north-central sierra of the Audiencia of Quito

Mita, mitayo. Forced-labor draft; drafted Andean laborer.

Mita de obras. Forced-labor draft for public works usually in Spanish urban centers.

Mita de obrajes. Forced-labor draft for textile mills.

Mitimaes. Loyal subjects of Inca empire sent to newly conquered areas in a military or didactic role. Term also used in southern Andes for economic colonists; in the northern Andes, the latter were called camayos.

Montaña. Subtropical area on lower slopes.

Obraje. Textile sweatshop.

Ocultos. Andean subjects who were hidden by their caciques during Spanish inspections and, therefore, not included in official censuses.

Oidor. Audiencia judge.

Originario. Andean who resided in his town of origin. Used in opposition to forastero.

Páramo. High-altitude eco-zone of north Andes characterized by barren plains.

Parcialidad. Administrative subunit of Amerindians, usually consonant with an ayllu (except in the case of crown parcialidades of vagabonds or forasteros) and under the leadership of a secondary authority called a principal.

Piso. Ecological niche associated with a particular altitude.

Principal. Leader or secondary lord of a principalazgo.

Principalazgo. Subunit of a cacicazgo, usually consonant with an ayllu or parcialidad, and entrusted to a leader called a principal.

Pueblo. Town or reducción.

Realengas. Lands designated as surplus and that had, therefore, reverted to the crown.

Reducción. A town in the countryside into which Amerindians were aggregated for administrative purposes and religious instruction; also used to describe the process by which Amerindians were aggregated into these towns, that is, the practice of "reducción".

Repartimiento. Large administrative unit of Amerindians who paid tribute to an encomendero or to the crown and performed the mita. Usually consonant in size with a cacicazgo.

Residencia. Official investigation into the administration of a royal official upon leaving office.

Rezagos. Back tributes officially entered in a separate accounting category for which the corregidor was not personally responsible.

Tambos. Supply stations along the highways which also served as inns for travelers.

Tianguez. Pre-Hispanic market system characteristic of the north Andes.

Tributarios. Andean men between ages 18 and 50 who were nominally responsible for providing tribute and corvee labor to the Spanish regime.

Vagamundo. Andean vagabond; often used synonymously with forastero.

Vaquero. Cowhand.

Vecino. A Spanish resident of a town or city who had voting rights on the town council.

Yana, yanacona. Andean who was not attached to a community and who was an official servant first of the Inca nobility and then of the Spaniards.

Visita. General administrative inspection.

Bibliography

Archival Sources

AC/Q   Archivo de la Curia, Quito
AGI   Archivo General de Indias, Seville
AMQ   Archivo Municipal de Quito
AN/Q   Archivo Nacional/Quito
AN/R   Archivo Notarial, "Juan Felix Proaño," Riobamba
ASF/Q   Archivo de la Orden de San Francisco, Quito
BC/A   Archivo del Banco Central, Ambato
BN/M   Biblioteca Nacional de España, Madrid
BPR/M   Biblioteca del Palacio Real, Madrid
RAH/M   Real Academia de Historia, Madrid

Published Sources

Alchon, Suzanne Austin. "Disease, Population, and Public Health in Eighteenth-Century Quito." In *"Secret Judgments of God": Old World Disease in Colonial Spanish America,* eds. Noble David Cook and W. George Lovell, 159–82. Norman: University of Oklahoma Press, 1992.

———. *Native Society and Disease in Colonial Ecuador.* Cambridge: Cambridge University Press, 1991.

Andrien, Kenneth. *Crisis and Decline: The Viceroyalty of Peru in the Seventeenth Century.* Albuquerque: University of New Mexico Press, 1985.

Arcos, Gualberto. "Evolución de la medicina en el Ecuador." Universidad Central del Ecuador *Anales* 61(October/December 1938): 1051–88.

Basile, David G. *Tillers of the Andes: Farmers and Farming in the Quito Basin.* Chapel Hill: University of North Carolina Press, 1974.

Bakewell, Peter. *Miners of the Red Mountain: Indian Labor in Potosí, 1545–1650.* Albuquerque: University of New Mexico Press, 1984.

Benítez, A., Sylvia. "Apuntes demográficos del cacicazgo de Sangolquí, siglo XVI al XVII." *Memoria* (Quito: MARKA) 2 (November 1991):59–90.

Bonifaz, Emilio. "Extractos de los libros del cabildo de Quito: 1534– 1657." *Museo Histórico* 17(April/June 1971):124–80.

Borchart de Moreno, Christiana. "Camayos, forasteros y vagamundos: Algunos datos sobre la migración en la región de Riobamba en el siglo XVII."

Paper presented at the Fifth Encuentro de Historia y Realidad Económica y Social del Ecuador, Cuenca, 17–21 November, 1986.

———. "Composiciones de tierras en el valle de los Chillos a finales del siglo XVII: Una contribución a la historia agraria de la Audiencia de Quito." *Cultura* (Quito) 2(September/December 1979): 139–82.

———. "Composiciones de tierras en la Audiencia de Quito: El valle de Tumbaco a finales del siglo XVII." *Jahrbuch fur die Geschichte von Staat, Wirtschaft und Gesellschaft* 17(1980):121–55.

———. "Origen y conformación de la hacienda colonial." In *Nueva historia del Ecuador*, vol. 4, ed. Enrique Ayala Mora, 139–66. Quito: Corporación Editora Nacional/Grijalbo, 1989.

———. "Las tierras de comunidad de Licto, Punín, y Macaxí: Factores para disminución e intentos de restauración." *Revista Andina* 12(December 1988):503–24.

———. "La transferencia de la propiedad agraria indígena en el corregimiento de Quito hasta finales del siglo XVII." *Caravelle* 34(1980): 5–19.

Burgos Guevara, Hugo. "El Guaman, el puma, y el amaru: Formación estructural del gobierno indígena en el Ecuador." Ph.D. dissertation, University of Illinois, 1975.

———. "La población del Ecuador en la encrucijada de los siglos XVI y XVII." International Congress of Americanists *Atti* 2(1972): 483–87.

Caillavet, Chantal. "La adaptación de la dominación incaica a las sociedades autóctonas de la frontera septentrional del imperio (Territorio Otavalo–Ecuador)." *Revista Andina* 3(December 1985): 403–19.

———. "La artesanía textil en la época colonial: El rol de la producción doméstica en el norte de la Audiencia de Quito." *Cultura* (Quito) 8 (January/ April 1986):521–30.

———. "La estructura básica de las sociedades autóctonas de la Sierra Norte de Ecuador en el siglo XVI (las "parcialidades" indígenas: unidades étnicas mínimas)." In *Reproducción y transformación de las sociedades andinas, siglos XVI a XX*, vol. 1, ed. Segundo Moreno Yánez and Frank Salomon, 173–96. Quito: Abya-Yala, 1991.

———. "Las jefaturas prehispánicas del norte del Ecuador: Formas de habitat y organización territorial." *Memoria* (Quito: MARKA) 2(November 1991):1–25.

Cardoso, Fernando Henrique, and Enzo Faletto. *Dependency and Development in Latin America*. Berkeley: University of California Press, 1979.

Carrera Andrade, Jorge. *El fabuloso reino de Quito*. Quito: Editorial Casa del la Cultura Ecuatoriana, 1963.

Carrera Colín, Juan. "Apuntes para una investigación etnohistórica de los cacicazgos del corregimiento de Latacunga, siglos XVI y XVII." *Cultura* 11(1981):129–79.

Cieza de León, Pedro. *The Travels of Pedro Cieza de León, 1532–50*. Ed. Clements R. Markham. New York: Franklin, n.d.

————. *Del señorío de los incas* (Segunda parte de la crónica del Peru). Buenos Aires: Ediciones Argentinos Solar, 1943.

Cline, S.L. *Colonial Culhuacan, 1580–1600: A Social History of an Aztec Town.* Albuquerque: University of New Mexico Press, 1986.

Cole, Jeffrey. *The Potosí Mita, 1573–1700: Compulsory Indian Labor in the Andes.* Stanford: Stanford University Press, 1985.

Cook, Noble David. *Demographic Collapse: Indian Peru, 1520–1620.* New York: Cambridge University Press, 1981.

Cook, Noble David, and W. George Lovell, eds. *"Secret Judgments of God": Old World Disease in Colonial Spanish America.* Norman: University of Oklahoma Press, 1991.

Cook, Sherburne, and Woodrow Borah. *The Aboriginal Population of Central Mexico on the Eve of the Spanish Conquest.* Berkeley: University of California Press, 1963.

————. *Essays in Population History: Mexico and the Caribbean.* Berkeley: University of California Press, 1971–79.

Coronel Feijoo, Rosario. *El valle sangriento: de los indígenas de la coca y el algodón a la hacienda jesuita, 1580–1700.* Quito: Flacso/Abya-Yala, 1991.

Cushner, Nicholas P. *Farm and Factory: The Jesuits and the Development of Agrarian Capitalism, 1600–1767.* Albany: State University of New York Press, 1982.

Deler, Jean Paul. *Ecuador: Del espacio al estado nacional.* Quito: Banco Central del Ecuador, 1987.

Deler, Jean, Nelson Gómez, and Michel Portais. *El manejo del espacio en el Ecuador.* Vol.1. Quito: Centro Ecuatoriano de Investigación Geográfica, 1983.

Dillehay, Thomas. "Pre-Hispanic Resource Sharing in the Central Andes." *Science* (1979) 204:24–31.

Espinoza Soriano, Waldemar. *Los cayambes y carangues, siglos XV y XVI: El testimonio de la etnohistoria.* Vol. 1. Otavalo: Instituto Otavaleño de Antropología, 1988.

————. *La destrucción del imperio de los Incas.* Lima, 1973.

————. *Etnohistoria ecuatoriana: Estudios y documentos.* Quito: Abya-Yala, 1988.

————. *Visita hecha a la provincia de Chucuito por Garci Diez de San Miguel en el año 1567.* Lima: Talleres Gráficos Quiros, 1964.

Estrada Ycaza, Julio. "Migraciones internas en el Ecuador." *Revista del Archivo Histórico del Guayas* 11(1977):5–26.

Evans, Brian. "Census Enumeration in Late Seventeenth-Century Alto Perú: The Numeración General of 1683–1684." In *Studies in Spanish American Population History*, ed. David J. Robinson, 25–44. Boulder: Westview Press, 1981.

————. "Migration Processes in Upper Peru in the Seventeenth Century." In *Migration in Colonial Spanish America*, ed. David. M. Robinson, 62–85. Cambridge: Cambridge University Press, 1990.

Farriss, Nancy M. *Maya Society under Colonial Rule: The Collective Enterprise of Survival.* Princeton: Princeton University Press, 1984.

Frank, Andre Gunder. *Capitalism and Underdevelopment in Latin America.* New York: Monthly Review Press, 1967.

Freile Granizo, Juan. *Numeraciones del repartimiento de Otavalo.* 2 vols. Otavalo: Instituto Otavaleño de Antropología, 1981.

Galeano, Eduardo. *Open Veins of Latin America: Five Centuries of the Pillage of a Continent.* New York: Monthly Review Press, 1973.

Gibson, Charles. *The Aztecs under Spanish Rule: A History of the Indians of the Valley of Mexico, 1519–1810.* Stanford: Stanford University Press, 1964.

————. *The Inca Concept of Sovereignty and the Spanish Administration in Peru.* Austin: University of Texas Press, 1948.

Glave, Luis Miguel. *Trajinantes: Caminos indígenas en la sociedad colonial, siglos XVI y XVII.* Lima: Instituto de Apoyo Agrario, 1989.

Gosner, Kevin. *Soldiers of the Virgin: The Moral Economy of a Colonial Maya Rebellion.* Tucson: University of Arizona Press, 1992.

Haskett, Robert. *Indigenous Rulers: An Ethnohistory of Town Government in Colonial Cuernavaca.* Albuquerque: University of New Mexico Press, 1991.

Horn, Rebecca. "Postconquest Coyoacan: Aspects of Indigenous Sociopolitical Organization in Central Mexico, 1550–1650." Ph.D. diss., UCLA, 1989.

Jijón y Caamaño, Jacinto. *Antropología prehispánica del Ecuador.* Quito: Prensa Católica, 1945.

Jiménez de la Espada, Marcos, ed. *Relaciones geográficas de Indias.* 3 vols. Madrid: Ministerio de Fomento, 1881–87.

Jones, Grant D. *Maya Resistance to Spanish Rule: Time and History on a Colonial Frontier.* Albuquerque: University of New Mexico Press, 1989.

Jurado Noboa, Fernando. *Sancho Hacho: Orígenes de la formación mestiza ecuatoriana.* Quito: Abya-Yala, 1990.

Kellogg, Susan. *Law and the Transformation of Aztec Culture, 1500–1700.* Norman: Oklahoma University Press, forthcoming.

Klein, Herbert. "Hacienda and Free Community in Eighteenth-Century Alto Peru: A Demographic Study of the Aymara Population of the Districts of Chulumani and Pacajes in 1786." *Journal of Latin American Studies* 7(November 1975):193–220.

Konetzke, Richard. *Colección de documentos para la historia de la formación social de Hispanoamérica, 1493–1810.* Madrid: Consejo Superior de Investigaciones Científicas, 1953.

Landázuri N., Cristóbal. "Territorios y pueblos: la sociedad pasto en los siglos XVI y XVII." *Memoria* (Quito: MARKA) 1(November 1990):57–108.

Landázuri Soto, Alberto. *El régimen laboral indígena en la Real Audiencia de Quito.* Madrid: 1957.

Lara, Jorge Salvador. "Apuntes para la historia de la población indígena del Ecuador." *América Indígena* 34(July/September 1974): 685–712.

Larrain Barros, Horacio. *Demografía y asentamientos indígenas en la sierra norte del Ecuador en el siglo XVI.* 2 vols. Otavalo: Instituto Otavaleño de Antropología, 1980.

Larson, Brooke. *Colonialism and Agrarian Transformation in Bolivia, 1550–1900.* Princeton: Princeton University Press, 1988.

León, Luis A. "Bosquejo histórico de las lenguas vernaculares del Ecuador y la educación bilingüe." *América Indígena* 34(July/September 1974):745–75.

———. "La mujer indígena en el régimen laboral incáico y colonial del reino y de la real Audiencia de Quito." *América Indígena* 35(November 1973):539–58.

León-Portilla, Miguel. *The Broken Spears: The Aztec Account of the Conquest of Mexico.* Boston: Beacon Press, 1962.

Libro de cabildos de la ciudad de Quito, 1575–1576. Descifrado por Jorge A. Garces. Quito: Archivo Municipal, 1935.

Libro de cabildos de la ciudad de Quito, 1593–1597. Quito: Archivo Municipal, 1935.

Libro primero de cabildos de Quito. Descifrado por José Rumazo González. Quito: Archivo Municipal, 1934.

Libro segundo de cabildos de Quito. Quito: Archivo Municipal, 1934.

Lockhart, James. *The Men of Cajamarca: A Social and Biographical Study of the First Conquerors of Peru.* Austin: University of Texas Press, 1972.

———. *The Nahuas after the Conquest: A Social and Cultural History of the Indians of Central Mexico, Sixteenth Through Eighteenth Centuries.* Stanford: Stanford University Press, 1992.

MacLeod, Murdo J. *Spanish Central America: A Socioeconomic History, 1520–1720.* Berkeley: University of California Press, 1973.

Martin, Cheryl English. *Rural Society in Colonial Morelos.* Albuquerque: University of New Mexico Press, 1985.

Mellafe, Rolando. "The Importance of Migration in the Viceroyalty of Peru." In *Population and Economics,* ed. Paul De Prez, 303–13. Winnipeg: University of Manitoba Press, 1970.

Minchom, Martin. "Demographic Change in Ecuador during the Eighteenth Century." *Cultura* (Quito) 24(1986):459–80.

Moreno Yánez, Segundo. *Sublevaciones indígenas en la Audiencia de Quito desde comienzos del siglo XVIII hasta finales de la colonial.* Quito: Pontificia Universidad Católica del Ecuador, 1985.

———. "Formaciones políticas tribales y señorios étnicos." In *Nueva historia del Ecuador,* vol. 2, ed. Enrique Ayala Mora, 9–134.

———. "Traspaso de la propiedad agrícola a la hacienda colonial: El caso de Saquisilí." In *Contribución a la etnohistoria ecuatoriana,* eds. Segundo Moreno Yánez and Udo Oberem, 245–75. Otavalo: Instituto Otavaleño de Antropología, 1981.

———, ed. *Memorias del primer simposio europeo sobre antropología.* Quito: Abya-Yala, 1985.

Murra, John V. *Formaciones económicas y políticas del mundo andino.* Lima: Instituto de Estudios Peruanos, 1975.

―――. "Historic Tribes of Ecuador." In *Handbook of South American Indians,* ed. Julian H. Steward, 2:785–821. Washington, D.C.: U.S. Government Printing Office, 1946.

Murra, John V., ed. *Visita de la Provincia de León de Huánuco, 1562.* 2 vols. Lima: Villanueva, 1967, 1972.

Murra, John V., Nathan Wachtel, and Jacques Revel, eds. *Anthropological History of Andean Polities.* Cambridge: Cambridge University Press, 1986.

Newson, Linda A. "Old World Epidemics in Early Colonial Ecuador." In *"Secret Judgments of God": Old World Disease in Colonial Spanish America,* eds. Noble David Cook and W. George Lovell, 84–112. Norman: University of Oklahoma Press, 1992.

Oberem, Udo. "El acceso a recursos naturales de diferentes ecologías en la sierra ecuatoriana (siglo XVI)." In *Contribución a la etnohistoria ecuatoriana,* eds. Segundo Moreno Yánez and Udo Oberem, 45–71. Otavalo: Instituto Otavaleño de Antropología, 1981.

―――. *Sancho Hacho: un cacique mayor del siglo XVI.* Quito: Abya-Yala, 1993.

―――. *Los quijos: Historia y transculturación de un grupo indígena en el Oriente ecuatoriano, 1538–1956.* Madrid: University of Madrid, 1970.

Ortegón, Diego de. "Descripción de la governación de Quijos, Sumaco y la Canela." *Cuadernos de Historia y Arqueología* 33(1973):3–28.

Ortiz de la Tabla Ducasse, Javier. "Las ordenanzas de obrajes de Matías de Peralta para la Audiencia de Quito, 1621." *Anuario de Estudios Americanos* 33(1976):875–931.

―――. "El obraje colonial ecuatoriano: Aproximación a su estudio." *Revista de Indias* 149–50(July/December 1977):471–551.

―――. "La población ecuatoriana en la época colonial: Cuestiones y cálculos." *Anuario de Estudios Americanos* 37(1980):235–77.

Patch, Robert. *Maya and Spaniard in the Yucatan.* Stanford: Stanford University Press, forthcoming.

Pease, Franklin. *Curacas, reciprocidad y riqueza.* Lima: Pontificia Universidad Católica del Peru, 1992.

―――. *Del Tawantinsuyu a la historia del Peru.* Lima: Instituto de Estudios Peruanos, 1972.

Pérez, Aquiles R. *Las mitas en la real audiencia de Quito.* Quito: Imprenta del Ministerio del Tesoro, 1947.

Phelan, John. *The Kingdom of Quito in the Seventeenth Century.* Madison: University of Wisconsin, 1967.

Porras Garcés, Pedro Ignacio. *Contribución al estudio de los valles Quijos y Misaguallí en la región oriental del Ecuador.* Quito: Fenix, 1961.

Powers, Karen. "Indian Migration and Sociopolitical Change in the Audiencia of Quito." Ph.D. diss., New York University, 1990.

―――. "Indian Migrations in the Audiencia of Quito: Crown Manipulation and Local Cooptation." In *Migration in Colonial Spanish America,* ed. David J. Robinson, 313–23. Cambridge: Cambridge University Press, 1990.

―――. "La migración vertical en la Audiencia de Quito: El caso de los quijos en el siglo XVI." *Revista de Historia Económica* (Quito) 2(December 1987):103–30.

―――. "Resilient Lords and Indian Vagabonds: Wealth, Migration, and the Reproductive Transformation of Quito's chiefdoms, 1500–1700." *Ethnohistory* 38(Summer 1991):225–49.

Ramírez, Susan. "The 'Dueño de Indios': Thoughts on the Consequences of the Shifting Bases of Power of the 'Curaca de los Viejos Antiguos' under the Spanish in Sixteenth-Century Peru." *Hispanic American Historical Review* 67(1987)4:575–610.

―――. *The World Upside Down: Cross-Cultural Contact and Conflict in Sixteenth-Century Peru.* Stanford: Stanford University Press, forthcoming.

―――. "Social Frontiers and the Territorial Base of Curacazgos," in *Andean Ecology and Civilization: An Interdisciplinary Perspective on Andean Ecological Complementarity,* ed. Shozo Masuda, 423–42. Tokyo, 1985.

Ramón, Galo. *La resistencia andina: Cayambe, 1500–1800.* Quito: Centro Andino de Acción Popular, 1987.

―――. "La cara oculta de la hacienda colonial: La visión andina en Cayambe, siglo XVII." In *Reproducción y transformación de las sociedades andinas, siglos XVI–XX,* eds. Segundo Moreno Yánez and Frank Salomon, 415–40.

Rebolledo G., Loreto. *Comunidad y resistencia: El caso de Lumbisí en la colonia.* Quito: Abya-Yala, 1992.

Renard-Casevitz, F. M., Thierry Saignes, and A. C. Taylor. *Al este de los Andes: Relaciones entre las sociedades amazónicas y andinas entre los siglos XV y XVII.* 2 vols. Quito: Abya-Yala, 1988.

Robinson, David, ed. *Migration in Colonial Spanish America.* Cambridge: Cambridge University Press, 1990.

―――, ed. *Studies in Spanish American Population History.* Boulder: Westview Press, 1981.

Romero Arteta, Oswaldo. "El indio quiteño en el siglo XVI." *Boletín de la Academia Nacional de Historia* 47(July/December 1964):212–23.

Roseberry, William. *Anthropologies and Histories: Essays in Culture, History and Political Economy.* New Brunswick: Rutgers University Press, 1989.

Rubio Orbe, Gonzalo. "Ecuador indígena." *América Indígena* 34(July/August 1974):581–604.

Rumazo González, José. *La región amazónica del Ecuador en el siglo XVI.* Seville: Estudios Hispanoamericanos de Sevilla, 1946.

Sahlins, Marshall. *Islands of History.* Chicago: University of Chicago Press, 1985.

Saignes, Thierry. *Los Andes orientales: Historia de un olvido.* Cochabamba: CERES, 1985

―――. *Caciques, Tribute and Migration in the Southern Andes: Indian Society and the Seventeenth Century Colonial Order.* London: University of London, 1985.

―――. "Las etnías de Charcas frente al sistema colonial (siglo XVII):

Ausentismo y fugas en el debate sobre la mano de obra indígena, 1595–1665." *Jahrbuch für Geschichte von Staat, Wirtschaft und Gesellschaft Lateinamerikas* 21(1984):27–75.

Salomon, Frank Loewen. "Don Pedro de Zámbiza, un varayuj del siglo XVI." *Cuadernos de Historia y Arqueología* 42(1975):285–315.

———. *Native Lords of Quito in the Age of the Incas: The Political Economy of North Andean Chiefdoms.* Cambridge: Cambridge University Press, 1986.

Salomon, Frank, and Sue Grosboll. "Names and Peoples in Incaic Quito: Retrieving Undocumented Historic Processes through Anthroponymy and Statistics." *American Anthropologist* (June 1986): 387–99.

Sánchez-Albornoz, Nicolás. *Indios y tributos en el Alto Perú.* Lima: Instituto de Estudios Peruanos, 1978.

———. "Migración rural en los Andes: Sipesipe (Cochabamba), 1645." *Revista de Historia Económica* 1(1983):13–36.

———. "Migración urbana y trabajo: Los indios de Arequipa, 1571– 1645." In *De historia a historiadores: Homenaje a José Luis Romero,* 259–81. Mexico: Siglo XXI, 1982.

———. "Migraciones internas en el Alto Perú: El saldo acumulado en 1645." *Historia Boliviana* 2(1)(1982):11–19.

———. "Mita, migraciones y pueblos: Variaciones en el espacio y en el tiempo— Alto Perú, 1573–1692." *Historia Boliviana* 3(1)(1983): 31–59.

———, ed. *Población y mano de obra en América Latina.* Madrid: Alianza Editorial, 1985.

———. *The Population of Latin America: A History.* Berkeley: University of California Press, 1974.

———. "El trabajo indígena en los Andes." *Revista de Historia Económica Ecuatoriana* 2(December 1987):153–81.

Santos Granero, Fernando, ed. *Opresión colonial y resistencia indígena en la Alta Amazonía* (Quito: Flacso/Abya-Yala, 1992).

Schroeder, Susan. *Chimalpahin and the Kingdoms of Chalco.* Tucson: University of Arizona Press, 1991.

Sempat Assadourian, Carlos. *El sistema de la economía colonial.* Lima: Instituto de Estudios Peruanos, 1982.

"Los sínodos de Quito del siglo XVI." *Revista del Instituto de Historia Eclesiástica Ecuatoriana* 3/4(1978):5–200.

Spalding, Karen. *De indio a campesino: Cambios en la estructura social del Peru colonial.* Lima: Instituto de Estudios Peruanos, 1974.

———. *Huarochiri: An Andean Society under Inca and Spanish Rule.* Stanford: Stanford University Press, 1984.

Stein, Stanley J., and Barbara H. Stein. *The Colonial Heritage of Latin America: Essays on Economic Dependence in Perspective.* New York: Oxford University Press, 1970.

Stern, Steve J. "Feudalism, Capitalism, and the World-System in the Perspective of Latin America and the Caribbean." *American Historical Review* 93(October 1988):829–72.

————. *Peru's Indian Peoples and the Challenge of the Spanish Conquest: Huamanga to 1640.* Madison: University of Wisconsin Press, 1982.

Tyrer, Robson Brines. *Historia demográfica y económica de la Audiencia de Quito: Población indígena e industria textil, 1600–1800.* Quito: Banco Central del Ecuador, 1988.

Vargas, José María. "Los cacicazgos." *Boletín de la Academia Nacional de Historia* 53(1970):250–64.

————. *Historia del Ecuador, siglo XVI.* Quito: Pontificia Universidad Católica, 1977.

Wachtel, Nathan. *The Vision of the Vanquished: The Spanish Conquest of Peru through Indian Eyes, 1530–1570.* New York: Barnes and Noble, 1977.

Wallerstein, Immanuel. *The Modern World System: Capitalist Agriculture and the Origins of the European World Economy in the Sixteenth Century.* New York: Academic Press, 1974.

Wightman, Ann M. *Indigenous Migration and Social Change: The Forasteros of Cuzco, 1570–1720.* Durham: Duke University Press, 1990.

Wolf, Eric. *Europe and the People without History.* Berkeley: University of California Press, 1982.

Wood, Stephanie. "Corporate Adjustments in Colonial Mexican Indian Towns, Toluca Region." Ph.D. diss., UCLA, 1984.

Zeitlin, Judith. "Ranchers and Indians on the Southern Isthmus of Tehuantepec: Economic Change and Indigenous Survival in Colonial Mexico." *Hispanic American Historical Review* (February 1989):23–60.

Zeitlin, Judith, and Lillian Thomas. "Spanish Justice and the Indian Cacique: Disjunctive Political Systems in Sixteenth-Century Tehuantepec." *Ethnohistory* (Summer 1992):285–315.

Zulawski, Ann. "Migración y mano de obra en un centro minero de los Andes: Oruro, 1683." In *Población y mano de obra en América Latina,* ed. Nicolás Sánchez-Albornoz, 95–114. Madrid: Alianza, 1985.

————. "Migration and Labor in Seventeenth Century Alto Peru." Ph.D. diss., Columbia University, 1985.

————. "Wages, Ore Sharing and Peasant Agriculture: Labor in Oruro's Silver Mines, 1607–1720." *Hispanic American Historical Review* 67(August 1987):405–30.

Index

Agreda, Pedro de, 34
Alchon, Suzanne A.: on epidemics, 17, 23, 185n20; on population increase, 7, 19, 22, 67, 78, 97, 169, 170
Amaguaña, 111, 113, 114
Amaguaña, Joseph Roberto, 159
Ambato, 36; location, 25, 52; migration from, 75, 76; migration to, 19, 22, 32, 62, 69; mitayos, 46; tribute collection, 101, 214n53
Anan Chillo. *See* Amaguaña
Argos, Rodrigo de, 143
Argos Guaraca, Augustín, 161–62
Auncibay, Francisco de, 32, 37
Ausentes: kin composition of, 54–55, 61, 64; late 17th century, 66–76; mid-17th century, 48–51, 53–66; rental of lands belonging to, 124–28; tribute arrears and, 129, 149; tribute fraud pertaining to, 100–103; types of, 11. *See also* Forasteros
Aybar, Ignacio de, 102
Ayllus, 12; as administrative units, 135; Chillos Valley, 21; incorporation of forasteros into, 38, 96; migratory styles, 54–55, 57–58, 59–64, 72–73; names of, 182

Bastidas, Alonso de, 84
Bonilla, Christóval de, 98
Borah, Woodrow, 6
Borchart de Moreno, Christiana, 74, 99
Bueno, Juan, 138–39
Buscador, 198–99n42

Cabezas Urcuquiango, Sebastián, 127–28, 129, 130, 131
Cacicazgos. *See* Caciques
Caciques: alliance with Spanish, 162, 165; Andean challenges to, 142–44, 147, 156–57, 158–67; deterioration of position of, 74, 149–50, 165; divestment of personal wealth of, 148–49, 166, 171; imprisonment of, 148, 149, 212–13n41, 213n46; intruder, 150, 151, 156–66, 171; knowledge of ausentes' whereabouts, 51, 73; personal wealth of, 202n6; principales, 97, 163; privatization of land by, 118; recruitment of private workforce by, 36–37, 109–10, 111, 112–13, 114–15, 116, 117, 118–19, 120–23, 132; rental of ausentes land by, 40, 124, 125–30, 132; role of, 107, 108, 202n3; "runaway," 149–50; Spanish imposition of, 97, 134–41, 142; survival of, 108–9
Caguasquí, 32
Caillavet, Chantal, 110, 136, 210n3
Cali, 25, 34
Calpi, 61, 62–65, 96, 181
Camuento, Marcos, 114–15
Cañari, 13, 27, 38, 83
Cañaribamba, 38
Cara, 13, 27
Carangue, 147
Caranqui, 13
Carma, 34
Carrera Colín, Juan, 118
Cartago, 34

Cayambe, 75, 121
Cayampi, 13
Chala, Joachín, 139
Chambo, 68, 69, 71–74
Chillogallo, 41, 113, 114
Chillos Valley, 21, 32, 83, 111, 112–14
Chimbo, 29; depopulation, 30, 46–47;
location, 52; migration from, 32;
migration to, 22, 62, 65, 69; tribute
avoidance, 94; tribute fraud, 101
Chimborazo, 80
Chunga, Juan, 146
Cieza de León, Pedro, 24
Contero, Andrés, 16, 26
Cook, Sherburne, 6
Cosanga-Píllaro culture, 28
Cotacache, 48, 50, 53, 182
Cotocollao, 40, 119
Cotton. *See* Textile industry
Cuenca: imprisonment of caciques,
149; location, 25, 52; migration
from, 38; migration to, 62, 69, 70,
71, 74, 76, 94; population, 18, 21;
population decline, 17, 37; tribute
collection, 101
Curi Argos, Gonzalo, 156–57
Cuxilago, Ynés, 155–56

Demographic control: imposition of
the state and, 81–82; transferred
from Andeans to state, 105; visitas
used for, 95–98. *See also* Manifes-
tación; Visitas
Dependency model, 4
Díaz de Pinera, Gonzalo, 24
Díaz de Zurbano, Sancho, 41
Disease, 17, 20, 23, 24, 30, 185n20
Duchinachay, Fernando, 162–63, 164

Encomiendas: cotton-textile economy
and, 112–13; migration from, 88;
migration to, 32, 37; as sources of
wealth and prestige, 88; tribute
fraud, 84–85; tribute from, 89–91,
98
Enzerma, 34

Epidemics. *See* Disease
Esquilache, príncipe de, 113, 198n33

Forasteros, 9; attempts to impose mita
on, 92, 197–98n32; change in
meaning of, 92–93; in crown
parcialidades, 87–95, 145–46,
197n21; exemption from mita, 7, 91,
197n21; imposition of mita on,
197n21; incorporation into ayllus of
place of residence, 38, 96; as intruder caciques, 152, 156–58;
number of, 15–16; pre-Hispanic
origin of, 122; recruitment into
private workforces, 110, 111, 132;
status of, 206n53; in textile industry,
77, 78, 111–14; upward mobility of
some, 152–58, 166. *See also* Ausentes; "Hidden" population

Galeano, Eduardo, 4
García Hati, Guillermo, 145
Garnica, Juan de, 162, 163
Garrochamba, 38
Gibson, Charles, 3–4
Glave, Luis Miguel, 9, 120, 123, 172,
195n44
Guaca: absenteeism in, 57–62; demo-
graphic profile, 179–80; depopula-
tion, 58, 193–94n17; marriage
patterns, 194n18
Guambahaló, 84
Guano, 84, 136–39, 142–44, 159
Guayaquil: location, 25; migration to,
69, 74; population, 18; population
decline, 24, 26; tribute collection,
101
Guerrero Salazar, Juan, 101
Gutiérrez Flores, Pedro, 83

Hacho, Sancho, 28, 205n44, 206n45
Haciendas: consolidation of, 74–75;
migration to, 46, 51, 79
Hati, Francisco, 83–84, 203n10,
215n70
Hati Zanipatín, Guillermo, 117, 118,
120, 145

ANDEAN JOURNEYS
Migration, Ethnogenesis, and the State in Colonial Quito

Karen Vieira Powers

This account of the native peoples of Ecuador in the sixteenth and seventeenth centuries shows how they not only resisted, adapted, and survived Spanish colonization but reinvented themselves as a culture. Offered are both a revisionist treatment of the demographic history of Amerindian Ecuador and a clearer understanding of North Andean ethnogenesis. Powers's study of Andean population movements in the Audiencia of Quito from 1535 to 1700 shows that native migrations account for a population increase in Quito during a time when contiguous areas experienced a rapid decline in Indian population.

Beyond reconstructing the movement of the native peoples, Powers also explores how migration changed the lives of Indians and Spaniards. The migratory flow from native communities to Spanish cities, textile mills, and haciendas resulted in a constantly mutating colonial world. For elite Spaniards, the migrations meant the near collapse of the tribute and forced labor system, while nonelite Spaniards were able to take advantage of the alternative labor supplied by the migrant Indians, resulting in social mobility and the formation of new classes. For Indians, the migrations were initially a survival strategy but ended in the decline of the traditional chiefdom. A key finding of the study is that Ecuadorean Indians achieved cultural survival by reconstructing Andean lifeways inside the sites to which they migrated.

"A truly outstanding, important work."—Susan E. Ramírez, DePaul University

Karen Vieira Powers is an ethnohistorian and a professor of history at Northern Arizona University.